MW01631551

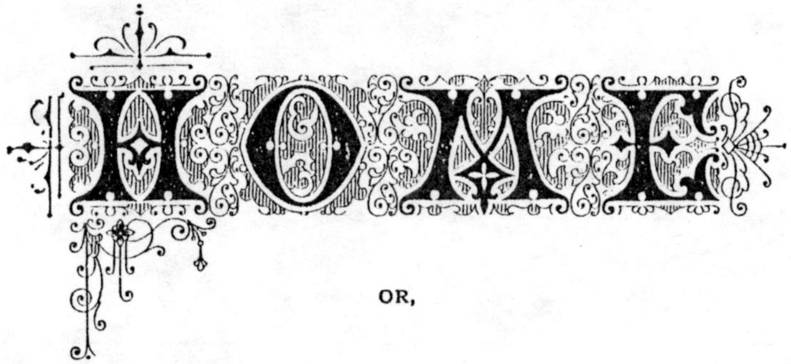

OR,

The Key to a Nobler Life

BY

C. E. SARGENT, A. B.

WITH LETTER OF INTRODUCTION

BY

MRS. LUCRETIA R. GARFIELD.

ILLUSTRATED.

Volume I.

KING, RICHARDSON & CO., PUBLISHERS,
SPRINGFIELD, MASS.
1888.

May peace be in thy home
And joy within thy heart.

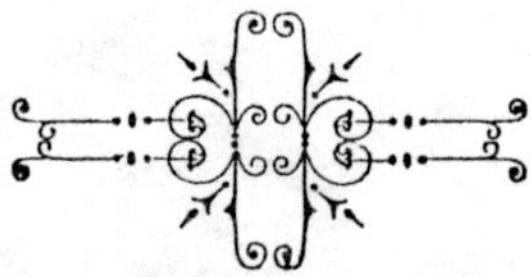

Archive Publishers, Heber City, UT 84032
www.archivepublishers.com

PREFACE.

THE reader will notice that we have confined ourselves in the treatment of this work almost exclusively to what is termed the "scientific method." We have not only regarded home itself as an institution of nature, but in the treatment of almost every subject we have tried to involve the exposition of some related natural law, because every relation of the home life is the outgrowth of some law of our nature or of our surroundings. It has been our aim to make this book a scientific treatise on the various phases of the home, and in this respect, so far as we know, it stands alone.

We have chosen to consider the various relations of the home life from this standpoint, from a conviction that society has come to need something more substantial than those mere expressions of sentiment, which, for the most part, constitute the books of this kind that heretofore have been given to the public. Many very entertaining books, however, have thus been produced, but the undisputed fact that all the while the old-time home love has been slowly but surely fading away, is sufficient proof that they have not accomplished the object for which they were written. It is true that the word "home" is one of the most poetic in human language, that the institution of home itself owes its origin to an innate sentiment, and that this emotion like all others grows and develops by its own action, so that such expressions of sentiment have their use; and the great number of those beautiful prose poems, that during the past few years have been offered to the public, show how deep and insatiable is this home sentiment. Yet in spite of all this, the street and the public hall are usurping the kingdom of the fireside, and the dark monster of Communism is creeping upon us. The restoration and preservation of the old home love and reverence by a more rational and scientific conception of the home relations, we believe, is all that can save society from wreck.

The home life is to the social life what the unvarying movement of the water wheel is to the clashing and discordant motion of the great factory. When the machinery stops or moves fitfully and unreliably the experienced machinist does not think, by merely lubricating the bearings, to remove the difficulty, but with lantern and wrench and hammer descends into the pit to see what ails the "great wheel."

There are certain diseases whose symptoms are chiefly or wholly local, but which, nevertheless, must be cured by constitutional remedies. Such is the character of most of those moral diseases that affect human society, and the remedies we have tried to point out are constitutional remedies. The one organ we have aimed to reach is that which is the most central and vital of any in the living body of society—the home.

Society is agitated to-day over the startling problem of divorce, and yet, with all its attendant evils, divorce must be regarded only as a *symptom* of a fatal disease that is preying on the vitals of society. Intemperance and licentiousness are symptoms of diseases that can be reached only through the organ of home.

What the home is, society will be. The moral corruption and the dark vices of the city would perish in a single night did not their cancerous rootlets reach down into the foulness of perverted homes.

Still, what a world would this be were it not for the institution of home! How would the streets of the great city be turbulent with lawless outcries at midnight did not the Great Father, through the kindly shepherd of a natural law, send his children at night, to the fold of home! How its divine protection hovers over the slow-breathing multitude like the shadow of a great wing!

This book is the product of one not hoary with experience, but of one who has tasted a little of the bitter water, and who has written from the depths of conviction. We hope that the public and the critics will receive his effort with feelings as kindly as those with which it is offered, and he will feel that from his soul a burden has been lifted.

S.

CONTENTS.

PUBLISHERS' NOTICE.

SPRINGFIELD, MASS., July 2, 1883.

TO THE READER:

Perhaps a word from the publishers of this volume would be appropriate right here. Since the date of the following introduction our author has graduated from college with high honors, and truly can we say that rarely does any institution of learning bestow its diploma upon one whose faculties are so broadly developed, or who has been more earnest in preparation for a life work in the service of mankind. Believing that the ministry of the following pages will ennoble the heart, purify the mind and elevate that sacred spot around which cluster our joys and our woes, we are

Most sincerely yours,

W. C. KING & CO.

THE FOLLOWING

LETTER OF INTRODUCTION

WAS ADDRESSED TO

REV. O. B. CHENEY, D. D., PRES. OF BATES COLLEGE, ME.

Cleveland O.
April 26th 1883

President Cheney

Dear Sir—

The table of contents of Mr. Sargent's book awakens interest at once in his work; but the reader will feel a new inducement to read the chapters to which these subjects introduce him when told that the author is yet a young man, still pursuing his College Course

To thoughtful men and women whose attention has been directed to these subjects the interest would not be in finding new ideas, but in the fact that our *young* men are beginning to think in the right direction - that they look to the true home as the great school in which the hope for humanity lies.

From all you tell me

I shall be glad to know of
Mr. Sargent's personal success,
and I hope for him a future
of continued growth and
usefulness.

With high regard

I am Very Truly Yours—

Lucretia R. Garfield.

MAN'S life's a book of history;
The leaves thereof are days;
The letters, mercies closely joined
The title is God's praise.

MASON

THE NATURE OF HOME.

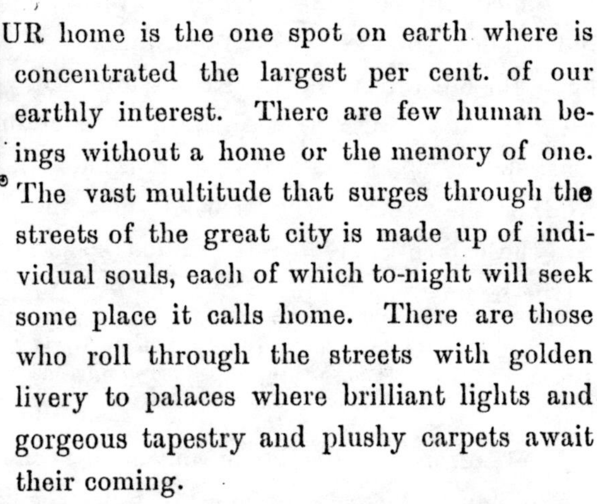

OUR home is the one spot on earth where is concentrated the largest per cent. of our earthly interest. There are few human beings without a home or the memory of one. The vast multitude that surges through the streets of the great city is made up of individual souls, each of which to-night will seek some place it calls home. There are those who roll through the streets with golden livery to palaces where brilliant lights and gorgeous tapestry and plushy carpets await their coming.

There are those who walk the frosty pavement with cold and bleeding feet, whose homes are in damp and dreary cellars, or in the rickety garrets of worn and wretched hovels. No lights, no music, no feasts await them, nothing but a crust and a bed of straw. And yet these places in all their wretchedness are the homes of human beings. There is still another class of homes, where has been answered the human heart's best prayer, "give us neither poverty nor riches;" where peace and joy and love and contentment dwell; where industry and frugality, with sunbrown hands and healthful appetite, sit at the board of plenty. But whether the home be a palace, a cottage, or a garret, it is home.

Home is in the soul itself; and, to a certain extent, is independent of outward circumstances. Of this inward home the outward is but the expression; and yet it is doubtful if the outward is ever a true expression of the inward, inasmuch as men's ideals always transcend their experience. Neither the wretched hovel where vice and hunger dwell, nor the palace where lies the gilded corpse of love can be a true home.

> "Home is the resort
> Of love, of joy, of peace and plenty, where
> Supporting and supported, polished friends
> And dear relations mingle into bliss."

Next to religion, the home sentiment is the strongest in the human heart. At the name of home the better impulse of every heart awakens. As the chord of the instrument is dead to every sound until its own harmonic chord is struck, when it vibrates and taking up the sound prolongs it as if it could not let it die, so many a darkened mind is dead to every appeal save that magic sound, "home!" The lives of thousands who have been snatched as brands from temptation's fire will testify to the magic power of a sister's early love, while the sudden remembrance of a mother's "good night kiss" has stayed the assassin's dagger. In the dark and loathsome dens of iniquity there are those whose lips have, for years, acknowledged their Creator only in oaths; whose eyes have shed no tears, and whose ears have heard only the blasphemies of drunken revelry. And yet could an unseen hand write upon those walls the words "Home" and "Mother's Love," lips would quiver, eyes would swim, and from the depths of many a soul in which the germs of truth and love had long since seemed dead, would burst the heart-rending confession,—

> "Once I was pure as the snow, but I fell,
> Fell like a snow-flake from heaven to hell,
> Fell to be trampled as filth of the street,
> Fell to be scoffed at, be spit on and beat;
> Pleading, cursing, begging to die,
> Selling my soul to whoever would buy;
> Dealing in shame for a morsel of bread,
> Hating the living and fearing the dead."

The powerful influence which the home sentiment exerts over the minds of men was shown in a striking manner a few years ago at Castle Garden, New York. Some ten thousand people had gathered there to listen to that sweet-voiced singer, Jenny Lind. She began with the sublime compositions of the great masters of song. Her audience applauded her with a respectful degree of appreciation. But at length, with sweetness ineffable, born of the holy parentage ot genius and passion, she poured forth that immortal song, "Home, Sweet Home." At once the irrepressible contagion of sympathy spread through that vast audience. Peal on peal of thunderous applause resounded, until the song was stopped by the very ecstasy of those who listened; and when the soft refrain was heard again, that mass of humanity was melted into tears; the great masters were all forgotten, while ten thousand human hearts knelt at the shrine of a poor and obscure outcast. Why was this? Was Howard Payne a greater genius than they? Must these mighty names yield their places to one whom the world has forgotten? No; it was simply because when sorrow laid his iron hand on the heart of Howard Payne, in his cruel grasp he chanced to strike that chord which vibrates to a lighter touch than any in the human heart save that alone swept by the master's hand.

"Home of our childhood! how affection clings
And hovers 'round thee with her seraph wings!
Dearer thy hills, though clad in autumn brown,
Than fairest summits which the cedars crown."

The rough experiences of the roaring, toiling, stormy world, may blot out all other images from the mind, but the picture of our early home must hang forever on the walls of memory, until "the silver cord be loosed or the golden bowl be broken."

The old man may not recall all the experiences, all the struggles and triumphs of his early manhood; but every feature of his childhood home, every little play-house that he helped his sister build, is photographed upon his heart's tablet and can never fade away. Perchance the golden light of eternity will not dim the brightness of that picture. Whatever else the heart may forget, it cannot forget the place of its birth; it cannot forget the little broken cart, the sled and the kite, the sister's fond caress, the brother's generous aid, the father's loving counsel, and the mother's anxious prayer.

It cannot forget the day when a chastening hand drew still closer the chords of love and bound the little circle in a common sorrow; the day when hushed footsteps were in the house, and the silent rooms were filled with the odor of flowers, and the garden gate swung outward to let a little casket through.

"That hallowed word is ne'er forgot,
No matter where we roam;
The purest feelings of the heart
Still cluster 'round our home.

"Dear resting place where weary thought
May dream away its care,
Love's gentle star unveils its light
And shines in beauty there."

But the ministry of home consists not alone in its fond memories and hallowed associations. It is the great conservator of good, the "seeding place of virtue." It is the origin of all civilization. The laws of a nation are but rescripts of its domestic codes. The words uttered and the doctrines taught around the fireside are the influences that shape the destinies of empires.

It is the influences of home that live in the life of kingdoms, while parental counsel repeats itself in the voices of republics. We would impress upon the minds of our readers this grand truth, and would that we might thunder it into the ears of all mankind, that a nation is but a magnified home. Parliament and Congress are but hearthstones on a grander scale. Those great and noble characters who have left a deathless impress upon the history of nations were not fashioned on battle fields, but in the cradle and at the fireside. They are those, moreover, who at every period of life, at every turn of fortune or adversity, have never forgotten the old home.

A mother breathes, under the canopy of a cradle, a prayer that her darling boy may be a conqueror in life's battle; that the hosts of sin may flee before the sword of his manly virtue, and from that cradle there arises a youth with that same prayer upon his lips, and in virtue's coat of mail he goes forth to battle. Harmless as the fall of snow-flakes, from his helmet drop the broken arrows of temptation's besieging armies. Fearlessly he marches through the dismal swamps of poverty and hunger and cold. With sweating brow he toils up the rugged steep of knowledge,

> Till full upon his vision gleams
> The prophecy of early dreams.

Humble and modest as a maiden he receives a nation's benediction with its crown. And when death's untimely visit drops the veil over life's grandest triumph, fifty million human hearts bow in the dust before the sable banners of a nation's sorrow.

When, think you, were fashioned the pillars of that colossal character? Did they spring up to meet the emergencies of fame and power? No! they were sculptured in the sacred quarry of the cradle with that chisel which only a mother's hand can wield. When we stand in the presence of art's grandest achievements we feel like bowing before that genius which can take from the hand of nature a block of marble and hew away the chips that hide a waiting angel. But the mother of Garfield took from the hand of God the unformed elements of a human character and shaped them into something it were blasphemy to compare with the proudest creation that ever leaped from the brain of genius—a God-like man.

> "O wondrous power! how little understood!
> Entrusted to a mother's mind alone,—
> To fashion genius from the soul for good."

No argument is necessary to convince us of the potency of home influence in shaping character. There are certain truths to which it is only necessary to call attention, and minds instinctively assent to them, and to this class, we believe, belong those general truths concerning home which we have mentioned. Indeed, they are recognized and taught in the trite maxims of every-day life. Napoleon understood well the nature of home and its mission when he said, "The great need of France is mothers." An old Scotch proverb says, "An ounce of mother is worth a pound of clergy." Mohammed said, "Paradise is at the feet of mothers."

Might not some American statesman say, "The throne of freedom's goddess is the hearthstone"? Our government is a grand experiment. Its ship is on an unknown sea and sails through unsounded waters. It is true that other governments have styled themselves republics, but with all of them there have been reservations that have made them republics only in name. Ours is the first experiment with a true republic. If we fail in this experiment, if our government falls, the world will hear the echo of that fall till the end of time as a dismal, warning sound. The victorious shout of error is the most dangerous sound that can fall upon the human ear. Rest assured that our government is no trifle. That ever restless spirit of liberty that to-day confronts the troubled principalities of Europe, is looking anxiously to the issue of our experiment. Mothers and fathers, that issue rests with you.

Your boys are soon to take the reins of this high mettled steed, America. A nation's only hope is in them, and their only hope is in you; and the instruments which God has put into your hands with which to fit them for this high office, are the influences of home. You to-day are writing on the yielding tablets of their hearts and minds the preface to the next volume of our nation's history. America should fear the disloyalty and contention of the fireside more than the nefarious plots of scheming politicians.

If your boys wrangle and contend at home, if they cannot discuss with dignity the little questions that arise in their daily intercourse with one another, be sure they will not honor the nation when they take their places in senate halls to discuss the great problems that confront the civilization of the nineteenth century.

Now, if home may be so powerful an influence for good, how important becomes the cultivation of the home sentiment. To be destitute of this sentiment is almost as great a misfortune as to be destitute of the religious sentiment. Indeed, we believe that one cannot possess a true and exalted love of home while there is wanting in his character that which when awakened may yield the fruit of a godly life. What a mighty responsibility rests upon him who essays to make a home, for the founding of a home is as sacred a work as the founding of a church. Indeed, every home should be a temple dedicated to divine worship, where human beings through life should worship God through the service of mutual love—the highest tribute man can pay to the divine.

If the home sentiment be one of the strongest passions of the human soul it was made such for a wise purpose. The affections of the heart all have their corresponding outward objects. We possess no power impelling us to love or desire that which does not exist as a genuine institution and necessity of nature. So this strong home sentiment only proves to us that the institution of home was divinely born. It is based in the very constitution of human nature, and so vital is the relation which it sustains to our needs, that every heart must have a home. It may not be of brick or wood or stone. It may not have a "local habitation and a name." But if not, out of the airy timbers of its own fancy the heart will rear the structure which it demands as a necessity of its being. We are aware that there are thousands who are *called* homeless; but their hearts' demand is at least partially met by the possession of an *ideal* home. The body may exist without a home, but the heart, never. The world called Howard Payne a homeless wanderer, yet kings and peasants have implored entrance at the vine-wreathed threshold of that home which he reared in the airy dreamland of poesy.

Another evidence of the divine origin of the institution of home is found in its obvious adaptation to the end it serves, and in the striking analogies which we detect between its functions and the general methods of nature.

Every growth in nature is nurtured and sustained through its early existence by a pre-existing guardian. The germ of the oak is nourished and protected by the substance of the acorn until it is strong enough to draw its food directly from the earth, and to withstand the tempest and the scorching sun. So it must be with the germ of that oak which is to wave in the forest of human society. And if we wish it to become a grand and noble oak, and not a hollow hearted deformity, we should look well to the protection and nourishment of its early years. We should see that there is the proper spiritual soil from which the little human germ may gather wholesome and strengthening food when it puts forth its tender rootlets into the great world without. The relation which the acorn sustains to the germ is precisely that which the home sustains to the child. If we were to suppose the germ endowed with intelligence, we should still suppose it ignorant of everything but the environments of the acorn. It would, of course, be all unconscious that there is a world without full not only of germs like itself, but of giant oaks. So the child is ignorant of the great outward world. The home is its little world and it knows no other.

Precious thought, that it never quite outgrows the blissful ignorance! We take on higher and broader views of life, but we are compelled by a law of our being to look forever upon our home as in some way the grand center from which radiate all other interests.

When the mother shades the windows of the nursery, she but unconsciously imitates the Creator of her child, who through the institution of home has shut from his feeble and nascent mind the flashing colors of the too brilliant world.

But not alone for childhood is the sacred ministry of home. It is the guardian of youth, a consolation amid the weary toils of manhood and a resting place for old age, where he, who is soon to lay off the armor, may find loving hearts and tender hands to guide his tottering steps to the water's edge.

Again, the mature mind is only that of a developed infant. It is still infantile with reference to the universe in its entirety. Nor can it ever fully comprehend the significance of life in the aggregate. Were we to attempt to dwell in the great temple of the world, we should become lost in its vast halls and mighty labyrinths. Hence it becomes necessary to reduce the scale of the world; to isolate the human mind, as it were, from the vastness of aggregate life. And this God has done in the institution of home.

"Home 's not merely four square walls,
Though with pictures hung and gilded:
Home is where affection calls,
Filled with shrines the heart hath builded!
Home! go watch the faithful dove,
Sailing 'neath the heaven above us;
Home is where there 's one to love!
Home is where there 's one to love us!

"Home 's not merely roof and room,
It needs something to endear it;
Home is where the heart can bloom,
Where there 's some kind lip to cheer it!
What is home with none to meet,
None to welcome, none to greet us?
Home is sweet,—and only sweet,—
Where there 's one we love to meet us!"

INFLUENCES OF HOME.

IT is a law of all initiate life that it is susceptible to outward and formative influences in an inverse ratio to its age. An ear of corn while it is yet green may have an entire row of its kernels removed, and when it becomes ripe it will show no marks of this piece of vegetable surgery. So the young child may have many a vice removed while he remains as plastic clay in the hands of those whose privilege it is to mold the character for eternity, and when he is old he will show no marks of the cruel knife of discipline and denial through which the change was wrought. But if he becomes old before the work is begun the scar will always remain, even if the experiment succeeds. A bad temper in a young child may be sweetened, but the acid temper of an old man reluctantly unites with any sweetening influences.

We find here a striking analogy to a physical law of our being. It is a well known fact that in early childhood the osseous tissues of the body are soft and flexible. The bones may be almost doubled upon themselves without breaking, but in the old the bones are so hard and brittle that they cannot be bent the least without breaking. We can make little or no impression upon them. They stubbornly refuse to respond to all influences. Surely it is true of the body, "As the twig is bent the tree's inclined." But it is no less true of the mind and soul. The disposition of an animal may be made just what we choose to make it by our treatment of it when young.

Who does not know that the disposition of the dog is almost wholly dependent on the manner in which the puppy is treated? This principle is recognized in the old adage, "It is hard to teach an old dog new tricks."

Whatever may be our views concerning the moral and spiritual relations of the human to the brute creation, it cannot be denied that the laws which govern the mental life of each are essentially the same. The difference is in quantity rather than quality.

What a grand virtue is patience! How charming in childhood! How sublime in manhood! Then let us learn a lesson from the ease with which patience is created or destroyed at will in the young animal.

The susceptibility of children to outward influences is largely due to their power of imitation, and this power was, doubtless, given them for a wise purpose.

Originality is not a virtue of infancy and childhood. Hence, if we would influence the acts of a child we should set him an example, we should act as we wish him to act. Patient children are never reared by impatient parents.

Most of the crime and misery of the world are due to the early influences of home. We may not be aware how small an influence may work the ruin of a child when he has inherited slightly vicious tendencies. By nature the disposition of a child is the sweetest thing in the world, and how beautiful, tender and sweet might become the lives of all if parents were conscious of these truths, and would act according to their knowledge. But they so often contaminate the sweet springs of childhood with the bitterness of their own lives, that we do not wonder that the old theologians so strongly believed in total depravity and innate sinfulness.

Infancy is neither vicious nor virtuous; it is simply innocent, and is susceptible alike to good and bad influences.

Its safety consists alone in the watchfulness of its guardians. The soldier has his hours of duty, but the parent in whose hands is entrusted the guardianship of an immortal soul is never off duty. When the baby is asleep all the household move softly lest they awake him; but when he is awake they should move and think and speak more softly lest they awaken in him that which no nursery song can lull to sleep again.

The young child is an apt student of human nature. You do not deceive him as you perhaps think. The knowledge of human nature, of the motives that impel us to actions, comes not from reason nor from observation. It is an intuitive knowledge and is always keen in the child. It acts, too, with far greater vigor between the child and parent, especially the mother, than between the child and others. Every look of the mother's eye is interpreted by her child with far greater accuracy than the most profound student of the anatomy of expression could interpret it.

The sharpest merchant may not detect the sign of dishonesty in the father's face so quickly as the child.

Parents, your child is the blank paper on which is to be written the record of your own lives. Be careful then what you allow to be written there, for the world will read it. Do you not see that through this principle by which you are instinctively *en rapport* with your child, an awful responsibility is thrown upon you? The secrets of your inmost soul are the copy which the trembling hand of your child is trying to write.

The word influence is the most incomprehensible, the most vast and far reaching in its significance, of all words. We seldom use it in any but a literal sense, but in every degree of its true meaning there is the shadow of infinity.

Philosophers tell us, not in jest, but in the profoundest earnest, that every footfall on the pavement jars the sun, and every pebble dropped into the ocean moves the continents with vibrations that never cease. Your hand gives motion to a pendulum, and in that act you have produced an effect which shall endure through eternity. The vibration of the pendulum as a mass ceases, but only because its motion has been transformed from mass motion to molecular motion. Had it been suspended in a vacuum and been made to swing without friction at the point of suspension, it would have vibrated on forever, but the friction which is inevitable, and the resistance of the air gradually bring it to rest, and we say the motion has ceased, but this is not true. The motion has not ceased, it has simply become invisible. At every vibration a part of the motion was changed at the point of suspension and in the air into the invisible undulations of heat and electricity. A moment ago the pendulum was swinging, but now infinitely small atoms are swinging in its stead, and the aggregate motion of all those atoms is just equal to the motion of the pendulum at first. These waves of atomic motion expand and radiate from the points of origin, extending on and on and on, past planets and stars, beating and dashing against their brazen bosoms as the waves of the ocean beat the rocky shore. This is not the language of fancy; it is the veritable philosophy, the demonstrated facts of science. Your will gave birth to motion communicated along the nerve of your arm to the pendulum, and that motion has gone past your recall, on its eternal errand among the stars. What a solemn thought! You are the parent of the infinite!

And yet this illustration but faintly shadows the awfulness of human influence. If a simple motion of your hand is fraught with eternal consequences, what shall we say of the influences of your mind? They shall live as long as the throne of the Infinite. Oh, that we might impress upon the minds of mother and father the awful truth that an influence in its very nature is eternal. Not a word or thought or deed of all the myriad dead but lives to-day in the character of our words and deeds and thoughts. We are the outgrowth of all the past, the grand resultant of all the world's past forces. Only God can measure the influence of a human thought.

"No stream from its source
Flows seaward, how lonely soever its course,
But what some land is gladdened. No star ever rose
And set without influence somewhere. Who knows
What earth needs from earth's lowest creature? No life
Can be pure in its purpose and strong in its strife,
And all life not be purer and stronger thereby."

A mother speaks a fretful word to a child at a critical moment, when just upon his trembling lips hangs the ready word of penitence, and in his eye a tear, held back by the thinnest veil through which a single tender glance might pierce. But the tender glance is withheld. The penitence grows cold upon his lip, the tear creeps back to its fountain, the heart grows harder day by day, until that mother mourns over a wayward child, the neighborhood over a rude boy, the city over a reckless youth, the state over a dangerous man, and the nation over the sad havoc of a dark assassin. Who can trace to its ultimate effect that fretful word through all its ramifications to infinite consequences? That word shall reverberate through the halls of eternity when planets are dust and stars are ashes.

Does any one doubt that the infinite results, in the form of modified thought, speech and action, yet to be experienced from the assassination of our late beloved president, are all traceable to the early influences of home?

Who can tell how much of that enormous crime must be shouldered by the parents of Guiteau? But if the ultimate consequence of the assassin's *evil* deed can never be estimated, neither can the *good* deeds of his victim. Truly may it be said of the immortal Garfield,—

> Such life as his can ne'er be lost;
> It blends with unborn blood,
> And through the ceaseless flow of years
> Moves with the mighty flood.
> His life is ours, he lives in us,
> We feel the potent thrill,
> And through the coming centuries
> The world shall feel it still.
>
> The web of human life is wove
> Not with a single strand,
> But every grand and noble man
> Holds one within his hand.
> And in that pulseless hand to-day
> There lies a strand of power,
> Whose gentle draft shall still be felt
> Till time's remotest hour.

Of all human influences those of home are the most far reaching in their results. The mutual influence of brothers and sisters may be almost incalculable. There are many men who owe their honor, their integrity and their manhood to the influence of pure minded sisters. Sisters usually have it in their power to shape the character of their brothers as they choose. There is naturally a pure and holy affection existing between brothers and sisters. It is natural for all brothers to feel and believe that, in some way, their sisters are purer and better than others, and sisters also believe that their brothers are nobler than the brothers of their associates. This sentiment is so universal that we cannot help believing it was ordained for a wise purpose. Of course there is the element of deception in it, but it is one of nature's wise deceptions. She deceives us, or tries to deceive us, when she paints what seems a solid bow upon the canvas of the sky. She deceives the superstitious and ignorant when she flings her chain of molten gold around the dusky shoulders of the night. But these deceptions are not such as to cast any reflections upon her integrity. So we may believe that this sweet deception which makes angels of sisters and heroes of brothers was divinely ordered to unite brothers and sisters in closest communion and to bring them both within the enchanted circle of home influence.

"I shot an arrow in the air,
It fell to earth, I knew not where.
* * * * * * * * * * * *
"I breathed a song into the air,
It fell on earth, I knew not where.
* * * * * * * * * * * *
"Long, long afterwards in an oak
I found the arrow still unbroke;
And the song, from beginning to end,
I found again in the heart of a friend."

BUDS OF PROMISE.

HOME as a natural institution has for its primary object the nurturing of those tender buds of promise which can mature in no other soil. But the human bud, unlike that of the flower, does not contain its future wholly wrapt up within itself, but depends more upon the hand that nurtures it. The rose bud, no matter in what soil it grows, no matter what care it receives, must blossom into a rose. No care or neglect, at least in any definite period of time, can transform it into a noxious weed. But on every mother's bosom there rests a bud of promise, and whether or not that promise shall be fulfilled depends upon her. Whether that bud shall blossom into a pure and fragrant rose or into the flower of the deadly nightshade, is at the option of the guardian. We would not, however, be understood as teaching the doctrine long since abandoned by the investigators of human science, that all are born equal as regards future possibilities. If men had known the subtle laws that govern the development of the human intellect, they perhaps might have traced the lightning's course through the infant brain of

Franklin, and have discerned in the nascent mind of Newton the unlighted lamp whose far-searching beams have since guided the human intellect through the trackless void of the night. And yet, had the guardianship of these minds been different, they might to-day be baleful blood-red stars in the firmament of guilt and sin. Homer, Shakespeare, Milton, Washington, Webster and Longfellow each lay as a little bud of promise on a mother's bosom, and yet that mother knew not that the world was to thunder with applause at the mention of her dear one's name. Knew not?

We will not, however, speak thus positively, for history furnishes much evidence that with the birth of such a bud there comes a hint of its promise; as it were, a letter to its guardian from the Creator.

So close is the relation between mother and child that to the spiritually minded mother there seems to come a premonition of her child's destiny. And yet this fact does not in the least lighten the burden of responsibility that falls on every mother at the birth of her child. Such a premonition, indeed, would always be a safe guide were it always given; but a mother, through lack of susceptibility dependent on temperamental conditions, may hold in her arms unawares, that which the world has a right to claim. Out from among the thrice ten thousand little children that swell the murmur in the school-rooms of the great cities, or with bare and sun-burnt feet patter up the aisles of those dear old school-houses that nestle among the hills and valleys, sacred urns that hold the childish secrets and hallowed memories of a thousand hearts, out from among these shall the angel of destiny select one and place upon his little head the crown of Longfellow and dedicate him to the service of his kind, and make him the sweet interpreter of star and flower.

Mother! shall it be your boy? Do you hear in your soul the gentle whisper? If you do, wherever you may be, may the benediction of humanity rest upon you. May your precious life be spared to watch the opening of that bud of promise. As friends and neighbors assemble to see the unfolding of the night-blooming cereus, so the world shall watch the unfolding of that precious bud.

Let every mother act as if she held a bud of promise. Let those who have not felt the premonition attribute it to their insensibility. Better a thousand times bestow your tenderest care upon an idiot, better believe that you hold the bud of genius and awake to bitter disappointment, than to learn in the end that you have failed to do your duty, and that a genius grand and awful like a fallen temple lies at your feet in the pitiful impotence of manifest but unused power.

But the buds of promise are not confined to the great geniuses. As we said at the beginning of this chapter, every infant is a bud of promise. It is not the Washingtons, the Lincolns, and the Garfields, that shape a nation.

They are the directing forces, like the man who holds the levers and valves of the engine. But, as after all it is the toiling, puffing steam that drags the train, so it is the great delving, toiling, sweating multitude that shapes the character of nations.

It was not her statesmen that made Greece grand. It was the character of the common people. The mightiest statesmen that the world has ever yet produced could not make a grand republic in the South Sea islands. What a nation needs is honest toilers; intelligent and scholarly farmers, cautious, scientific and temperate railroad engineers, learned blacksmiths, and healthy, intelligent and pious wood choppers.

Thus every mother is the guardian of a bud of promise, and whether she will or not must hold herself responsible for the blossom, and let her not hasten to rid herself of that responsibility. That bud will open soon enough. No bud develops so rapidly as a human bud. Let it remain a bud just as long as possible. The rose acquires its perfume while its petals are folded, and the longer it remains a bud, the sweeter will be the blossom.

Again, it is the most rapidly developing bud that soonest fades. Then do not pull apart the tender petals of that bud of promise in order to hasten its unfolding, lest in an hour of sadness you should say:—

"And this is the end of it all:
Of my waiting and my pain—
Only a little funeral pall
And empty arms again."

There can be nothing more destructive to the promises it contains than to attempt to open a rosebud with any other instrument than a sunbeam.

The world is full of the withered buds of human promise that have been too early torn open by the thoughtless hand of parental pride.

The crying sin of American parents is their unwillingness to let their children grow. They wish to transform them all at once from prattling infants into immortal geniuses. They have more faith in art than in Nature, in books and school rooms than in brooks and groves.

Young children should not only be kept from school, but they should be taught at home very sparingly and with the greatest caution in those things which are generally considered as constituting an education. Many suppose that the injury of too early mental training results solely from the confinement within the school room, but this is a great mistake. The injury results chiefly from determining the expenditure of nervous energy through the brain instead of through the muscular system. Your young child must have no thoughts except those which originate in the incoherent activity of his childish freedom.

All others he has at the expense of bone and muscle, lung and stomach, and ultimately at the expense of his whole being. The solution of a mathematical problem is as much a physical task as the lifting of a weight. The passion of the orator and the devotion of the saint are both measured by the potentialities of bread and meat.

So that those who try to fill their little children's minds with "great thoughts" and who teach them to meditate upon the great realities of life, thinking thereby to make them grand and great, are not only defeating their own ends, but are destroying the foundations of future possibility. They are turning to loathsome foulness the sweetest perfume of those buds whose undeveloped petals they are so rudely tearing apart.

The social forces of the present age are such as to render young children peculiarly liable to precocity. Mentality has acquired such an impetus through hereditary influences that the minds of infants early commence that fatal race of thought, which results in the wreck of so many thousands of human bodies. Thoughtfulness in youth, and even in childhood, when the physical system has become strong enough to be aggressive in its relations to the natural forces, cannot be too strongly urged. But infantile thought is not only useless, but is a great evil, and usually involves an irreparable waste of life force.

There are two great evils whose indirect influence upon the world cannot be estimated.

The one is the overfeeding of infants, and the other is the unnatural and abnormal activity of the infant mind; and the one evil enhances the other, for there is nothing that so interferes with digestion in the young child as thought.

Wendell Phillips in speaking of the evils of American precocity, with his characteristic and humorous hyperbole, tells us that the American infant impatiently raising himself in the cradle begins at once to study the structure and uses of the various objects about him, and before he is nine months old has procured a patent for an improvement on some article of the household furniture.

> "Who can tell what a baby thinks?
> Who can follow the gossamer links
> By which the manikin feels his way
> Out from the shores of the great unknown,
> Blind, and wailing, and alone,
> Into the light of day?
> Out from the shore of the unknown sea,
> Tossing in pitiful agony,—
> Of the unknown sea that reels and rolls,
> Specked with the barks of little souls—
> Barks that were launched on the other side,
> And slipped from heaven on an ebbing tide!
> What does he think of his mother's eyes?
> What does he think of his mother's hair?
> What of the cradle-roof that flies
> Forward and backward through the air?
> What does he think of his mother's breast,
> Bare and beautiful, smooth and white,
> Seeking it ever with fresh delight—
> Cup of his life and couch of his rest?"

CHILDHOOD.

ALL animals are born in a somewhat helpless condition, but none so helpless as the human being, hence its necessity for the tenderest care. Throughout all nature it is the function of the mother to exercise a special care over the young. The mere intellectual desire for the child's welfare is not sufficient to insure that degree of attention which it requires; for the most intelligent, and even Christian mothers are sometimes utterly neglectful of their children, while the selfish and narrow minded are frequently very tender in their attentions. Why is this? It is simply because the mother love, or more properly, the parental love, is not the outgrowth of a sense of duty. It is an instinct which we possess in common with the brute. It is a significant fact that throughout the whole animal kingdom the parents possess this instinct just in proportion to the helplessness of the offspring.

The home is a universal institution, and exists among the lower animals the same as with the human. It was, doubtless, designed to meet the necessities arising from the helplessness of offspring. The young lion could not accompany its parents in their search for food, nor could the eaglet soar with its mother into the heavens. Hence the necessity of an instinct that should prompt the lion and the eagle to select and prepare a proper place in which to leave their young while they may attend to the duties imposed by their mode of life. So reason may tell us that it would be far better for us to take good care of our children, and to provide for them a suitable home, but our observation of those in whom the instinct is weak convinces us that mere reason seldom produces this result. While the intellect tells us what we ought to do, it gives no impulse to do it; but instinct gives the impulse, the desire to do, and when the instinct is in a healthy condition we may rely on the intellect of Him who implanted the instinct, for the fitness of the acts to which it prompts us. Indeed, it is a law of our being that reason cannot perform the office of an instinct. It may tell us that we ought to breathe incessantly, but there are few of us who would not forget the duty were it not for the instinctive impulse.

Without the home instinct, the legitimate desire for novelty which all possess would be left unbalanced, and the whole human race would wander from place to place, and the world would become one mighty caravan. Without the instinct of parental love, the child would be held in the same esteem as any other person who should give us the same amount of trouble. And since it is a law of our selfish nature that unless provision is made by special instinct, we cannot love that which gives us only pain, the child's lot on earth would indeed be an unenviable one. But the instinct transforms all the pain and trouble into joy, so that the parents are not only made willing thereby to incur all the troubles and anxieties which their children bring, but are even made to take positive delight in incurring them.

The home instinct and that of parental love are closely allied, and so intimate is their relation that we cannot doubt that they were bestowed with reference to each other. It is true that many other blessings, even the sweetest joys of life, are rooted in the home instinct; but these are all secondary and subsidiary to the one grand end, the home of childhood.

Home is the only place where childhood can develop. It is there only that are to be found those influences which are necessary to fertilize the character of the child and cause it to blossom and bear the fruit of a noble life. Why have nearly all great men had homes illustrious for their beauty, and the purity of their influences? The answer is to be found in the fact that the soil of home contains just those elements required for the growth and development of the child's body, mind and soul.

Notice closely the figure, the face, the features, the voice of that little street waif. Why is his frame so small and shrunken? Why are his features all crowded and pinched? Why do his eye, his walk, his voice and his manner suggest shriveled precocity? For the same reason that an apple which has been early detached from its stem will become early ripe, but never developed. Subject it to whatever treatment we may, it will shrivel up and become insipid, fit symbol of the boy who was early dropped from the home into the street.

The home is the garden where buds become fruit. How important then that the garden be kept free from weeds, while it is enriched with affection and exposed to the sunlight of joy. How slight an influence may serve to blight that opening bud.

The child is as impressible as he is helpless. He is simply the raw material of a character to be fashioned by the silent and imperceptible influence of his surroundings. And it is this which

"Plants the great hereafter in this now."

Silently as the falling of snow-flakes the character of that child is forming. We cannot see the bud unfold, and yet we know that to-morrow it will be a rose. So our perception cannot follow the growth of the child's character, and yet we know that day by day its forces are gathering and that soon he will become to his anxious parents a joy or a sorrow.

Children are much more easily influenced by example than by precept. A child may be told repeatedly that dishonesty is sinful, yet if he detect dishonesty in father, mother, sister or brother, he will imitate the example.

You may as well tell him that sinfulness is dishonest, for he knows no difference. Both terms are meaningless to him.

Most of the thieves, robbers and murderers of the next generation are now little innocent children in the arms of mothers. How should mothers shudder at this thought! The first evidence of passion or of evil intent, the first manifestation of dishonesty, should alarm the mother like the cry of fire in the night.

> "The summer breeze that fans the rose,
> Or eddies down some flowery path,
> Is but the infant gale that blows
> To-morrow with the whirlwind's wrath."

Mothers! you cannot watch the formation of that child's character with too critical an eye. By watching, however, we do not mean that suspicion and doubt which are so fatal to the free open confidence of the child, but that, without which, all your efforts in his behalf will be fruitless. Better a thousand times that the child, even in his tender years, should gaze full upon the hideous face of sin, than that the silken cord of confidence be broken, that binds him to a mother's heart. Liberty is the only atmosphere in which a human soul can grow. Strict literal watching is both unnecessary and injurious. Confidence between mother and child may become so perfect that the child cannot commit a wrong without confessing it. Your watching then should be directed to the maintenance of this confidence, which can be ensured only by putting the child upon his honor, for honor grows only by being exercised. With this confidence between yourself and your child you will at all times be conscious of his moral condition. You will feel in your very heart the first dawnings of evil thought in him. And remember that it is necessary you should know the evil thoughts as soon as they dawn, for the conflagration that scourges with its fury great cities is less dangerous at its onset than the first evil thought in the heart of youth.

> "Crush the first germ ; too late your cares begin
> When long delays have fortified the sin."

But by nature the young child is innocent, and positive influences for evil must be brought to bear upon him before he can become otherwise. With his half divine nature he recoils from the very sight or sound of that which is wrong. Yet he is so imitative and so susceptible that his danger is nevertheless imminent, and the fact that he may more readily imitate the good than the evil should not relax parental vigilance.

Young children and even infants comprehend far more than people generally believe. They cannot express their mental operations by the use of language. Their thoughts are expressed only by their actions, and how vague an idea of the thoughts of the profoundest thinkers should we have if our only clue to them were the mere outward acts of their author. Were actions the only interpreters of human thought, the world would appear to us like a vast insane asylum.

Happiness is the only food on which the child can be fed with profit. Sorrow is sometimes an excellent thing for those whose spiritual digestion is sufficiently strong, but children never should be fed on this diet. Sorrow ripens, but joy develops a soul. But let us not entertain that foolish and cruel notion so prevalent, that hard knocks, disappointment, constant work and little recreation are necessary to develop the character of a child. Some one has given the following beautiful piece of advice to mothers: "Always send your little child to bed happy. Whatever cares may trouble your mind, give the dear child a warm good-night kiss as it goes to its pillow. The memory of this in the stormy years which may be in store for the little one will be like Bethlehem's star to the bewildered shepherds, and welling up in the heart will rise the thought, "my father, my mother loved me!" Lips parched with fever will become dewy again at this thrill of useful memories. Kiss your little child before it goes to sleep."

"Ah! what would the world be to us
 If the children were no more?
We should dread the desert behind us
 Worse than the dark before.

"What the leaves are to the forest,
 With light and air for food,
Ere their sweet and tender juices
 Have been hardened into wood,—

"That to the world are children;
 Through them it feels the glow
Of a brighter and sunnier climate
 Than reaches the trunks below."

HOME TRAINING.

THE training of the child necessarily begins with the body, for the young child must be regarded chiefly as a young animal. The animal is the first to be developed, and in every well born and healthy child the manifestations of animality will precede those of intellectuality. One has said, "If you would make your child a good man, first make him a great animal." The child's prospects of future greatness are measured in part by his stomach and lungs.

The most important period of a child's training, then, is that period during which he is an animal. Nature's method seems to be to form first a powerful physical system, and then on this as a foundation to rear the intellectual and the moral. If the physical is diseased the mental cannot be healthy. The most important element in a great man is a great body, great in health, in vital stamina, and in its capacity to become the foundation for the mind.

In view of these facts it becomes of paramount impor tance that the mother have a knowledge of physiology.

No woman has any moral right to bear the honored name of mother till she possesses such knowledge. We would not place a delicate machine in the hands of one who was ignorant of its structure. Not that the mother should be a physician, for she generally practices medicine too much. It is as important that she should know how to let her child alone, as to know how to take care of him. It is not necessary that she should know just what to do for him when he is sick. It is much better for her to know what not to do for him. It is the doctor's duty to cure him when he is sick, but it is the mother's duty never to give the doctor an opportunity to display his skill in this direction. Let every mother remember this fact, that the cry of a sick child is the tell-tale that convicts her of sin. A child never cries unless its mother has wronged it. A healthy child is always angelic. No parent has any business with any but a healthy child, for wholesome food in proper quantities never deranged a stomach. Pure air never diseased a lung. A human eye was never blinded by the diffused sunlight. Teeth never decayed through grinding pure and wholesome food.

No child, unless his appetite has been pampered by a foolish mother, will ever crave that which it is necessary to withhold from him. Nor will his appetite ever require to be urged. No rational person will contend that reason should usurp the place of instinct in the matter of eating and drinking. Those delicate conditions of the system in which it accepts or rejects nourishment are entirely beyond the ken of reason. Through the whole animal kingdom, including man, there is an instinct which tells its possessor just what kind of food and how much its system requires. No tests of science could determine this. Tyndall may exhaust all his resources in trying to determine whether or not a given robin has eaten enough to meet the requirements of its physical nature. At his best he can only estimate it, but the robin knows exactly.

We have known a mother to urge her little baby to sip from her own cup of tea, and have seen her appear quite grieved because the little creature with pure mind and pure body instinctively rejected the proffered beverage of sinful men. And after being defeated in her attempt to poison and vitiate his taste, she would exclaim, "I fear my child is going to be eccentric." Some mothers are almost terrified at seeing their child eat a piece of bread without butter, although writers on hygiene, whose books are within the reach of all mothers, are agreed that butter is one of the abominations of civilization. It is not our intention to write on the subject of health or diet, but so long as butter, spices and other unnecessaries are admitted to be evils, it seems unpardonably foolish, not to say wicked, to urge the young child to use them, especially since he does not desire them, and shows by his actions that he would much prefer not to have his food polluted with such stuff. Let the mother refrain from pampering her child's appetite, or else be willing to take the consequences when that same appetite, diseased and perverted by her own hand, shall bring him home reeling and staggering to her frantic arms. That mighty army of one hundred thousand who are annually marching down to drunkards' graves were, for the most part, we believe, trained for that awful march by mothers.

It is admitted by all that alcohol is repugnant to the unvitiated taste of man or beast. No child with instincts pure from the hand of God will taste of alcohol. It is not until his appetite has been depraved by Mrs. Winslow's Soothing Syrups and other abominations. All these must first be forced down his throat by the stern exercise of parental authority before he learns to tolerate alcohol in any form. The child's instinct is God's argument and it is unanswerable. If it be true then that a healthy instinct rejects alcohol, how shall we account for the almost universal appetite for it? There can be but one explanation, some almost universal depraving agency; and what can this be but the wrong physical training to which mothers subject their offspring.

The problem of home training to-day covers the problem of intemperance. So long as children are growing up with a taste for the nostrums with which babies are universally poisoned the world will be full of drunkards.

But it is not alone the poisonous nostrums which deprave the appetite. The cookies, candies, sweetmeats and the thousand products of human depravity and a luxurious civilization conspire to destroy that pure instinct which God designed to be a perfect guide as regards the quantity and quality of our food. We do not understand how Christian mothers can consistently express their faith in God while their acts show that they distrust the wisdom which gave the child this instinct.

The little child is fed on flesh, pickles and highly seasoned food till he becomes sick; then of course he cries. That breaks the mother's heart and she gives him a cooky to stop his crying before he goes to bed. She cannot bear the idea of her child going to bed hungry. The cooky may give him the colic, but what of it so long as he is not hungry! She cannot tell whether he has the colic or the headache, but if he cries he must have some medicine. It is of but little consequence what it is so long as it is medicine. We have actually heard mothers when questioned as to why they gave their babies a certain kind of medicine, answer that they "wished to give them something and didn't know what else to give them." We presume it never occurred to them to give the baby the benefit of the doubt.

The disposition depends upon the condition of the stomach. If that be sour, the disposition will be sour also. Many a good child has had his disposition spoiled with cake and candy. A tendency to all forms of depravity may result from a diseased condition of the digestion.

Every form of sin may originate with the stomach. Almost all of the suicides result from the mental disease of melancholy. This disease is known by all physicians to be the direct result of an affection of the liver, and the liver and stomach are so related that the one cannot be affected without the other. Hence a wrong physical training of a child may lead to suicide.

The habit of dwelling perpetually on the dark side of life, as the melancholy person does, results in the perversion and depravity of the whole mind. Thus every sin may originate in the stomach.

There are mothers who would regard the withholding of sweetmeats from their children as cruelty. It is hard to believe that such persons exist, but observation forces the fact upon us. Such mothers, of course, can appreciate no higher enjoyment than that of eating and drinking, and they feel perfectly contented so long as their children are eating something that tastes good. They never stop to question whether the physical pleasure which a piece of highly spiced mince pie yields their child can compensate for the physical, intellectual and moral depravity that may result from it. The mother who gives her child candy, cakes, etc., simply for the pleasure of the child, without regard to their effect on his health, whatever may be the character of her outward life, is in spirit a sensualist.

It is customary for mothers when their children get angry and scream, to give them something that tastes good to eat. Now this is a two-fold evil. It is both a physical and moral evil. It is a physical evil because it tends directly to produce dyspepsia. The human stomach cannot perform its functions properly while the mind is angry. The adage, "Laugh and grow fat," is founded in true philosophy. In order for digestion to be performed in the most perfect manner there must be at the time of eating a sense of peace and joy pervading the mind, making the very consciousness of existence delightful. All have observed that the dyspeptic men are those who are fretful and cross at the table. The tea is too cold; the coffee is too weak; the steak is cooked too much or not enough; the potatoes should have been baked instead of boiled; there is too much saleratus in the biscuit; or there is some trouble with something—enough to cast a shadow over the whole meal and cause the whole family to sit in gloomy silence.

This is not so much because dyspepsia tends to make people cross at their meals, but because being cross at meals makes them dyspeptics. Many men have become incurably diseased by eating when they were angry, and the mother who gives her child a cooky to stop his crying is laying for him the foundation of a life of suffering.

Again, such a practice is morally wrong because it rewards a child for being angry. In this way he learns, whenever he wishes anything, to scream and cry until his wish is gratified. He soon acquires such a habit that he does this even though no one be near to grant the wish.

This is his first lesson in rebellion against an unseen power. As he grows older the screaming is changed into cursing, and thus originates the habit of profanity. Men swear chiefly because their mothers gave them cookies to stop their crying. When mothers learn the secret of home training, all the vices that now curse the world will die out for want of soil in which to grow.

All children are overfed. There is no danger that any child will starve so long as its mother loves it, but there is great danger that it will be fed to death.

But, says the mother, how shall I avoid these evils? How shall I keep my child's appetite healthy? And when he screams and will not be satisfied with anything but a peppermint, what shall I do? These are honest questions. No mother willfully injures her child by knowingly depraving his appetites and thereby all his passions. It is, of course, through ignorance and not malice.

The remedy is the most easy and natural thing in the world. Simply let the child alone; that is all. Children have a divinely given right to be let alone, but this right has never been granted by man. Your child will keep his own appetite healthy if you will let him. When he screams for that which it is not lawful for him to have, the treatment is very simple, let him scream. The human mind acts from motives and never without them. The child screams either to make you yield to him, or from a feeling of revenge because you do not yield.

Now the only way to prevent a mental act is to take away the motives which prompt to the act. Hence the way to break a child of the vice of screaming is to remove these two motives. The first you can remove by showing him that your word is law. When you have commanded him to do or refrain from doing a certain thing, make him understand that you will not revoke your order and that further pleading will be in vain.

The second motive, that of revenge, may be removed by proving to him that it "doesn't work." Show by your indifference that his loud crying does not give you the least inconvenience. You can accompany the music with the humming of a careless tune. He will see by this that his scheme of vengeance is defeated, and there will be nothing left for him to do but to stop crying and amuse himself as best he can. If it is time to put your little child to bed, do not coax him to go and then be conquered by coaxing in return. Do not be conquered at all. In the first place, you should not tell him to go to bed till you know that it is time for him to go, and not till you are determined he shall go. It is not necessary that you be arbitrary. There is no objection to arguing with him, if your command at the time is not fully understood by him. Try to convince him that he ought to do as you tell him. In every instance the import of the word *ought* should be kept before his mind. But if he still resists, use the argument of force, paying no attention to his cries and screams.

We do not write thus coldly and unfeelingly from any lack of love for little children. There is nothing in the wide realm of being so lovely and pathetic as a young child. There is no eloquence that can equal its prattle. No mother can love her child too much. It is not the intensity of the mother's love that we would condemn, but the unwise and injudicious direction of that love. And when we say the child should be let alone, we do not mean that he should be coldly neglected, but simply that he should be allowed to grow and develop in the soil of his own childish freedom; that his body should be left chiefly to the care of its own instinct, while the mother watches the process with delight. Mothers usually make much harder work taking care of their children than the necessities of the case require. Most mothers may learn a valuable lesson from the cat. See how she takes care of her kittens. She does not doctor them; she manifests no anxiety for their physical welfare. She simply watches the kitten's growth, and doesn't assume any higher prerogative. She brings a mouse and lays it before the little savage, but she does not urge the case in the least. If the kitten does not want it, she does not say, "I'm afraid my little darling is going to be sick. Can't he eat it anyway? Please eat it for mamma." O no, she just eats it herself, and does not seem to have the least fear that nature will forget to bring back her child's appetite. Nor does she seem to resent the kitten's refusal to accept her offer, but the next mouse is usually eaten with a relish. Thus the cat is wiser than the human mother, for she is wise enough to entrust to nature those things which she herself is not wise enough to do. The world has yet to learn that the little children are its physical and spiritual teachers. When Christ would name the greatest in the kingdom of Heaven he said, "Who so humbleth himself as this little child, the same is greatest in the kingdom of Heaven," thus making it a kingdom of little children. There was philosophy in that beautiful reply of Christ. All sin consists simply in the acts that are prompted by instincts which have been depraved. Children's instincts are least depraved, for they are nearest to the source of all purity. Hence the child's heart must always be the truest symbol of Heaven.

We do not belong to that school whose motto is "spare the rod and spoil the child." We believe that untold evil has resulted to the world from that false philosophy, and we are glad to know that the world is rapidly discarding it. To say nothing of the morality, or rather immorality, of the doctrine, it is entirely unnecessary. How foolish to break the sweet spell of confidence by beating and striking, when the little heart can be melted in penitential grief by a word! Why use sticks and clubs when the child does not fear them half so much as he does his mother's grief! Hyenas snarl and *growl* and strike, and some mothers snarl and *scold* and strike. Isn't the analogy almost humiliating?

But this method of treatment does not accomplish the desired result. Whipping a child does not and cannot produce any desirable internal change of character. It may modify the outward acts. It may also produce an internal change, but only for the worse; only that change which comes from perpetually harboring a feeling of hatred and revenge. A blow struck upon unregenerate humanity can awaken but one feeling, and that is the feeling of resentment. The child always resents a blow, whether it comes from his parent or from a playmate. He cannot easily be made to acknowledge in his heart that the punishment is just; and while he believes that it is unjust he will feel rebellious, and no one will contend that a rebellious feeling can do much toward elevating the character. The feelings of anger, hatred and physical fear are among those which we have in common with the brutes, and while we are under the dominion of these feelings we cannot rise much above the brute. All know how utterly depraving anger is to the whole mind, and the effect of physical fear is nearly as bad. Some who have been thought noble have been known when brought face to face with death upon the ocean, to rudely snatch a life-preserver from a helpless woman; thus showing how physical fear may paralyze the sense of honor and every other noble sentiment of the soul. Now what is true of the man under the influence of an intense fear is also true of the child under the influence of a less intense fear. It is the nature of fear, whether great or small, to repress all that is God-like and arouse all that is demoniac. You cannot inflict corporal punishment on a child without filling his little heart with fear. It is a well known fact that under a cruel and tyrannical teacher the pupils rapidly become vicious and untrustworthy. This is simply because of the moral repression resulting from constant fear. Then do not frighten the children. Every argument that can be deduced from the wide range of human nature forbids us to inflict corporal punishment on children.

"But," says the disciple of the rod, "the child can be made to acknowledge the justice of the punishment, and ought not to be punished until he does acknowledge it. By the proper argument he may be made to feel that he deserves to be punished." Very well; then he does n't need to be punished. The object of punishment of course is to induce penitence, and if the child becomes penitent before the punishment, he certainly does n't need to be punished. Who would punish a child after he had acknowledged that he ought to be? Think of the mother who could whip her child after he had laid his head sobbing on her bosom and said, "Mamma, I ought to be whipped!" And yet, according to the admission of even the Solomon school, he should be willing to say this before he ought to be whipped. He must be made penitent before the punishment can have any but an evil effect.

The whole truth is expressed in these two facts. First,

we ought not to punish a child till he sees and acknowledges the justice of the punishment; and second, when he sees and acknowledges the justice of the punishment, he does n't need it. Thus the doctrine of the rod is crowded out entirely. There are no circumstances under which it is proper to use it.

The object of all training is to develop character, and not merely to secure outward obedience. A child may be a model of obedience, and yet with every duty which he outwardly performs he may mingle an unuttered curse.

With a horse or dog the prime object is to secure outward obedience. We care but little about the moral character or the spiritual destiny of our horse, so long as he obeys the whip and stops when we say "whoa!" But what parent could say this of a child! The true mother cares less for the outward act than for the inward. It is not so much her object to make the child obey her commands as it is to make him obey the commands of his own conscience and the spur of duty. If the child is internally obedient to his own conscience, he will develop a noble character even though he should disobey every parental command.

Let every parent remember that there may be a vast difference between outward and inward obedience, and that either may exist without the other. The child may not cherish any feelings of hatred toward his parents, nor have any definite sense of rebellion, yet if he obeys simply because he fears to disobey, while he cannot feel that the command is just, he experiences, only in a less degree, all those evil results that come from harboring the sentiments of hatred and revenge. This obedience is outward and not inward.

But how shall the stubborn boy be trained who seems incapable of responding to any other appeal than that of the rod? Let us suppose a case, the most difficult that we can conceive, and see if there are any points where our doctrine would fail in practice. Suppose a mother requests her boy to go to a neighbor's house on an errand. The boy wishes to play ball and stubbornly refuses to go. What shall that mother do? "Give him a good sound thrashing," the Puritan mother would say. But even if she can do it now, she will certainly lack the physical power in a short time, and then what shall she do? "Turn him over to his father," some one may say. A year or two more will place him beyond the authority of his father, then what is to be done? Here the resources of the "rod" school become exhausted. He has defied the authority of force, and has triumphed. The rod system, like some systems of medicine, works well in those cases which need no doctoring. As a rule the rod arouses the very passion which led to the commission of the offense, the very one we wish to allay. The secret of governing a child is to soothe those faculties whose unrestrained action gave rise to the offense, and at the same time to call into action the restraining faculties, those which would have prevented the commission of the offense had they acted at the time. One of the principal restraining faculties is conscience, or the sense of obligation. Now all are supposed to possess this faculty in some degree. Those who do not, are morally deformed; they are monstrosities, and their treatment involves something more than the subject of "home training." We are not giving directions for the management of the insane, nor the morally idiotic, but for the management, training and development of those who are fit to be entrusted with their own freedom, those who are free agents and who are capable of becoming men and women.

Now let us see how this doctrine will work with the stubborn boy we have just supposed. He of course is under the influence of anger, the very passion which the mother would excite still more if she were to attempt to punish him. Hence she must cool this passion by arousing the sense of obligation. Let her appeal to his honor. He has honor, but it is suppressed for the time by anger. He loves his mother unless he is a fit subject for the penitentiary, and in that case he does not come within the jurisdiction of any system of home training. A system must be devised expressly for him. Perhaps it may be advisable for her to do the thing herself which she has commanded the boy to do, or perhaps it may be well to call his sister and send her on the errand, with the understanding that it is not just for her to be compelled to do it. When he remembers that his little sister has performed a duty that was not hers but his, he will feel a little uncomfortable in the region of conscience. He should be reminded, perhaps, during the evening, that he is under moral obligation to another who has performed a duty that he refused to perform. It should be talked of for a long time, and his conscience should not be allowed to rest till he has paid the moral debt. No precise rule can be given as to the way in which his conscience should be appealed to in every instance. Circumstances may vary so that any attempt at this would be impracticable. The mother should be so well acquainted with the nature of the child as to be able to appeal to any sentiment at will, under any and every varying circumstance.

Some may object to this because it defers obedience too long. But a disobedient, ungrateful and stubborn boy should be regarded by parents as a misfortune, and they should be happy if they succeed in securing obedience at all, even if it requires days to secure obedience to a single command. But if this method is practiced with the child from his infancy, he will not become a disobedient and stubborn boy. We have supposed an extreme case in order to anticipate and fortify ourselves against the argument arising from such cases.

But we are well aware that many a good old mother who has wielded the rod for thirty years, will, in her just egotism, point to her noble sons and daughters as a triumphant refutation of these views which she will be pleased to call trash. Nor would we disregard the well-earned practical knowledge of these grand women. Their egotism is pardonable. Yet we shall modestly claim that they are liable to be mistaken in some of their views of life, and when they oppose our doctrine and style it theory, we shall reply that the doctrine of moral accountability is a theory, but it is one that appeals so strongly to the common sense and intuition of mankind as to be independent of the argument of actual experience.

We would not contend that injudicious training is sure to spoil a child, neither will the wisest training always serve to develop a noble character. The children of noble mothers will sometimes be noble in spite of wrong training. Men have developed powerful lungs who through their whole lives have breathed hardly a breath of pure air. Men have had strong digestion who have abused their stomachs, and intemperate men have died of old age. But these are the exceptions and not the rule. For one who desires to live a long life it would not be safe to be intemperate simply because a few have lived to be old in spite of intemperance. Neither is it safe to follow a wrong system of training because some mothers of the rod persuasion have reared a family of noble children. Such mothers transmit to their children healthy bodies and sound minds and good morals, and they would have developed into noble men and women under almost any system of training. Besides, the occasions for punishing such children occur at intervals so rare that little injury can result.

In the training of the child, physical culture should precede all other kinds; next should follow the training of the affections. He should be taught to love only the good and to hate all that is bad. After this the intellect should be trained. Not however by sending him to school to sit all day on a hard seat where his feet cannot touch the floor, and where he learns to say "A." Little children are usually sent to school when they should be romping through the woods and pastures. Of course we do not condemn the common school system, yet there are many features of it which tend greatly to neutralize the good. It were infinitely better for the race to live in barbaric ignorance with sound and healthy bodies, than in the grandest civilization with bodily weakness and physical impotency; for a barbaric race may become civilized, but a race of physical weaklings is doomed to extinction. And it cannot be denied that the common schools, especially in the city, are rapidly sapping the physical stamina of the civilized world, and this is especially true in hot-headed America.

Children should be educated at home by the parents; at least till they are well developed physically. It is safe to send a boy to school when he has become so strong physically that no teacher can suppress his buoyancy and make a man of him.

Studiousness on the part of young boys and girls should be regarded by parents as a more dangerous symptom than hemorrhage of the lungs. Indeed, these are often symptoms of the same disease.

There are many and strong arguments for educating children at home. In the first place, the mother is the natural teacher of the child. The eagle does not send her little ones to school to learn to fly, nor does she employ a governess, but chooses to perform the duty herself. The spiritual sympathy between mother and child enables the mother to minister to the individual wants of the child as no other teacher can. There are locked chambers in every human soul, but in the child's there are none to which the mother does not hold the key.

The public school tends to destroy the individuality of the pupil, to crush out all his originality and force his mind, whatever may be its natural tendency, into the common channel. Civilization tends directly toward physical and mental diversity, and individual peculiarities, but the public school does not recognize this fact.

Low down in the scale of life we notice but little diversity. A flock of birds seem all alike. We cannot detect any difference between two foxes of the same age and sex, but dogs and horses differ, because for ages they have been under the modifying influences of man until their condition corresponds to that of the civilization of man. In the early ages men differed from one another far less than they do at present. Civilization and a tendency to diversity are so closely dependent on common causes that whatever hinders the one hinders also the other. Of course we would not contend that the common schools retard civilization, although in this respect they certainly have a tendency to retard it.

In the public schools all are compelled to take the same course, regardless of their individual peculiarities of talent. If a pupil is by nature poorly endowed with the mathematical talent, he must go through just as fast but no slower than the others. The explanations that suffice for those who are mathematically inclined must suffice for him also. No provision is made for taste or talent.

But this is not the case when the children are educated at home. Every peculiarity of talent may be provided for. Then there is a great source of pleasure in the education of one's own children. It tends to perpetuate the authority which parents ought to have over their children. If the child has been educated by his parent he will never cease to have the highest respect for that parent. This is a strong reason why parents should educate themselves and keep pace with their children in all their studies; for although dutiful children will always respect their parents however ignorant they may be, yet intelligent parents, those capable of instructing their children, will be respected still more. Then, if for no other reason, the children should be educated at home, to maintain the authority of the parent and the respect of the child.

Let the mothers of our country, as far as possible, pattern after that mother who not only trained the bodies of her boys and made them physical heroes, but trained their affections and made them moral heroes. Nor, indeed, did her care cease here! She has trained them intellectually, fitted them for college, and sent them forth to meet on life's arena those intellectual heroes who have been trained at the hands of honored masters.

Men shall feel in this a beauty and a pathos to the end of time, whenever the historian shall turn for a moment from the crimson pictures of national strife to narrate the simple story. Can those boys ever cease to respect that mother? Can they ever cease to reverence her very name?

Perhaps it is not generally known that we worship God with the same faculty with which we honor our parents. Now the children of such mothers as we have considered must feel perpetually a sense of honor and parental reverence. This strengthens and develops the faculty with which God is worshiped. Hence we see why the children of such parents are usually religious. The unwritten life of one such woman is a stronger argument than all the silver irony of prostituted genius.

There are, of course, but few mothers or fathers who can fit their boys or girls for college, and this is not necessary in order to apply the doctrine we have advocated. There are but few boys and girls who go to college. Nor is it necessary to keep the children home from school. The mother can superintend the education of a child even while he is in school. The teacher's function should be something more than merely listening to the recitation of the pupil. But this is nearly all that the average teacher does. Hence the mother has a wide field even while her child is in the public school.

There seems to be a growing tendency on the part of mothers to entrust the training of their children to the hands of hired nurses. This is a great error. In the first place, its breaks the current of divine magnetism between mother and child which ought to make the mental pulses of both beat in unison. Again, it has a tendency to diminish filial reverence in the child. By separating him from his mother at that tender age in which the links of the eternal chain should be forged, we render it almost impossible for him to love her as he ought. This is not to be wondered at, for the modern fashionable mother sees her child only as a visitor would see it. The child must be dressed up as if to entertain strangers, and when he begins to cry he is carried away at once by the nurse, while the mother makes another appointment. Perhaps one of the most striking manifestations of God's mercy to the race is seen in the fact that comparatively few offspring are born of such women—if the license of literature will permit us to use the word woman in this connection. Better a thousand times that the world should be populated from the slums than from such sources.

> "The mother in her office holds the key
> Of the soul; and she it is who stamps the coin
> Of character, and makes the being who would be a savage
> But for her gentle care, a Christian man."

REWARDS AND PUNISHMENTS.

THE rewards and punishments of home should be analogous to those, if not identical with them, which God has already instituted as natural rewards and punishments. There should be little or nothing artificial in the rewards or punishments of home.

If a child is bribed to do his duty by some promise of reward, he is likely to acquire the fatal habit of performing virtuous acts from low motives. The approval of conscience is the natural reward for the performance of one's duty. If an artificial reward is substituted for this, the motive is transferred from conscience to some selfish faculty, and the whole moral character becomes depraved. Hence no reward should ever be given for the mere performance of duty when it is clear to the child that it is his duty. In some cases where the desired act seems to be an act of self-sacrifice on the part of the child, and one which he does not understand to be particularly his duty, it is perfectly right and often wise to offer rewards. But if he is hired to do those things which his own conscience plainly tells him he ought to do, he will learn to act in such cases from the motive of the reward, and not from that of conscience. But during this time conscience must lie idle for want of something to do, and God never lets a talent lie in a napkin without depreciating. Although conscience might have prompted him to the same act, yet if it be not the determining motive he cannot experience the approval of conscience. Conscience deals with motives, not with acts, and, like every other function of our being, grows by exercise. The food of conscience is its own approval, and in order to secure its approval it must afford the ruling motive.

Whenever a reward is offered, an appeal should not be made at the same time to the sense of duty. It should pass simply as a trade, and the child should not be reminded that there is any right or wrong about it. These are the only circumstances under which it is proper to offer a reward to a child.

We would not have it understood, however, that rewards should be given only for those acts which conscience cannot approve. Such acts, of course, should never be required nor performed at all. Rewards should be offered only for good deeds, those which the conscience of the child, if it were to act at all, would approve. All we mean is simply that a base reward should never be made to supplement conscience in such a way as to become the ruling motive. If it be found that conscience is acting at all, do not offer a reward to complete the motive and make it strong enough to rule his act, but try to stimulate conscience to a still higher degree of action, until its motive becomes sufficient of itself to produce the desired result.

As a rule the reward when given should appeal to the mental rather than the physical. It should be something which has a tendency to stimulate the thinking or inventive powers rather than something which merely satisfies a physical want. It is generally better to give a book than a drum, although there are far meaner rewards than a drum. Candy and sweetmeats should never under any circumstances be offered. That which is unfit for an adult is surely unfit to constitute a reward for a child. It is a fact that the world makes its greatest efforts in response to the demands of sensual gratification. Is it unreasonable to suppose that the foundation of this evil is laid in childhood through the pernicious practice of rewarding children with sweetmeats?

A toy steam engine or some machine which will stimulate the constructive or inventive faculty is, perhaps, the most appropriate present which can be given to a boy.

There are circumstances, however, under which it would be improper to give such gifts. In case the child is already too much inclined to mental activity, no present should be given which will farther stimulate the intellect.

At the present time there are many cases of this kind, especially in the cities. For such precocious children a cart or sled or a pair of skates would be a far more appropriate gift than a book or even a steam engine.

But the worst and most injurious practice connected with the subject of rewards and punishments is that of bribing children with promises that are never meant to be fulfilled. It happens in many cases that this is the child's first lesson in falsehood. All promises made to children should be conscientiously fulfilled, for the whole life and character of the child may be changed by a single repudiated promise. Let no parent assume the fearful responsibility of giving his child the first lesson in dishonesty.

The punishments of home should be, as far as possible, natural. They should consist chiefly if not wholly in pointing out and making a direct application of the same kind of punishment which nature herself inflicts for the same offense.

For instance, the natural punishment which Nature has appended to the sin of falsehood is the suspicion and distrust of our fellow men. Hence when a child tells a falsehood, he should be made to feel that he has done that for which he deserves the suspicion of the whole family. All eyes should be turned upon him with a pitying distrust.

Nature's punishment for selfishness is a withdrawal of the sympathy and love of society, and in addition thereto the defeat of its own ends. Selfishness is always defeated in the end. Hence when a child has encroached upon the rights of his brothers or sisters through selfishness, the sympathy of the family should be withdrawn, while at the same time he should be prevented from reaping the benefit which he anticipated from his selfish act. The other children should be made to feel that he is actually unworthy of their society. In certain cases, perhaps, he should be banished from the society of the family and even shut up in his room, as a severer punishment and as a more direct and literal application of that principle which is involved in the banishment to which society always dooms the selfish man. God has made society on such a plan that it cannot tolerate selfishness. He has also arranged our nature so that the very best thing for the selfish man is to have society shun him. It is the medicine that will cure him if he is curable.

Now is it not safe to follow God's method in punishing the child for selfishness at home? Who will come so near to challenging the wisdom of God as to style this "idle theory"? If the child be defeated in his selfish purpose by the parent, and he is banished for an hour or a day, as the case may be, from the sympathy of the family, he will come to feel by no process of logic, perhaps, but by the force of habit and association, that such conduct on the part of others is the necessary and inevitable accompaniment of his selfishness, that it is founded in the everlasting relations of his social nature. When he becomes a man he will receive the same kind of punishment from society if he still persists in his selfishness. He will then perceive that the punishment is rational and inevitable, and that the relation between it and the offense is constant and necessary. If any other method is pursued the child will in the course of his life be subjected to two kinds of punishment for the same offense, one an arbitrary and the other a natural one. The human mind is unable to perceive any necessary relation between the crime of selfishness and the pain inflicted by an angry parent with a birch stick. There is no logical relation between them, and as a natural consequence the child rebels, at least spiritually, and hence is made more selfish than before. He will be more and more selfish as he grows older, and when he comes to receive the natural punishment from society for his sin, he will rebel against that from the mere force of habit. He will come to hate society. He will be cold and cynical. He will come to entertain a morbid sentiment of ill will toward society, and, spurred on by the feeling that the world owes him a debt, he may be led to commit some dark and dreadful crime against his fellowmen. It is not impossible that a large per cent. of the pirates, robbers, and murderers are such because of the unwise and illogical relation between the offenses and punishments of their childhood.

One has truthfully said, "Caprice or violence in correcting will go far to justify the transgressor in his own eyes at least; he will consider every appearance of injustice as a vindication of his own aggression." Who has not seen a confirmation of this among school boys? Often a boy is whipped by a teacher when if properly managed he would willingly express his sorrow for the offense. But after the whipping he goes sullenly to his seat muttering to himself, "I'm glad I did it." He is glad he did it because he feels that his teacher has wronged him, and that in a certain sense the offense which he himself has committed makes them even. Human beings, and especially children, when under the influence of anger, are not very reasonable, and are not inclined to take very impartial views of subjects.

But it may be said that he ought to look at it differently; that he has no right to look at it so partially; that the case is plain if he will look at it rightly. Very well, but if he doesn't look at it rightly, the facts of the case are of no benefit to him, and he receives all the injurious results to his moral nature that he would receive if the facts were on the other side of the case.

There is no possible human act that is not right or wrong; if right it is self rewarding, and if wrong it is self-punishing. It is the function of human authority to teach the transgressor wherein his transgressions punish themselves.

"A picture memory brings to me:
I look across the years and see
Myself beside my mother's knee.

"I feel her gentle hand restrain
My selfish moods, and know again
A child's blind sense of wrong and pain.

"But wiser now, a man gray grown,
My childhood's needs are better known,
My mother's chastening love I own.

"Gray grown, but in our Father's sight
A child still groping for the light
To read his works and ways aright.

"I bow myself beneath his hand;
That pain itself for good was planned,
I trust, but cannot understand.

"I fondly dream it needs must be,
That as my mother dealt with me,
So with his children dealeth he.

"I wait, and trust the end will prove
That here and there, below, above,
The chastening heals, the pain is love!"

THE FIRST BOTANY LESSON

THE FIRST LESSON.

AMUSEMENTS FOR THE HOME.

THE human mind demands amusement. One of its constituent elements is a love of fun. No innate demand of the mind can be denied without injury. Amusement and fun are as essential to the growth and development of the young mind as sleep, or any form of exercise. Hence we have no sympathy with that system of home government which suppresses this element in the children. Such systems are suicidal, and one can hardly help doubting the genuineness of that religion that imposes perpetual melancholy as one of its tenets. It has been said that Christ never was known to laugh but often to weep, and if he foresaw the existence of that creed that suppresses laughter as one of the cardinal vices, it is no wonder that he never laughed. But there is no evidence that he did not laugh. The character of his mission was such as to render any record of his lighter moments entirely out of place. It is, however, a well known fact that Christ was of a thoughtful, serious cast of mind, and even if it could be proved that he never laughed, the fact would have no weight as an argument against laughter among us. We are not expected nor required to follow his example in all things, for this would be impossible. Marriage is a divine institution and imposes obligations upon us from which Christ by virtue of his nature and work was exempted.

Were it not for the superstitious folly of so many people, what we have said on this phase of the subject would be entirely superfluous. Probably but few Christian people at the present day would openly acknowledge that they have conscientious scruples against laughter, yet there are thousands of stern fathers who virtually suppress all laughter in their homes, as a religious duty. They would not acknowledge to themselves even that they believe laughter to be wrong in the abstract, and yet somehow or other they manage to resolve every occasion for laughter into something that ought to be suppressed.

It is the duty of the parents to make home pleasant and agreeable, and even to furnish occasions for merriment and fun, as much as it is to furnish food and shelter. Children should not be required to remain quiet and sedate during the long evenings simply because the stern father wishes to read the newspaper. If he wishes to read aloud something that would be interesting to the children, it is proper to do so. All parents should consider themselves under obligations to furnish at least one paper or magazine expressly for the children. Not one of the ponderous and somber journals of Zion, but one full of light jokes, interesting stories, and such information as children desire and can appreciate. Of course the father and mother are to be allowed time to read their religious and political papers, and their scientific books; but the children's right in this respect must not be encroached upon. It will not hurt the father or mother to read aloud from the "Youth's Companion" or some other paper of similar character, or, perhaps, what is better still, they can lay aside their own paper and listen and be interested while one of the older children is reading.

Reading aloud by parents and children is one of the most useful sources of amusement in every home. In addition to the amusement, valuable information would be obtained, also healthful vocal exercise and elocutionary drill.

Another source of amusement, peculiarly appropriate for the home, and one of which we never tire, is music. The money spent for a musical instrument is not thrown away. Every home should contain some such instrument, and there are but few families that cannot afford a piano or an organ. There is something in the nature of music that tends to evolve harmony in the hearts of those who jointly produce it or listen to it. There is something of philosophy in the oft quoted words of Shakespeare:

"The man that hath no music in himself,
Nor is not moved by concord of sweet sounds,
Is fit for treasons, stratagems, and spoils."

It is probable, however, that the author used this word music in the broadest sense of poesy, yet even in its restricted sense there is the semblance of truth. The world presents us with many examples of grand and noble souls that are deaf to the pleadings of the harp, and yet the fact remains untouched that music is the language of the highest souls. Eloquence holds a wand for the soul's lofty moods, and yet there is an altitude in whose rarefied atmosphere the soul is dumb, and in the frenzy of despair seizes the harp and the viol. From these spiritual beatitudes on whose hushed summits the veil is rolled back, there comes no message save in wordless strains.

We cannot stand beside a friend in the presence of music without feeling the ties grow stronger. The spirit's invisible arms clasp each other. Neither can we stand beside an enemy without feeling the timbers of hatred that have braced our souls apart, give way, and before we are aware our spirit proclaims him friend.

How peculiarly appropriate, then, as a home amusement, is music. As well might you drive love from home as to exclude music. Let the boys learn to play the violin; and let the girls play the organ or piano. Let the home be a perpetual temple of song.

A silent home, where there is no music nor reading and but little conversation, is a dull and sad place for the young. Children do not like to stay long in those places where their only entertainment is their own thoughts.

There is nothing worse for a child than subjective thinking, thinking of his own thoughts. It leads to habitual melancholy, and this state is so thoroughly unnatural for a child that it cannot exist without enfeebling both mind and body. Those who commit suicide will be found in almost every instance to be those who were led to subjective thinking during the long winter evenings of their childhood.

A boy cannot maintain health of body without laughter, merriment, and fun. We have every reason to believe that a lamb would not maintain its bodily health and grow to be a mature animal if it were prevented from running and frolicking.

Most especially does the feeling of merriment assist the digestive function. This idea is already prevalent among the people, and yet there is too little abiding faith in the medicinal virtue of fun. Our meals should be scenes of uninterrupted merriment. It is a fact universally acknowledged that the American people eat too rapidly for the good of their health. Now there is nothing that checks rapid eating like fun and merry conversation. One of the evils of Puritanism, which we have not yet outgrown, was the idea that cheerful conversation is unbecoming at meals. The children were taught to eat in silence at the second table, under the awful superintendence of their parents, who had eaten up all the good things. The eating up of the good things, however, was not half so cruel as it was to compel them to put on long faces, and be men and women, and eat in silence. The free ventilation, the hard work, and the simple fare which they enjoyed prevented them from having the dyspepsia. But we cannot tell how thoroughly their stomachs and livers were prepared by such treatment at meal time, to give the dyspepsia to the next generation. It is not at all an extravagant belief, that much of the dyspepsia of to-day had its remote origin among the Puritans in their cruel suppression of childish mirth at the family board. There are families in which the Puritanic idea is still prevalent, that "children should be seen but not heard." We have no sympathy with that doctrine. Such an idea could have originated only in parental selfishness. In the days of our grandfathers the children were, indeed, pitiable creatures. But we are gradually becoming more civilized on this point. The same principle in human nature that has given rise to societies for the "prevention of cruelty to animals" has so modified our sentiments toward children that we no longer regard them as so many wild beasts put into our hands to be tamed. Children are now allowed to spend most of their time in the pursuit of fun and to laugh at meals.

Parents should mingle with their children in their sports and games. It is not unbecoming to a mother or a father to play with a child, but, on the contrary, it is quite becoming; and in so doing a parent is discharging one of the highest duties that have been imposed upon him. This is not the task it may seem to be. There is something in the relation of parent and child that makes the parent take positive delight in that which delights the child. Every mother knows this to be true. There is that in the experience of every one which testifies to this. We all feel an interest in those things which interest the ones we love. This principle has an influence even over the senses. Articles of food which we do not ordinarily like, when eaten in the presence of a loved one who does like them, actually become savory to us. We are made by this principle to fall into the same line of thought and feeling with those we love. And hence the mother experiences almost as much delight from playing with a cart as does her child. This same principle doubtless accounts for the fact that all animals play with their young. This is Nature's argument. The cat and dog, however old and dignified, almost continually play with their young; so does the lion, and probably all wild animals. Animals that cannot by any other possible means be induced to manifest the slightest degree of playfulness, are full, or appear to be full, of fun and frolic while rearing their young. Do not these facts proclaim a natural law? Playing with children is a subject of more importance than most people are aware of.

The oldest of a family of children often has a bad disposition, and it is doubtless due to the fact that it had no older playmates. It seems to be a law of the child's nature that in order to properly develop he requires an older playmate.

The younger members of the family are provided for in this respect by the older ones, and accordingly their dispositions are better, and their minds are usually more symmetrically developed. Now, if parents would heed this law and become the intimate associates and playmates of their children while they are young, no such disparity of disposition and character would be found.

The chief reason why so many children become dissatisfied with their home and desire to leave it at the earliest possible opportunity, is because they have not had happy homes; and unhappy homes are seldom looked back to with tender thoughts in after years. But let them keep the old time feeling in their hearts that "there's no place like home," and when the hour of reunion draws nigh with its glad tidings and joyful welcome they will not send the cruel telegram of two words, "business pressing," but will come with open hearts and smiling faces, bringing back again the same feeling that they carried away, that "there's no place like home."

But children are not the only beings that require amusements. All require it, even the aged. Absolute rest is not the thing required by the father when he comes home from the shop, the office, or the store. Human beings need but very little of that kind of rest beyond what they get during the hours of sleep. If there could be found a vocation in which all the faculties should be exercised alike, those engaged in such a vocation would require no amusement beyond what would necessarily result from exercising the faculty of mirth equally with the other faculties. But the relations of human life afford no such vocation, hence the wisdom of making special provision for amusements.

Suppose we have a complicated machine, only a part of which is in action, half of the wheels remaining motionless. Now suppose we discover that the machine is wearing out in that part which is constantly exercised. What shall we do to maintain the symmetry of the machine and prevent it from becoming in a short time useless? Will it be sufficient to simply stop the machine a few hours or days and then start it again? Surely not, for half of it is now actually rusting out from the want of being used. One half needs rest and the other part needs action in order to check the process of destruction. Hence the only way to accomplish the desired result is to stop the part that has been continually running and start the other part.

This illustration explains the whole philosophy of amusements and recreations. Man does not need to rest, but simply to start up the other half of his vital and mental machinery, and home furnishes the only adequate motive power.

"Frown not, when roistering boys or toss or strike
The bounding ball, or leap or run or ride
The mastered steed that, as the rider, loves
The rushing course, or when with ringing steel
The polished ice they sweep in winter's reign;
All pleasing pastimes, innocent delights,
That gladden hearts yet simple and sincere,
Let love parental gather 'round the home,
And consecrate by sharing ; let it watch
With kind, approving smiles each merry game
That quickens youthful blood, and in the joy
That beams from crimson cheeks and sparkling eyes
Its own renew, and live its childhood o'er."

HOME SMILES.

SMILE is the most useful thing in the world in proportion to its cost. It costs absolutely nothing, but its utility is often beyond estimation. It comes as the involuntary and irrepressible expression of a sentiment that lies at the basis of human society. Smiles constitute a part of our language. There seem to be certain combinations of words that require to be supplemented with a smile before they can have any meaning to us.

The human soul, shrouded in the mysteries of personality, yearns to know the essence of other souls, as it were, to touch a hand in the dark, and smiles are the electric flashes that illumine the wide gulf that separates individualities.

There is a mystery in what we call acquaintance. Acquaintance, however, is not the proper word, but since human language affords no apter one we shall be obliged to use it. Why should we say that we are acquainted with this one and not with that one? Acquaintanceship does not consist in a knowledge of an individual's peculiarities of character or disposition, for we sometimes feel acquainted with persons whose minds are sealed books to us. We cannot understand them. Their thoughts are mysterious and unfathomable, and they always seem to take a turn which was wholly unexpected to us and which we cannot account for, and yet we feel perfectly acquainted with them.

There are others whose minds are as transparent as glass. Their mental operations are performed, as it were, in the sight of all. We can almost anticipate their very thoughts, and yet we would not think of speaking to them because, as we say, we are not acquainted with them.

Acquaintance is not a conventionality of society, for it may be observed in those rude and primitive communities where the mere conventionalities of society have little weight. It is more strongly manifested in little children even before they can talk than in older people. This shows that whatever acquaintance may be, it is natural and not artificial. In what then does it consist? What passes between two souls when a third party says, "this is Mr. ——, Mr. ——"? There is usually some form of salutation, as the bow or the shaking of hands; although there is nothing of a permanent or essential nature in these, for the mode of salutation differs in different nations and communities. The Turks fold their arms across the breast while bowing; the Laplanders touch their noses; and in Southern Africa they rub their toes together.

But there is one act that accompanies all these different

modes, one rite that never varies. It is the smile. The philosophy of acquaintance is wrapt up in the philosophy of the smile. When two smiles have met, two souls are acquainted. A smile is the sign that a soul gives when it would examine another soul.

Every soul in the universe lives alone. There is a dark curtain dropped before the window of its house which hides it from the view of all. Every one has felt his loneliness even in the midst of crowds. Souls cannot come into contact, but they can draw aside the curtain from the window. To smile is to draw aside the curtain. The fondest souls can do no more. Even lovers must caress through a window.

At home, these curtains should often be drawn aside, for there is nothing so fatal to a home as to have its members become unacquainted with each other. And there is nothing so difficult as to renew the acquaintance of brothers and sisters, when once it has been lost. When they begin to be restrained and self-conscious in each other's society; when they begin to review with indifference those phases of life over which they once smiled and wept together,—they are unconsciously, perhaps unwillingly, cutting each other's acquaintance. There is no sadder sight on earth than that of a brother and sister who are unacquainted. The coldness and reserve that springs up between the members of so many families originates in a lack of "smiles at home."

By smiles we do not mean that which takes the place of loud laughter when the occasion is insufficient to provoke us to more noisy demonstrations. Nor do we mean either the transient smile with which one regards the ludicrous, or the habitual smile that often accompanies a low degree of thought-power. There is a smile that originates neither in the sense of the ludicrous, nor in thoughtlessness. Like certain articles of dress such smiles are becoming on all occasions. They sit with equal grace upon the brow of joy and of sorrow. They seem as appropriate when they wreathe the mother's thoughtful face as when they live in the dimpled cheek of laughing girlhood, or with their magic play transform the eyes to twinkling stars.

These are the smiles with which we would adorn every home. We would set them as vases of flowers in every house.

Smiles should be the legal tender in every family for the payment of all debts of kindness, and each member should be willing to take this currency at its face value; for its value is beyond the reach of those disturbing influences that shake the world of commerce. And, what is better than all, it can never be demonetized, for it bears the immutable stamp of the divine government.

Let the members of the family, almost as often as they meet, greet each other with a smile, for eyes that meet in full gaze without a smile soon grow cold. The mother, if she would keep the confidence of her son, must be lavish of her smiles. Mothers often weep in the presence of their sons on account of the anxiety that they feel for them. This is a great error, for in the first place it leads a young man to conceal that which he believes would displease his mother. This is often the beginning of a fatal reserve. Besides, it causes him to feel that his mother has not confidence in him, and that however much she may love him she fears to trust his honor.

The smile is nature's cure for the disease of bashfulness. This disease is simply the fear which one soul experiences in approaching another. But the smile is an instinctive effort to suppress the fear and to know the soul.

A knowledge of this principle would be of great service to those having the charge of bashful children. Strangers should always encourage a smile in a bashful child. Such children should be met with smiles rather than with words. The smile is the only form of salutation that a bashful child can use. He cannot speak to a stranger in audible language, but if the stranger will consent to use the language of smiles he may almost always gain quick admission to his confidence. When the bashful child smiles and blushes and hangs his head in the presence of strangers, there is great hope that he will outgrow the infirmity, for the smile is an instinctive effort to overcome it. But where the child is not inclined to smile there is little hope, and the malady usually degenerates into moroseness and oddity.

The habitual smiler is never a dyspeptic. Smiles promote the general health and are especially fatal to any disease of the stomach or liver.

Smiles also promote the growth of the religious sentiment, because they cannot thrive without a constant sense of obligation to others. Especially do they tend to cultivate benevolence, for every smile is a gift, and benevolence grows by giving. There are few souls that can "smile, and murder while they smile." None indeed can murder, while they smile from the heart. There may be the same movement of the facial muscles, but smiles are not merely contractions of certain muscles. They are mental acts.

The actor may give the outward expression of a smile, and murder while he smiles, but the words of the great dramatist are not true of a single human soul except the smile be spurious.

> "Sweet is the smile of home; the mutual look
> Where hearts are of each other sure;
> Sweet all the joys that crowd the household nook,
> The haunt of all affections pure."

JOYS OF HOME.

JOY is the natural and normal condition of every human soul. To be genuine and permanent it must depend chiefly on internal instead of external conditions. Every natural function both of the body and of the mind is attended with pleasure and never with pain, unless it be the penalty for a broken law. If walking is not pleasurable, it is because there is some trouble with the physical system. If daylight does not bring to the eye positive pleasure, it is because the eye is diseased and there is a maladjustment between it and the light. The difficulty is always on the part of the eye and never on the part of the light. When the song of birds, the sighing of the breeze, the rippling of the brook, the chirping of the insect and the thousand voices of nature do not bring to the ear and soul the exquisite sense of divine harmony, it is because sin with rude hand has broken the chords of the spirit's harp. We always hear music at second hand, just as we see beauty. Hence it has been said that "beauty is in the eye of the gazer, and music is in the ear of the listener.'

There is philosophy in this saying, for all the music that we hear is that which the soul itself produces when it responds to the myriad voices from without. These sounds and voices from nature, God's great orchestra, must be reproduced by the soul's response before they can become music to us. It is not the music without that we hear, but the spirit's imitation of it.

If, then, the soul be tuned to the same key so as to give a true response, rest assured that our lives will be filled with harmony and joy, for God's hand never strikes a discord.

The secret of human joy, then, is to keep the spirit's harp in tune. To the spirit whose harp is out of tune, the clouds are but unsightly rags with which the mantle of the sky is patched; the mountain in its grandeur is but an eminence that is hard to climb; the sublime thunder of Niagara is but a loud noise that makes it difficult to sleep; while the songs of birds, the patter of the rain, the laughter and the voices of the woods are but the troublesome prattle of Nature's children.

Joy cannot be bought with gold. There is but one thing that Nature will take in exchange for it, and that is obedience to the divine laws of our being. Joy is the only legitimate and necessary product of every normal and healthy function. It is absolutely impossible for any function of our being, if healthy and normal in its action, to produce anything but joy, no matter what may be the outward conditions. The truest and highest joy is a product of health, and is but partially dependent on external conditions.

Nature aims at no other grand result than that of joy. She has created the myriad varieties of fruit for the pleasure of the palate. For the joy of the eye she has painted on the earth's green canvas the gentle hints of heaven, and bathed the picture in the liquid silver of the sunlight. For the ear she has filled the earth with harmony divine. For the joy of our social and domestic natures she has instituted the home, the fireside and society. For our intellectual nature she has filled the universe with problems, the solution of which gives us exquisite pleasure. For our spiritual nature she has given the heavenly reward of an approving conscience. Thus is joy the eternal aim of Nature.

On whom then rests the blame when life's joys are tarnished and its sweetness turned to bitterness? Whom shall we blame for the strained and weakened eye that makes the sunlight painful? Whom shall we blame for the overwrought brain that makes causation and all problems irksome? Whom shall we blame for the seared and deadened conscience that makes duty a task and honor a burden? We fancy that the conscience of none of our readers is yet so far deadened that he will not quickly answer, "I myself am to blame."

The clamor for joy and pleasure, then, when rightly interpreted, is a universal call to duty, for the reward of duty is unalloyed joy. 'Tis a call to study and mental discipline; for the fruit of culture, like that of duty is joy and only joy. It is a call to physical obedience and to the cultivation of health; for joy is the necessary and inseparable accompaniment of these, and without them it cannot exist. Let the reader remember this one fact, that obedience to the physical, intellectual and moral laws of our being is the only condition that Nature imposes upon us, and when this one condition is complied with she will shower upon us joys untold. She will make the breath of morning a source of exquisite delight. The very consciousness of existence will thrill us with that joy which all have felt at rare intervals, undefinable, and too subtle for any analysis. External objects and conditions seem to play no part in the program. At most they are only the occasions and not the causes of the joy. We look into the face of a friend or out over the sheen of a lake and we feel an unutterable joy coursing through all the channels of our being, and welling up in gurgling laughter; and we cannot for our lives tell why we laugh. The joy that comes to perfect health with the sweet intoxication of the morning dew, is "the purest and sweetest that Nature can yield." Such is the bountiful reward of Nature for obedience to her laws.

We have dwelt thus at length on the laws that govern the emotion of joy because they have an important bearing on the subject of which we are treating.

The fireside is the only spot where it is possible to obey all the laws of our being: hence it is the only spot where supreme joy can exist. Domestic joy is the only joy that is complete.

Truly has the poet said:

> "Domestic joy, thou only bliss
> Of paradise that hath survived the fall."

Man may cultivate his intellect and derive pleasure from obedience to its laws, even though he may not have a home. He may derive a joy from obedience to the laws of his moral nature while he is a hermit or a wanderer. He may even derive some enjoyment from partial obedience to the laws of his social nature. But all enjoyment from this source must be partial, because all obedience to the social law must be incomplete outside the domestic circle. The family is the truest type of society.

But without a fireside man's domestic nature, from which he derives by far the largest amount of his earthly enjoyment, cannot but remain cold and entirely inactive. This department of his nature can be kept alive only by the heat of the hearth-stone. The home is the place where all the joys of life may exist in their ripest fruition.

Even the intellectual nature, which is the farthest removed from the sphere of domestic influence, cannot be developed to its fullest possibility outside of the home; for the boy requires in the first stage of his intellectual development the wholesome spirit of rivalry and emulation that exists among children of the same household. In every stage he needs the stimulus of honest commendation, and this comes in its purest and most useful form from the members of the same family.

The joys peculiar to the moral and spiritual nature must be only partial, and far below what this part of our being is capable of yielding, unless it be cultivated in the sanctuary of home. Conscience must be kept sharp by the pathetic appeals of little children, by the tender looks and anxious words of mothers and sisters, and by the nice adjustments of domestic obligations.

What a plea do we find in these facts for the institution of home, and how much is signified by "the joys of home!" No words of ours are necessary to impress that significance upon the minds of those who are the members of happy families. With what feelings of delight do such look forward to the evening hour when the family, overflowing with joy, shall gather around the board with mirth and laughter. How the father's heart thrills at the sudden thought that the hour is near when he shall meet his loved ones; when he shall leave his care and troubles all behind, and sit in his easy chair, or recline upon the sofa, and watch the fire-light dancing on the wall and hear the merry voices of the children, or listen to the sweet music of his daughter's voice. Can heaven yield a sweeter joy than this?

But the joys of home are not to be measured by actual

domestic felicity, for home has joys independent of this. There is joy in the very thought that one has a home. There is joy in the poetry with which the divine artists of time and memory conspire to paint the old homestead.

Joy is heightened and pain is lightened by being shared, but home is the only place on earth where they can be fully shared. Everywhere else there is a reserve that makes our joys and pains peculiarly our own. At home the heart may be opened, and all that it knows and feels may be known and felt by others.

The joys of home are the only ones of which we never weary. We grow tired of those joys that come from mingling promiscuously in society. We tire of the exciting pleasures of trade and commerce. We tire of gazing at the marble fronts and gilded palaces of the great city. We shut our eyes and close our ears in weariness and disgust even at the sights and sounds of the public park. But we never grow tired of mother's song, although the birds in the park may weary us. We may leave the art gallery satiated, but the old pictures on the walls of home are ever new.

Let us then cherish the joys of home, for their perennial freshness hints at their eternity. The child, who with his playmates, wanders from his home over the hill and meadow, when he wearies of his sports and games, turns at nightfall to his home to lay his little weary head upon his mother's breast. So when we shall weary of the little sports and games of earth, may we find our homeward way back across life's meadow and up the hill to the threshold of the home eternal, and lay our weary heads upon the bosom of the Divine, forever and ever.

"Sweet are the joys of home,
And pure as sweet; for they
Like dews of morn and evening come,
To make and close the day.

"The world hath its delights,
And its delusions, too;
But home to calmer bliss invites,
More tranquil and more true.

"The mountain flood is strong,
But fearful in its pride;
While gently rolls the stream along
The peaceful valley's side.

"Life's charities, like light,
Spread smilingly afar;
But stars approached, become more bright,
And home is life's own star.

"The pilgrim's step in vain
Seeks Eden's sacred ground!
But in home's holy joys again
An Eden may be found.

"A glance of heaven to see,
To none on earth is given;
And yet a happy family
Is but an earlier heaven."

EDUCATION OF OUR GIRLS.

THE education of woman is among the foremost problems of the nineteenth century. It is something more than a social problem. It is a civil and political, a moral and religious problem as well. Inasmuch as the presence of woman constitutes one of the chief charms and benefits of society, and inasmuch as it is she who far more than man gives character to society, her education and culture are a social problem.

But into her care have been entrusted the nation's future statesmen, those who are soon to be clothed with authority and to make laws for the government of mankind. Hence her education becomes a civil and political problem. Not only is she entrusted with the guardianship of the intellect and character of the world's statesmen and philosophers, but her gentle presence, as she bends over the cradle, and the silent influence of her daily life are shaping the entire moral character of the coming generation; and thus does the education of woman become a great moral problem.

Again, since she shapes the moral character of the world,

and since the eternal destiny of man depends upon the character in this life, it follows that her education becomes the profoundest spiritual and religious problem.

In view of these momentous facts what should constitute the education of our girls? Human life is short and its powers of endurance are limited. None of us can reasonably hope to accomplish all that our imagination may picture to our minds as desirable. We cannot appropriate the great sea of knowledge. We surely cannot do better than Sir Isaac Newton, who picked up only a few pebbles on the shore. But whether we are able to pick up one or many of these pebbles we should select only those whose size and shape best adapt them to our purpose.

We have no argument to offer against the study of those branches which utilitarians are wont to condemn as involving a waste of time and energy. We have no sympathy with this utilitarian idea. We pity the man who is able even to distinguish between beauty and utility. That mind which does not see the highest use in Niagara is but poorly developed and poorly educated. Nature has drawn no line between the beautiful and the useful. On the contrary, she has purposely blended them in an indistinguishable union. Every apple tree is first a vase of flowers and then a golden fruit basket. A blossom is the preface to every useful product. Before Nature can allow even a potato to grow and ripen she places the divine seal of beauty on it in the form of a little flower. That little flower, which is made the necessary condition of the potato's development, was placed there to teach us that there is a use in beauty and a beauty in use. Hence we would not condemn the study of music and the fine arts. The history of music is the history of human development. It has been the sensitive gauge that has marked the civilization of every age and nation. The music that charmed the undeveloped and savage ear of the past would be to us but rude noise, and perchance the divinest harmony that wafts our spirit starward may be but discord compared with the symphonies that echo down the aisles of coming ages. Music is not altogether an art; it is a science as well, and viewed in its highest aspect it becomes the grand exponent of that universal and divine harmony which every properly developed soul has felt, and which gives credence to that sweetest of all mythologies, "the music of the spheres."

Thus while we cannot speak too highly of the *science* of music as a means of soul development and heart culture, yet as a mere outward accomplishment it cannot be denied that it usurps a disproportionate amount of time and energy, and we would unhesitatingly condemn that method of study which would reduce the science and art of music to a mere system of finger and vocal gymnastics. It is a fact which the observation of almost every one will confirm, that the present method of musical instruction has a direct tendency to take the soul out of music, and leave it, like the poetry of Pope, a mere shell from which the living creature has departed. The modern masters of song seem to have forgotten the prime object of music, viz., to move the heart and lift the soul. They exhibit their powers to us as the circus rider exhibits his, and they expect us to applaud them for their skill in execution; if we do not they attribute our indifference to the "lack of culture."

Life is too short and its duties too momentous for a girl to spend years in acquiring proficiency in the production of a mere sound, and one in which, in spite of her culture, she is discounted by the ordinary canary bird. Music should be made an instrument and not a toy.

All this may be true, says the mother, but how shall I educate my daughter? It is easy to generalize and to criticise existing systems; but what is the particular method which I must follow in order to avoid this criticism?

In the first place, it is necessary to have a just view concerning woman's place in the economy of society. It is useless to give advice in regard to the higher education of woman to those who covertly or otherwise regard woman as an inferior being, whose highest and most legitimate function is to swing a cradle through the air twelve hours a day. We would not express other than the tenderest sentiments concerning the divine mission of motherhood. But has the reader ever asked himself what it is that makes motherhood so divine? Is it not, after all, that which lifts woman above motherhood, that can make motherhood divine? We are pained when an eminent writer gives weight to expressions like the following: "The great vocation of woman is wifehood and motherhood." Would the author object to a slight change in the latter part of the phraseology so as to make the expression applicable to man? Would those who think that the quoted words express a fine thought be offended with the following? The great vocation of man is husbandhood and fatherhood? The moment we exalt motherhood to the rank of a prime object, that moment does it descend to the level of the function involved, and the divine mother becomes simply a mammal of the genus "homo."

All there is of divinity in motherhood is derived from the divinity of womanhood. Why does the artist always paint that kind of motherhood which suggests to our minds the condescension of the divine to the human? It is not the motherhood, but the condescension to motherhood, that makes it divine and beautiful. Whatever heightens and glorifies woman's nature then renders more beautiful and more divine the mission of motherhood. It is the seminary that sanctifies the nursery.

We hope the world has heard the last of that sickly sentiment concerning "woman's sphere," "The hand that rocks the cradle rules the world," etc. If that hand were permitted to take hold of the world a little more directly, it would not at all interfere with its ability to rock the cradle. The female robin must feed and care for its young, but it finds time each morning to sing its little hymn of praise upon the tree-top to its Maker. So woman may rock the cradle sufficiently each day and yet find time to glorify her God with her intellect.

We would see the little sister and brother hand in hand enter the primary school; we would see them together promoted to the grammar school; we would see them struggling on through the course all unconscious that there is any radical difference in their mental constitutions; we would see them graduate from the high school together, and together enter the university, and here through four years of intellectual conflict we would see them stand side by side in that fiercely contested arena, and with tongue and pen and brain compete for those prizes whose winning foreshadows life's success. We would see them both at the graduating. exercises, fearlessly giving to the world a specimen of their thought and eloquence,

"Mid the sweet inspiration of music and flowers."

Nor would we see them part here; but with brave hearts enter the same profession. We see no good reason why women should not serve their kind as lawyers, doctors, and ministers. It is true there are objections and hinderances incidental to their sex, but these we believe are fully counterbalanced by those qualifications in which they must be acknowledged even superior.

In medicine, it is fast coming to be the opinion of the

world that woman, whatever may be her incidental disabilities, is by nature even better endowed than man with some of the peculiarities of talent that prophesy success. One of these peculiarities is that intuitive insight which, when supplemented by scientific knowledge, leaps to right conclusions with the certainty of an instinct. It is in moments of emergency that woman's mind betrays its peculiar fitness for the medical profession. All must admit that she is the natural nurse, and it is almost an adage among physicians that "as much depends upon the nursing as upon medical skill." We would not, of course, make this claim for woman with reference to all professions. It is not the general superiority of woman that we seek to prove, but simply that for the profession of medicine, at least, she has some special qualifications.

But we would not deny that she may with equal propriety enter almost any of the other professions, and in this we are confident that we only anticipate the tide of public sentiment. How eminently do her sincerity, morality and spiritual mindedness fit her to point the world to nobler endeavors and higher ideals.

Many of the arguments which prove her fitness to minister as a physician to the diseased bodies of mankind also go to prove her special fitness to minister as a moral physician to their diseased souls.

Why then should our talented and ambitious girls lament that there is no field open for them. There are very few professions open to their brothers, which they may not also enter if they will but have the courage, not the immodesty, to step aside from the conventional path which the hand of society has marked out for them. But while woman possesses so many of the qualities requisite in the professions, there are still few women who are adapted to a professional life, and the same may be said of men. Hence a professional education cannot meet the requirements of the great mass either of girls or of boys. "The greatest good to the greatest number" should be our motto. We must go, then, to the little farm-house and the little cottage beneath the hill. Not that the farm-house and the cottage are the abodes of intellectual weakness. On the contrary, history shows that the world's great minds, like wheat, potatoes and apples, are usually produced on farms, yet it cannot be denied that the mass of the people, those to whom we wish to speak, are symbolized by the farm-house and the cottage.

What, then, shall constitute the education of the common girl who is destitute of the ambition and, perhaps, the talent to become great and useful in any professional capacity? We answer, in the first place, that her education should be as varied and perfect as possible. If for no other reason to enable her properly to educate and rear her own children. Whatever grand truths are planted in the mother's mind take root in the next generation, and there grow, blossom, and shed their perfume on the world.

The child receives the mother's very thought by intuition. If the mother's mind is weak and narrow in its range, the child is affected by this fact long before it finds any meaning in the mother's words. But if the mother's mind is cultured and refined by study until her thoughts are grand and far-reaching, the child's soul will grow and expand under the mesmeric influence of these thoughts, as the plant grows under the influence of the sun.

Again, education, or the refinement and organic improvement resulting from education, is transmitted from mother to child. Who cannot tell by the looks of a little boy whether his mother was educated or not? The child of the educated mother will have a finer grained organism; he will be handsomer, will have more regular features than the child of the ignorant parent. As a rule he will acquire the use of language at an earlier period. He will also generally be found more open and frank in his manner, and more susceptible to moral and spiritual influences.

How grand and comprehensive, then, becomes the theme of woman's education. To the parent no question can be more important than how shall I educate my daughter? If it is impossible to educate both let the son go uneducated, and educate the daughter. The importance of the son's education may be, indeed, beyond estimation; yet that of the daughter is even more important.

Many parents believe that the virtue of their daughters

will be more secure if they remain in general ignorance; but the frightful statistics of our great cities show this to be a terrible mistake. It is a fact that cannot be denied, that the ranks of that army which parade the streets of the great cities at midnight, in painted shame, are filled from the country. Few are natives of the city, notwithstanding the dangers and temptations of city life are far greater than those of the country.

There can be but one explanation of this fact. The superior educational facilities of the city afford a salutary and restraining influence in the form of mental culture. The city girl is better educated than the country girl, hence she has a stronger character.

Both may be innocent, for innocence may live comfortably with ignorance, but virtue and ignorance cannot long endure each other's society. A young kitten is innocent, but it has but little character; and we could not call it particularly virtuous. There are thousands of human kittens whose virtue consists only in the innocence of ignorance.

"Pulpy souls
That show a dimple for each touch of sin."

Let every mother and father remember that there is no virtue in ignorance, even ignorance of sin. If you do not give your boy an opportunity to use his muscles he will soon cease to have any muscles. So there can be no virtue without temptation; if you do not give your daughter an opportunity to use her virtue in the resistance of temptation, it is to be feared that she will soon cease to have any virtue.

A certain woman had a choice plum tree, the fruit of which she was anxious should ripen. The birds had carried away all but one, and over this she bound a cloth. It was safe from the birds, but while she shut it from them, she shut it also from the sunshine and the storms which alone could ripen it, and it withered away and fell.

The mother should teach her daughter above all things to know herself.

The man was unwise, who, fearing that his bird-dog would acquire the habit of killing barn fowl, shut him up during his puppy-hood and secluded from his sight every kind of bird. When he released him to test the merits of his system of education, the dog rushed at the fowls and killed them all before his master could call him off.

Would he not have acted more wisely had he taught the young dog to discriminate between barn-fowl and wild-fowl? As it was he did not educate him, but attempted to suppress an inborn instinct.

Equally unwise is the mother who keeps, or tries to keep, her daughter in ignorance concerning those things which she has a divinely given right to know. Let her direct her daughter's intuitions as nature unfolds them, but never attempt to suppress them, for sooner or later there must come a revelation.

Whatever may be true concerning the question of woman's rights; whether or not she has a moral right to participate in the civil government of society, we will not here attempt to discuss.

A concession of her rights, however, as interpreted by the strongest advocate of woman's suffrage is not at all inconsistent with the undisputed fact that woman finds her highest mission at the altar of home. Nor does this fact interfere with what we have already said concerning the inconsistency of making wifehood and motherhood the prime object of life.

The doctrine of woman's rights can never be proved by contending that she is not by constitution and nature calculated to pursue a somewhat different object in life from that which man pursues, or at least to pursue the same by somewhat different methods.

If it could be shown that men and women should both engage in the cultivation of the soil, it would be still undeniable that woman is best adapted to the more æsthetic portion of the labor, and man to the rougher and heavier portion. If a flower garden or nursery were placed in the midst of rough stubble, none would deny that it would be natural for the man to mow the stubble, while the woman should tend the garden in its midst. This would be true even if it should be shown that woman should help to till the soil.

So if it should be shown that woman has a moral right to participate in the solution of social problems, which we are not by any means prepared to deny, it would still be true that it is her most natural function to have particular charge of the little nursery, home, in the midst of the rough stubble of human society.

Woman's education, then, is necessarily very imperfect, unless it be largely in the line of that which best becomes her nature.

She should have, emphatically, a home education, and this means something more than a knowledge of the dust-pan and broom.

It means something more than a mere knowledge of the daily routine of housekeeping, in the popular sense of that word. Woman holds in her hands the physical health of the world. Three times each day our lives and health are at the mercy and practical judgment of woman. Nay, more, for the world's character is largely what its food makes it. Indirectly, then, she exerts a modifying influence over our loves and hates, hopes and fears, joys and sorrows.

Whoever controls a being's stomach controls that being's destiny. What, then, can be more important than that girls should be educated in cookery and the related sciences, chemistry and hygiene? This, then, is what we mean by a home education for girls, that they should be taught both through the wisdom and experience of mothers, and also through the medium of books, how to engage in the noble occupation of housewife with the best advantage to mankind.

Such an education cannot be obtained solely from practice in the kitchen. The whole mind must be expanded and disciplined by a study of nature and her laws. No woman can possibly fulfill, in the best manner, her duties as housewife without a good general education.

"Three years she grew in sun and shower;
Then nature said, "A lovelier flower
On earth was never sown;
This child I to myself will take;
She shall be mine, and I will make
A lady of my own.

"Myself will to my darling be
Both law and impulse; and with me
The girl, in rock and plain,
In earth and heaven, in glade and bower,
Shall feel an overseeing power
To kindle or restrain.

"She shall be sportive as the fawn
That wild with glee across the lawn
Or up the mountain springs;
And hers shall be the breathing balm,
And hers the silence and the calm,
Of mute insensate things.

"The floating clouds their state shall lend
To her; for her the willow bend;
Nor shall she fail to see
E'en in the motions of the storm
Grace that shall mold the maiden's form
By silent sympathy.

"The stars of midnight shall be dear
To her; and she shall lean her ear
In many a secret place,
Where rivulets dance their wayward round,
And beauty born of murmuring sound
Shall pass into her face."

EDUCATION OF OUR BOYS.

AN education does not necessarily mean the discipline of a college course. In the present condition of society, that advantage is, as a matter of necessity, reserved for comparatively few. In its true significance education means something more than the ability to unravel the involved constructions of a dead language; something more than a proficiency in mathematics and the physical sciences; something more, even, than can be reaped from the most laborious toil of the human intellect. It is a drawing out, a developing and strengthening of every element, every faculty, every power of body, mind and spirit. It is such a condition of the whole being, resulting from a constant refinement, that the several powers shall observe the highest economy in their separate spheres, while the power of co-ordinated action shall be rendered more perfect. One may so cultivate and strengthen the muscles of his little finger that he may be able to support with it twice his weight; while the main muscles of his body are so weak that he may not be able to lift half his weight. You could not call such a man a strong man. So one may cultivate his mere intellectuality till he becomes the brilliant center of the world's admiration, if such were possible; but you cannot call him educated if he is vicious, if his anger is uncontrollable, if he is a drunkard or a glutton, if he is stubborn, if he is unconscientious, if he is irreverent, if he is spiritually blind, if he is selfish, if he is dead to the appeals of human want and suffering.

An education on this broad basis should be the life-work of every human being.

We would not by any means be understood as undervaluing the education of the intellect. The importance of the education of a power is commensurate with the importance of the power itself, and certainly no power of our being can be of more importance than the intellect. A college education is within the reach of every young man who possesses the ambition for it, even though he may possess neither friends nor money. There are hundreds of students in this country who are paying their own way through college by their own energy and labor. In most of our colleges, a young man of activity and determination may earn during the vacation enough to pay his expenses during the term. So that he who thirsts for knowledge has no legitimate excuse if he does not avail himself of a college education. None should ask us to bring other evidence than the illustrious triumphs of a Garfield. There never yet was occupation so low, nor obstacle so broad and high as to defeat the resolve of a human soul. No fierce monster of opposition ever reared its hydra head in the path of a human endeavor,

> That would not shrink and cower
> Before the dauntless power
> Of a fearless human will.

There are those who are conscious that they were richly endowed by nature with noble gifts, but who have failed in life through their own indolence. It is customary for these to comfort themselves in their sad retrospection by repeating these melancholy lines :—

> "Full many a gem of purest ray serene
> The dark unfathomed caves of ocean bear;
> Full many a flower is born to blush unseen
> And waste its sweetness on the desert air."

Do those lines prove that truth is not an essential element of poetry? No, for they are believed and felt to be true by mistaken souls, and in that way they perform the function of truth. They convey, or rather seem to convey, a solemn truth to those who have unwittingly surrendered life's argument to the merciless opponent of circumstances by the unwise concession of their own weakness.

But let us put this doctrine to the practical test. We have said that an education does not necessarily mean the discipline of a college course. Indeed, all are not so constituted that a college education would bring them the greatest good even intellectually. Nor would we be so radical as to deny that circumstances may defeat the purpose of merely going to college, but the circumstance of poverty is not a valid excuse. At any rate, all may become well educated. Those men are almost numberless who have become great and useful by the light of a pine torch, who have learned the science of mathematics with a stick for a pencil and the ocean beach for a slate. But suppose we meet the barefoot boy in the street picking rags, what word of advice have we for him? He will listen to all our fine talk about the grand possibilities which this free and glorious republic offers to the poorest and the lowliest; he will listen to the story of those great souls who have climbed to glory over fence rails and canal boats; and when we have finished he will meet us with the question, "What shall I do and how shall I begin?" Let us see if we can answer these questions. As the first step toward the desired result, he can pick up a rag, just as he has been wont to do, and examine it, not as heretofore with the simple purpose of determining whether he shall put it into one or the other of two baskets; but he can make it the text-book with which to begin an education. He can ask those older and wiser than himself what it is made of and how it is made. They will point him to the great mill yonder, where, if he tells his purpose, he can gain admission and learn something of the mechanical principles involved in the manufacture of the rag. If he continues to make inquiries until he can trace a piece of cotton through all its transformations, till it comes out a piece of fine bleached cotton, he has surely begun an education in earnest. He can save a penny a day for a few days and buy a primer, and with that primer under his arm he may politely accost any lady or gentleman with these words, "I am determined to make the most of myself. I want to learn to read. I have bought a little book. Can you give me any advice or help?" There is not a man or woman in all that great city with a heart so hard as not to be melted to sympathy by that appeal. He would be astonished at the amount of love and sympathy and philanthropy in the world which he before had considered so cold and heartless.

Young man; boot-black; rag-picker; obscure farmer boy; or dweller in the dingy haunts of the city; remember that Freedom's goddess holds over your head a crown. She never crowns a royal idiot; she scorns fine clothes and gloved hands, and she never puts that crown on any but a sweaty brow.

> From every lowly cottage roof,
> However poor and brown,
> From every dusty hovel, points
> A hand at glory's crown.

Although it is true that men can be good farmers or mechanics without being able to read or write, yet we believe that the greatest possible number of these classes should be liberally educated. We often hear it remarked that one is very foolish to spend so much time and money in procuring an education if he intends to make no use of it, the remark implying that if he intends to enter no profession the time and money thus spent are wasted.

We have no sympathy or patience with that view of life. Man is above the brutes chiefly because he knows more. It is a greater sin to take his life than that of a brute, because he has more life to take, because his faculties are more God-like and more powerful.

Now education means simply making these faculties powerful and God-like, and nothing more. Hence an educated man is more a man than an uneducated one. It increases the humanity of man and adds to our very being. So that if one is to spend his life in idleness gazing at the clouds, it is a duty he owes to himself, to the universe and to God, to make the most of himself by acquiring a liberal education.

Knowledge, like virtue, should be an end in itself. Think of a mother teaching her children to be virtuous because their prospects of financial success would be greater! We should pity the moral weakness of that mother. We all instinctively recognize virtue as a sublime object and end in itself. It is a part of that God-like nature of which we boast, it is a part of our very immortality. So is knowledge. Why then should we talk about knowledge and education simply as means to facilitate the accumulation of dollars and cents? Let no mother teach her boy such sophistry.

The capacity of the soul for enjoyment is just proportionate to its interior development. Knowledge is to the mind what health is to the body, it makes more of us.

Education is the handmaid of religion. The statistics of every community will show that criminals are taken from the ranks of the ignorant. If the best and highest minds do not in some way associate knowledge and religion, why are all our colleges and seminaries under the direct supervision of the Christian church? Education has transformed the savage into the Christian. The wide gulf that stretches between the beastly cannibal and the God-like Christian man has been bridged by the invisible cables of education, and away into the infinitely potential future shall stretch this golden bridge, till the farther end shall rest upon the massive masonry of the eternal.

Education was divinely instituted. Nature is the school mistress whom God employs to educate his children. This sweet and patient teacher knows how to win our hearts so that study becomes a pleasure. Everywhere she has placed before our eyes an open text book with such fascinating pictures that we cannot help reading the description of them. She found us with the beasts. Patiently she has conducted us through the primary school of the savage and barbarian, through the grammar school of war and bloodshed, till we have entered with her the high school of modern civilization. She will lead us triumphantly through and admit us into her vast university. There she will show us mysteries that would blind us now. In her laboratory we shall learn the awful secret of being. When we have graduated here she will lead us proudly up and present us to the Great Master, at whose side we shall sit and under whose tuition we shall turn our eyes starward and forever and forever shall study the infinite of infinites.

> "The heights by great men reached and kept
> Were not attained by sudden flight;
> But they, while their companions slept,
> Were toiling upward in the night."

BOOKS FOR THE HOME.

SOME one has said that "to thoroughly know one book is to have a key to all libraries."

The vast battalion of books that fill the shelves of our great libraries is almost appalling to behold, alcove upon alcove piled into the very domes of colossal buildings. Think of what they contain: the crystallized thought and wisdom of the centuries, and yet where shall we begin to make an analysis of that wisdom. We may call for a given book, but we find that book laps over on both sides of its subject.

Figuratively speaking, it leaned for support both ways upon its shelf. One subject is dependent upon another so that we cannot thoroughly know a single book in all that great library without knowing all. The classification may be admirable, yet it is after all but the classification of the dependent parts of a sublime and incomprehensible whole. How despair seizes the lover of wisdom, how hopeless seems his task, when he gazes upon those awful records of human thought. His feelings may be defined as those of mental strangulation. As we sit beneath the great dome and watch the men and women, with noiseless footsteps and with the anxiety of thought upon their faces, glide in and shift their burdens and pass out, how appropriate seems the metaphor that would make the library a vast sea, in which these men and women are strangling and in their mad despair letting go of one straw and grasping at another, vainly struggling to rise above the overmastering flood for one breath of thought that is yet unspoken, or to speak a word that is yet unwritten.

Since, then, we cannot compass the range of human thought, since we must be content with single links from an unbroken chain, the problem for us to solve becomes this, viz., where shall we break that chain, what books shall we read? This is one of the problems which parentage imposes, and, perhaps, there is no more vital one which parents are called upon to solve. As the body is chiefly what its food makes it, so is the mind. It is true that the infant mind has its positive mental proclivities, which cannot, and surely should not, be eradicated, yet they may and should be guided, and thus prevented from producing mental excrescences upon the character. The books of a family, not less than the training of the parents, shape the destiny of the children. The books of a family, however, we regret to say are not always solely those which are on exhibition in the book-cases and on the table of the drawing-room. There are in too many families books that are not on exhibition at all, books of which the parents are ignorant, books that are read only by lamplight, while the parents suppose that no lights are in the house. Parents! if you knew the books that, while you are sleeping at midnight, your children are reading by that dim light which casts its glimmer into the street, you would blush with shame.

Books are advertised in our daily newspapers under the veil of pathological philanthropy, to which the advertiser dares not put his name. Boys are directed to send so many postage stamps to a post-office box, to which there are many keys. A hint to the wise is all that is necessary. We will not enlarge upon this class of literature which disgraces the civilization of our age. But, like the "pestilence that walketh in darkness," none knows or feels it till it breathes its fatal breath into his face. This hellish literature lies piled mountain high in the dark and subterraneous caverns of society, and under the added gloom of midnight it is read by the baleful torches of lust. Our public schools are flooded with books that the teacher never sees. They constitute the text books from which the lessons are learned and recited without the aid of a tutor. Perhaps it is impossible to wholly eradicate this social evil. No parent is sure that his child has not already been contaminated. But parental vigilance is the only remedy that falls within the province of this work.

We have said enough concerning the books that should not be read. We come now to a more difficult task, viz., to determine what books should be read.

Of course we can give no definite list of books which should be read by each and every one. Courses of reading, however, have frequently been marked out, but we have little faith in the wisdom of such a method, unless the tastes and inborn mental tendencies of the individual for whom the course is marked out can be consulted. That evil feature of our public educational institutions which tends to destroy the originality and individuality of the child and student by forcing all casts of mind into a common mold, is strong enough already without helping on its bad effects by recommending the same course of reading for all. We do not mean by this, of course, that the parent, teacher, and guardian should not advise those under their charge with reference to the selection of books. We do not deny the wisdom of marking out a course of reading, if it be done with express reference to the mental peculiarities of those for whom it is intended, and by some one who is thoroughly conversant with those peculiarities.

Let parents study the minds of their children. Every parent should know enough of the general principles of mental science to enable him to make tolerably good intellectual and moral classifications. Until he does, he should hesitate before he attempts to pilot a human mind up the perilous rapids of childhood and youth.

Suppose a parent perceives that his child is greatly interested in shells, fossils, beetles, and all those things that pertain to zoological science, and that when his eye for the first time falls on a book devoted to this science, he is delighted beyond measure. Could there be anything more unjust and foolish than for that parent to withhold all such books from his child and to mark out a course of reading which should consist largely of psychological works, and books in which he is not at all interested, and compel him to toil through them. It is not, however, impossible that the child may possess a taste for both classes of books which we have mentioned, but if he has not already evinced a taste for both, it is surely the duty of the parent to ascertain the facts of the case before he compels him to read those books for which he has evinced no taste. If the boy is continually disposed to marshal his little playmates and march them around the house to the music of a tin pan, he will be a good candidate for West Point, and will probably be found to possess a latent love of history, and may perhaps become an historian. If he is disposed to spend much of his time in the work-shop making his own toys, he will delight in natural philosophy and in the biographies of great inventors. Parents should be able to interpret these outward indications of innate talent, and, regarding them as the cries of a hungry mind, should be quick to furnish the proper food. If the boy who is inclined to invent and to use tools, be compelled by his parents to study history most of the time, instead of natural philosophy, he will very likely conceive a general dislike for all kinds of reading.

But if he be allowed first to read and study those branches that lie along the line of his taste and talents, he will not only acquire a taste for reading, but by such a course he will also early develop a strong individuality. Every mind should be first developed in the line in which it earliest evinces an unmistakable tendency.

This secures a stability of purpose and an individuality that no after course or promiscuous reading can destroy. The mind may then be brought into shape, as it were, by supplementary reading. Nor will this be difficult, but on the contrary, very natural, since it will have first acquired a taste for reading.

Every book in the great library is the record of some man's individuality, and when you have read the book you have read the man. Books differ as men differ. A person may associate with a hundred different people of that character which one meets every day upon the street, and not be conscious of the modifying influence which they exert over him. But he may afterwards meet a single individual in whose silent presence he will feel the tumultuous thrill of a molding influence. The meeting of such people is a crisis in one's life, and he is never the same afterwards.

So with books. We may read alcove after alcove of the books that make up the body of a public library, and never feel that we have read anything. The largest library that adorns the great city is almost useless after a scholar has carried home an armful of books. "Of the writing

IN THE LIBRARY.

EVENINGS AT HOME.

of many books there is no end." But of the writing of great books there has hardly been a beginning.

If one wishes to cultivate his social nature and improve himself generally by mingling in society, he cannot do it to the best advantage by going to the circus or the theater. All will admit that the most effectual way is to select a few choice associates better than himself.

Now since a library is but a proxy for society, the same rule holds good in respect to it. Read the few great books; books that work revolutions in our natures, and burn themselves into our memory and become a part of ourselves.

We do not mean that every child should read Plato, for Plato would be the same as no book at all to a child. "Robinson Crusoe" and the "Arabian Nights" are great and revolutionary books from a child's standpoint, and when he has grown stronger, "Pilgrim's Progress" and "Paul and Virginia" are also great and revolutionary. A few such books await him at every stage of his development, so that no one need read any but the great and good books. We have used the word few with reference to good books in a relative rather than an absolute sense. Of course there are in all libraries very many good and great books, but when compared with the mass they are certainly few.

But how shall you determine whether a given book be worth reading or not? By what means are you to be certain that you have selected one of those few? By the testimony of your own soul. If the book throws your whole being into the wild tumult of mingled thought and aspiration, if it lifts you till you feel, in the sweet deception of the hour, that the wings of your own spirit leave their shadows upon the star-lit heights, and you almost wonder that you yourself have allowed those grand words to remain so long unsaid, look no farther. You have found the book you were looking for, and it bears the divine imprint of genius.

All books, whether great or small, are but attempts to translate that one great book which lies open before humanity, the star-and-flower-writ book of Nature. There are many imperfect translations and poor commentaries, and thrice happy is he who can read the original without translation or commentaries.

"Books are not seldom talismans and spells,
By which the magic art of shrewder wits
Holds an unthinking multitude enthralled.
Some to the fascination of a name
Surrender judgment, hoodwinked. Some the style
Infatuates, and through labyrinths and wilds
Of error leads them, by a tune entranced.
While sloth seduces more, too weak to bear
The insupportable fatigue of thought,
And swallowing, therefore, without pause or choice,
The total grist unsifted, husks and all.
But trees and rivulets, whose rapid course
Defies the check of winter, haunts of deer,
And sheep-walks populous with bleating lambs,
And lanes in which the primrose ere her time
Peeps through the moss that clothes the hawthorn root,
Deceive no student. Wisdom there and Truth,
Not shy, as in the world, and to be won
By slow solicitation, seize at once
The roving thought, and fix it on themselves."

EVENINGS AT HOME.

THE evening hours are the holy hours of home life. They are the hours in which there is the freest play of all the hallowed influences that come from the domestic relation; the hours in which the radiant forces of the home are focalized and brought to their highest efficiency.

There is really just as much sunshine on a cloudy day as when the sky is clear, but the sickly growth of vegetation during cloudy weather proclaims its ineffectiveness. So the home may exert just as much actual influence when its sunshine is intercepted by the clouds of care and busy toil; when the merciless dispatch with which "father's" dinner must be prepared, or with which some of those many labors inseparably connected with the home life must be performed, has so absorbed the time and energy of the family that each member seems to be an illustration of the "survival of the fittest." Under these circumstances the home may send forth as large an amount of influence, and yet such influence cannot reach the lives and characters of those who have a claim upon it. Such may be called latent influence.

It is only when the "day is done" that home exhibits its sweetest and serenest life. It is when the sun has gone down that the home influences become actual and potent.

In opening the tender buds of young characters, the light from the hearth-stone is far more efficient than the sunlight.

The distinctive characteristics of the home life are manifested most strongly when the labors of the day are ended and the family gather round the fireside for the evening. One hour of evening home life is worth a month of the ordinary daily experience. It matters little where our days are spent if we spend our evenings at home.

Man's soul is not receptive during the day, for its attitude is not favorable. The labor of the day puts the mind into that attitude in which it resists the shaping influences of life. Labor itself is in part a process of spiritual resistance, so that the soul that toils is comparatively safe from the snares of temptation.

During the hours of labor we are also less susceptible to good influences as well as to evil ones. The whole being puts itself upon the defensive while it toils. Satisfied with its own condition, it refuses to be changed by outward influences. In this principle we find the explanation of the adage "idleness is the parent of vice." The evening is the hour when crafty Satan preaches most eloquently. It is also the hour at which he can gather the largest and most attentive audience. In our great cities Satan's churches are crowded every evening.

But, fortunately, the evening hour is also the hour in which the good angel can gather his largest audience, and he who would baffle Satan's influence must preach in the evening. The evening is the hour when the protecting power of home is greatest; it is the hour when its protection is most needed. We see a divine wisdom in this. The only hour in the day when the laboring young man is vulnerable to temptation is when his labor is ended and the mind relaxed, and just at this needed hour the home exerts a doubled influence. Parents need not be at all anxious concerning the character of their boys who from choice stay at home evenings, but they should never feel at ease concerning those who desire to spend their evenings away from home.

We do not mean that children should never go away from home evenings. The evening is a very proper and agreeable time to visit our neighbors, and children should be allowed frequently to spend the evening with their neighbors' children. This is only a transfer of home influence. They are at home in one sense when at their neighbors' home, or at least they are surrounded by home influences.

It is an excellent practice to allow children, even when

very young, to visit their neighbors' children alone in the evening. The reason of this may not at first be obvious, but we think that upon reflection every parent will perceive the wisdom of it.

In the first place, it is a mild lesson in self reliance and independent action, which every parent should try to develop in the minds of his children.

Again, all children who are to develop into noble men and women must sooner or later be brought into contact with temptations to every form of improper action, and the earlier this process commences, and the more gradually they encounter the temptations of life, the better for their welfare. And, certainly, sending children to their neighbors' alone in the evening, thus putting them upon their own sense of propriety, and subjecting them to the little temptations to trifling breaches of etiquette, which always present themselves when little children gather in groups, is one of the most judicious methods of applying this principle. It is not well for parents in such cases to be over strict in regard to the hour of the children's return. It is far better to teach them to exercise their own sense of propriety in this matter.

Let them be taught that it is a gross breach of good manners to stay much beyond a certain hour, perhaps nine o'clock.

But this is far different in its effect from commanding them to start when the clock strikes nine. In the one case they are compelled to go home by an inward sense of propriety, and in the other by an outward sense of authority. It is always a cross for children to leave their playmates, and if they can just as well be taught to make this sacrifice through their own sense of propriety, their parents should certainly rejoice in this early opportunity to give them a practical lesson in self denial. If the child is compelled by an outward authority located at home, to withdraw from a pleasant associate, he is quite likely to conceive a dislike for that authority and for the place toward which it constrains him.

Then let the children visit. Let the parents visit in the evenings. Let all the members of the family feel that the home is not a prison. This is the only way in which children can be taught to love home and to feel that home is the best place to spend their evenings. You cannot make them feel this by compelling them to stay at home evenings. If a child has acquired a distaste for home, the evil must be corrected by the use of mild stratagem.

One of the strongest arguments for the habit of spending the evenings at home is found in the opportunity which they offer to the young for self-improvement.

Horace Mann once wrote a beautiful truth in the form of an advertisement, "Lost, yesterday, somewhere between sunrise and sunset, two golden hours, each set with sixty diamond minutes. No reward is offered, for they are gone forever."

We would like to have the ordinary young man of twenty-five look over our shoulder while we do a little figuring. We mean that young man, however, who is always complaining because he hasn't time.

We mean that young man who is mourning because he hasn't an education, who would have gone to college could he have spared the time.

We want to show him how many of those golden hours set with diamond minutes he has thrown away since he was sixteen years old. It is nine years since then, and in each of those years there were three hundred and sixty-five evenings. Setting aside the fifty-two Sunday evenings, which, however, might be employed to advantage without violating the fourth commandment, then taking out fifty-two evenings more, one for every week, for visiting and entertaining visitors, there will remain two hundred and sixty-one. Now each one of these two hundred and sixty-one evenings contains four of those golden hours. Hence in one year he throws away one thousand and forty-four hours. During the nine years from sixteen to twenty-five, he throws away nine times this number, or nine thousand three hundred and ninety-six hours.

Just think of it. The average college student spends about four hours a day in study. There are five days in a week in which he studies, making twenty hours a week. Thirty-eight weeks constitute the college year, making seven hundred and sixty hours which he studies in a year.

There are four years in the college course. Hence in his whole course he studies four times seven hundred and sixty, or three thousand and forty hours. This is less than a third as many as the young man may throw away between the ages of sixteen and twenty-five. Should not every such young man feel indignant with himself? Time enough spent on the street corners, in the stores, in the hotel, or in the bar-room, to go through college three times. Nine thousand golden hours gemmed with five hundred and forty thousand diamond minutes, gone forever.

Perhaps it may seem even cruel in us to remind the young man of his terrible loss, but it is never too late to do better. A noble endeavor can never be too early or too late. We would not cause any young man a useless painful regret. He cannot profit by mourning over spilt milk, but if he will keep his pan right side up for five years to come he can go through college yet, and graduate when he is thirty years old, and have the honor of presenting to himself his own diploma.

But not alone for the opportunities for culture which they afford are evenings to be prized. The evening in the happy home is a fragment of heaven, we cannot afford to lose it. The ineffable joy that human nature is constituted to experience at the evening hour around the golden altar of home, is a symbol and a prophecy of that which every truly and interiorly developed soul has reason to believe is in store for him. It is the only place where each and every faculty and power of mind and body may legitimately act, and with that divine spontaneity that feels no pressure nor restraint. When reason acts through the day it is spurred to action by the necessities of daily duty, and the pleasure which all organic activity, both mental and physical, is intended to produce is lost in the mad whirl of life's tumultuous conflict. The same is true of that innate tendency to mathematical computation which is capable of conferring so much pleasure by the revelations it gives of the universality of divine law and order. But when these powers act amid the cheerfulness of the evening entertainment at home, in the playful solution of problems and puzzles, they act with that spontaneity and accompanying pleasure on their own account which hints at their origin and their destiny. This same principle applies to every power of being. Who does not still carry in his mind the sweet pictures of happy evenings at home, when all the family sat by the fire, mother with her knitting, and father with his stories of prouder days, while the kitten gambolled upon the floor or played with the ball of yarn that fell from mother's lap, and while the fire-light moved upon the wall like the waving of a white wing in the darkness,—as if heaven could not permit so much joy upon the earth without having its representative there? Now mother tardily rises to light the lamp, and the children gather round the table with slate and pencil to grapple with those little tasks and problems that only sweeten life's remembrances.

How indelibly through all the change-freighted years this picture remains upon the canvas of the soul. Unlike the perishing works of genius, time never bleaches the canvas nor turns the picture pale. Gaze on that picture, O youth. Nor turn your eyes aside when Temptation with perfumed robes sweeps past thee in the tumultuous rush of beauty's carnival. When we turn our eyes from the soft colors of a beautiful picture, to gaze upon the brilliancy of the electric light, and then turn again to view the picture, how dim the colors, how blurred is the whole picture till we have steadily and persistently gazed for a long time.

Learn a lesson from the analogy that exists between the spirit's eye and that of the body. That sweet picture of your home, O youth, gleams not brilliantly but softly and forever in the evening fire-light. Reflect before you turn your eyes from that soft fire-light to gaze long upon the splendors where beauty glides 'neath lights that dazzle.

"Gladly now we gather round it,
For the toiling day is done,
And the gay and solemn twilight
Follows down the golden sun.
Shadows lengthen on the pavement,
Stalk like giants through the gloom,
Wander past the dusky casement,
Creep around the fire-lit room.
Draw the curtain, close the shutters,
Place the slippers by the fire;
Though the rude wind loudly mutters,
What care we for wind sprite's ire?

"What care we for outward seeming,
Fickle fortune's frown or smile?
If around us love is beaming,
Love can human ills beguile.
'Neath the cottage roof and palace,
From the peasant to the king,
All are quaffing from life's chalice
Bubbles that enchantment bring.
Grates are glowing, music flowing
From the lips we love the best;
O, the joy, the bliss of knowing
There are hearts whereon to rest!

"Hearts that throb with eager gladness—
Hearts that echo to our own—
While grim care and haunting sadness
Mingle ne'er in look or tone.
Care may tread the halls of daylight,
Sadness haunt the midnight hour,
But the weird and witching twilight
Brings the glowing hearthstone's dower.
Altar of our holiest feelings!
Childhood's well-remembered shrine!
Spirit yearnings—soul revealings—
Wreaths immortal round thee twine!"

SELF CULTURE.

CULTURE is the constant elimination of useless movements, and the attainment of increasing economy in the expenditure of our forces. The Indian has plenty of strength, but the white man of half his weight and strength, who has acquired the art of boxing, is more than a match for him; and this for the simple reason that the Indian has not yet learned to eliminate the movements that do not count. He is a spendthrift as regards forces. But the white man, by means of patient culture, has learned to omit all useless movements, and to expend his forces in that manner and at that time and place in which they will tell the most. He does not bend a joint or contract a muscle that does not produce some desirable outward result.

It is easy to detect an uncultured person in society; for example, when he attempts to walk across a hall or drawing-room in the presence of spectators. It is not because he does not perform all the movements necessary to take him to the other side, but because he performs certain other movements that interfere with, or obstruct the essential movements; such as the turning of the head from side to side, accompanied by a wasteful expenditure of thought in the form of a painful consciousness that people are gazing at him. There is in his blush a wasteful expenditure of vital forces in compelling the blood to the surface. All such movements are uneconomical because they produce no desirable or useful result. Nature has agreed to give us a positive dislike for all such movements, and we call them awkward. She has also made us susceptible of a positive delight from witnessing economical movements, and at her suggestion we call them graceful. Graceful movements, then, are simply economical movements. If the person referred to should walk across the hall with the least possible expenditure of vital and mental force, the movement would necessarily be graceful. Civilization is but aggregate culture, and since culture is the spirit and essence of economy, we see why it is that the science of political economy has always developed itself simultaneously with civilization. Indeed, civilization and political economy are one and the same.

Such, then, is the nature of culture in the abstract. Let us follow out the principle in its application to our physical, mental, and moral natures, and see whether we can find in it anything that shall be of use to us in the development of our lives and characters. Our muscles are cultured when we can use them with no waste of force. Our intellects are cultured when we can solve a problem or arrive at a conclusion by the shortest and most direct route of logical deduction. Our moral nature is cultured when duty becomes a graceful and economical movement in the soul; when the useless movements of sin are eliminated; when all our spiritual forces are concentrated, and it no longer becomes necessary to divide the force by detailing a squadron to guard the harbor of love and duty against the pirate fleets of selfishness. When we can say "Thy will be done," without a diverting and wasting struggle with ourselves. The reason why certain men have been able to accomplish such wonderful results in the field of thought and investigation is because, through long toil and patient culture, they have learned to concentrate the mental forces by eliminating all useless thoughts. Like the bee, which always takes a straight line, they have acquired an intellectual instinct by which they are enabled to take the shortest, directest, and consequently most economical line of logic links between their intellectual standpoint and the solution that they crave. And he who can do this, he who can take the shortest road, can surely go farther and accomplish more in the same time than he who is compelled to hunt out his path, to travel through all the by-ways, the briers, the brambles, and the underbrush, and at last, perhaps, lose his way altogether in the vast swamp of intellectual uncertainty.

All culture in its ultimate analysis is necessarily self culture. Culture when used as a verb always means to afford the conditions for self-direction or self-development. If we attempt to culture a horse or a dog we accomplish the result only by inducing him to make certain voluntary movements in the direction of our will. But if he does not choose to act according to our will, all culture ceases until he becomes willing to obey. We cannot culture anything that has the power of volition. Hence, when we break a colt, or train a dog, he cultures himself at our suggestion. And thus it is that all the culture we receive in this life must be self culture. Teachers may suggest, but we must execute; they may advise, but we must do the work.

The sense in which we have used the word "culture" is not very different from that in which we have used the word "education" in the chapter on the "Education of our Boys." Indeed, all that we have said by way of definition in either chapter might have been said with equal propriety in the other. We will allow the one to supplement the other.

The words educate, train and culture are, for all practical purposes, synonymous, and may be used interchangeably.

In our chapter on "Home Training" we have presented some similar thoughts concerning the importance of training or cultivating the physical, intellectual, and moral nature in the proper order, and in the right way. That, however, was intended chiefly for advice to parents concerning the management of children too young to attempt self culture. But the primary constitution does not change. What the child requires, the youth and young man require, only, perhaps, in larger quantities and in different proportion. Hence in this chapter we shall aim to give such helpful advice as will enable young men and women to continue the process that their parents helped them to begin. They may now call it self culture, to denote a higher stage of the same process. The first and chief aim of self culture, as of all education, should be symmetry. The undue strengthening of one part or faculty, to the neglect of another, is not culture, but according to our definition it is the reverse, for it destroys that power of co-ordinate action and economical expenditure of effort in which culture consists. No power of mind or body exists independent of other powers, and no one can be unduly strengthened without peril to the other and weaker ones. If the stomach be enlarged by overeating, while the lungs be kept weak and small, the whole body will become diseased and the mind also; for a sound mind cannot exist in an unhealthy body. The stomach, being large, will crave a large amount of food, but the lungs, being small, cannot furnish oxygen enough to oxidize the carbon that is furnished to the blood by the stomach; so the system becomes clogged; corrupt and troublesome ulcers appear, and perhaps consumption, and all because the stomach was enlarged. Not because the lungs were not cultivated, but because the stomach was cultivated alone, as if it were an independent organ. Similar disasters follow the independent and separate training of any of the other physical powers. If the stomach, the appetite, the lungs, the liver, the kidneys, the circulation, the skin, and the muscles be all cultivated together, the more they are cultivated the better. It is absolutely impossible to carry that kind of culture to excess. But if we cannot cultivate all, it is far better not to specially cultivate any of the physical functions.

It is a well known fact that circus performers are very short lived; and yet we would naturally expect them to live to a very old age. How full and powerful their lungs are! How agile! How almost marvelous the strength of their muscles! How erect they are! What free play all the internal organs must have! They are compelled by their employment to live temperately; their food is that which is recommended by the highest medical authority; they sleep in well ventilated rooms. It would seem that if earthly immortality were possible, the professional gymnasts should possess the boon.

But instead the average duration of their lives is very short. How shall we account for this paradox? Simply by that principle just named, which demands the symmetrical and proportionate development of all the functions. They carry training of the muscles to such an extent, that like wasting fire they consume their vitality. In spite of all hygienic regimen and temperance, their training is not symmetrical, although it may appear to be such. The human body is a delicate machine, and no wheel can be made to turn faster or slower than it was intended to turn without tearing off the cogs. But it is often found that in the same individual certain vital organs even without special culture are larger and more powerful than others, and this is doubtless the reason why many apparently healthy people die young. It is because they are born with some of the vital organs powerfully developed, while others are weak, and the strong ones consume the vitality that the weak ones have not the energy to appropriate. It should be the first object of culture to balance the powers by cultivating the weak and restraining the overaction of the strong. After this most desirable result has been secured, all the functions should be trained alike, and the whole carried to the highest possible state of culture. It is usually an easy matter to ascertain what organs of the body are weak, and what strong, but in case the facts are not obvious, a physician should be consulted, who should be requested to test all the vital organs; not to doctor them, but to measure their strength. If the brain and nervous system are predominant, much muscular exercise should be taken, while the mental powers, and especially the imagination, should be restrained. If the reverse is true, the brain should be forced to act, and the tendency to muscular action should be held in check. If the muscles are stronger than the frame-work of the body, then great care should be used not to exercise the muscles to their full extent, for such a practice would be sure to strain the body and injure the vital organs. This condition is oftener seen in women than in men; hence women frequently injure themselves by lifting. If the muscles are weaker than the frame-work, then little injury can result from the full and unrestrained use of the muscles. But Nature is very kind to those who are too ignorant to ascertain their own weaknesses. She has so constituted us that the best and most useful form of exercise is that of walking or running. And that is just the kind of exercise that the necessities of life compel us to take the most of. This form of exercise actually has a tendency to balance the organic developments, for it brings into action every organ of the body, and in such a way as to benefit the weak ones relatively more than the strong ones. For instance, if the lungs are weak and the muscles strong, then the lungs will be the first to say stop; and they will say so just at that moment when they have received the greatest possible amount of good from the running.

The lungs will have received just enough exercise to do them good long before the muscles have had enough to test their endurance, or to strengthen them much. If the muscles are weak and the lungs strong, then the muscles will control the amount of running, and adapt it to their own particular needs. Long before the lungs have received exercise enough to do them much good, the muscles will have received just enough to do them the greatest possible amount of good. Thus we see how it is that running is the best exercise in the world, and, to a certain extent, relieves us of the responsibility of ascertaining which are our weak organs, for it will pick them out for us and make them strong. People both walk and run far too little. It is, perhaps, impossible for human beings or animals to be born with all their organs in a state of perfect balance, and running seems to be Nature's means of balancing them, for she gives the young of all animals, the human species included, an irrepressible impulse to run almost continually, and during that age, too, in which their organs are most easily modified.

As a rule, children need no other physical culture than their own freedom. A child in the woods for one day will do more in the direction of curing an organic weakness than all the doctors of Christendom.

We have spoken thus minutely on the subject of physical culture because physical culture is not only the basis of all culture, but the same general directions which we have given, are as applicable to intellectual and moral culture as to physical.

Symmetry is the one idea that should be kept prominently in view in all forms of culture. But the laws of the mind are such as to allow considerable margin for variety's sake. One need not be equally gifted in all his mental powers in order to be symmetrical. It is not necessary that he be able with equal facility to play the violin and calculate an eclipse. He may be born with such a latent talent for music as to render this not only the most pleasant but also the most profitable occupation of his life, and still violate no essential law of symmetry. But if he possesses the talent to such a degree as to become its slave, while his whole mental energy is absorbed by the one passion, and he is left to feel that there is nothing else beside music to render life worth living, he has passed the limits which the law of variety allows him and has become unsymmetrical. His musical faculty should be restrained, while other faculties should be called to the front and compelled to act. This is a hard task and one which is not very frequently accomplished, for the very reason that the difficulty itself is of such a character as to prevent the person from seeing things in their true light. When one talks to him about the grandeur of science and the beauties of philosophy, he listens with impatience to such foolishness. The same is true of all forms of disproportionate mental development. Nothing but a knowledge of the mental economy will enable one, under these circumstances, to see himself as he is. When one looks upon himself from the standpoint of mental science, he eliminates the bias of his own feelings resulting from his strongest tendencies, and sees himself as others see him. It is very often the case that one can be made to see his own mental defects in no other way than by a study of mental science.

There is one law of great importance that should not be lost sight of either in physical or mental culture. It is the law of periodicity. It is in recognition of this law that the professional gymnast is required to practice at just such an hour each day. In some way which we cannot fully understand, the muscles instinctively adapt themselves to the conditions of periodical activity, so that when the appointed hour arrives it finds them in that particular condition which enables them to derive the greatest possible amount of good from a given amount of practice. The law operates precisely the same in the mental economy. A music teacher who has had much experience will insist that the pupil practice at the same hour each day.

It is not essential that we should advise more minutely with reference to the education of the mental powers, since the needed advice may be found in the chapter devoted expressly to that subject.

Moral culture involves no different principle from that of intellectual culture, and the cardinal idea of symmetry is as applicable to this form as to the two forms we have already considered. The same is true of the law of periodicity; the saint who prays at regular periods will grow in the instinct of prayer and faith, while he who prays only when he finds it convenient will find that the intervals grow constantly wider. It is necessary, however, to keep constantly in mind the fact that the only legitimate condition of him who lays claim to moral culture, is that of the complete supremacy of the moral sentiments over the passions. All sin originates in passional supremacy, while out of the ceaseless and often equal conflict between the moral impulses and those of the passions, grow all the enigmas of human conduct. A person in whom the latter condition exists will remain alike to his friends and foes an unsolved problem. He will be both very good and very bad. When under the dominion of the excited passions he may be a fiend; but an hour later he may be a saint. The saddest condition for a human being is that in which the passions and moral sentiments are so equally balanced that neither can gain a permanent victory over the other.

When the moral sentiments and the passions are both predominant at intervals, the moral sense becomes capricious and cannot be depended upon. The person becomes distrustful of his own good resolves, and his character loses all stability and permanence. Either condition is bad enough, but on the whole we regard the relation of equality between the passions and the morals as the most dangerous and destructive.

So deplorable is this condition that we would even regard the permanent ascendency of the passions as a lesser evil.

Such a condition offers little hope of recovery, for the passions and moral sentiments both grow by their occasional victories, the one as fast as the other, and both are weakened by their occasional defeats, the one as much as the other. The remedy for this condition is to make the intellect an ally for the conscience. It should be required to devise means to keep the passions out of temptation. When the passions are not aroused by the presence of temptation, they are not difficult to manage. Ordinarily, however, temptation is a source of strength, uniformly, indeed, if it be resisted. But this condition is not always fulfilled, and in the case we are considering it is almost sure not to be fulfilled, so that the intellect should see that temptation is never allowed to be present, and should seek those places, occasions, and influences that appeal to the morals. By persisting in this course a long time the moral nature will gain a permanent victory, and then the vigilant restraint may be removed, the fetters may be taken off from the passions, and they will recognize their master.

"When gentle twilight sits
On day's forsaken throne,
'Mid the sweet hush of eventide,
Muse by thyself alone.
And at the time of rest
Ere sleep asserts its power,
Hold pleasant converse with thyself
In meditation's bower.

"Motives and deeds review
By memory's truthful glass,
Thy silent self the only judge
And critic as they pass;
And if thy wayward face
Should give thy conscience pain,
Resolve with energy divine
The victory to gain.

* * * * * * * * * *

"Drink waters from the fount
That in thy bosom springs,
And envy not the mingled draught
Of satraps or of kings;
So shalt thou find at last,
Far from the giddy brain
Self-knowledge and self-culture lead
To uncomputed gain."

SUNDAYS AT HOME.

WHETHER we regard the Sabbath as divinely appointed or as growing out of the instincts and necessities of man's moral and spiritual nature, the experience of man has demonstrated that it sustains a vital relation to our highest welfare.

Hence no work dealing with the varied phases of domestic life would be complete without a chapter on "Sundays at Home."

With the exception of the few hours supposed by all civilized people to be spent in public worship, the day is not in any sense a public day, but, on the contrary, it is the most private of all days. It is a day when the loud tumult of public affairs is hushed, and each individual becomes a world in himself. It is a day of personal meditation. A purely public day, like the Fourth of July in the United States, bears little relation to the home life. It is from the fact that Sunday is the most private of all days, that we here make it a subject of special consideration; in order, if possible, to determine what purpose in the economy of home shall be subserved by this important period called the Sabbath. It constitutes one seventh of our entire existence, and of no other seventh do we spend so large a part at home. For the small part that is devoted to public worship by no means equals that consumed on other days by labor and those duties which partially or wholly isolate us from the influences of home.

How, then, shall we employ the Sunday at home? How shall we secure for it a place among the higher ministries of home life? This, of course, will depend somewhat upon the views we hold concerning the nature and object of the Sabbath. It is not our purpose to discuss the subject in its theological aspect, but simply to compel it, if possible, to yield a contribution to the lessons of home life. And yet it is impossible to do even this without taking some definite ground as to the religious significance of the day. It is useless to contend that the Sabbath has no religious significance, for to divest it of such significance, would be, in the nature of things, to abolish it altogether. If it be claimed that the Sabbath was born of human instincts, still it was of the religious instincts, and to prove that it was thus born would be to claim for it a Divine sanction. We believe that the religious nature of man and the institution of the Sabbath are complementary, the one to the other. But whatever origin may be claimed for the Sabbath, and whatever purpose it was primarily intended to serve in the economy of civilization, we have no reason to believe that it was intended for a period of "suspended animation" or of physical and mental stagnation. Jesus rebuked the too close and Pharisaical observance of the Sabbath, and taught, both by precept and by example, that man was not made in order that he might observe the Sabbath, but on the contrary, that the Sabbath was made in order that man might have the privilege of observing it. Man was made first and the Sabbath was adapted to him, although we believe that the natural law on which the Sabbath is based is coeval with the history of creation.

If, then, the Sabbath originated in the religious instincts of man, it is inconsistent and foolish to contend that it should not be observed as a day of special religious exercise. But the question still arises, what constitutes special religious exercise? and by what method is the desired result best attained? The now generally recognized law that disagreeable or painful action always weakens instead of strengthening the faculty involved, is directly opposed to the Puritanic observance of the Sabbath; for how can a child be submitted to more intense mental torture, than to be compelled to spend a whole day where he is not allowed to smile, where all conversation is suppressed, except that which is absolutely necessary, and where even that is conducted with semi-whispers in the unmistakable tone of reverence and awe. The Sabbath in too many homes is a day to be dreaded by the children. The observance of it required is so strict as to be painful, and hence weakens instead of strengthening their moral and religious nature. The effect of such forced action is almost always far worse than no action at all. This law obtains with reference to every power of our being, but its action is most obvious with reference to the moral and spiritual faculties. These must act from choice or they cannot be strengthened. Hence the question becomes a most delicate one, "How shall the Sunday be spent at home?"

Perhaps no further advice to the intelligent parent is required than that he should be guided in all cases by this great law, that every action, in order that it may strengthen the part acting, must be accompanied with pleasure, instead of pain.

In the first place, let the Sunday at home be divested of all needless solemnity; let it be a day of cheerfulness and social enjoyment, a day of music both instrumental and vocal, a day of conversation and reading. Let the children be taught to think and to meditate on the great problems of life and the vast concerns of eternity, not in a solemn, awe-inspiring way, but in a manner consonant with good judgment and common sense. Let them be encouraged to engage in respectful discussions among themselves, on these questions. Thus will they early develop a tendency to think and hold opinions of their own, while yet the parents' superior wisdom may detect and point out fallacies in their reasoning. There is little danger of sophistry and false conclusions in these arguments if the parent is watchful, and seeks constantly to set the young thinkers right, not by an *ipse dixit*, nor even by "thus saith the Scripture," but by convincing their reason with superior logic. When one begins to doubt any doctrine, whether intellectual or religious, he naturally conceives a dislike for any authority which disputes his ground, unless the authority is enforced by reasons which his own intellect is compelled to acknowledge as conclusive. Superior logic is the only authority which a questioning mind naturally receives with good grace. Hence, if you do not wish your child to hate the Bible, do not attempt to silence all his questions by the mere quotation of Scriptural texts, but first, calmly and kindly lay bare the fallacy in his argument, and then show him, if you choose, how your own argument accords with Scripture.

But it may be asked, why not teach the child to trust? why cultivate a tendency to question, by harboring the argumentative disposition? There is, it is true, a period in early childhood when unquestioning trust is natural and proper. But let us remember that when the child reaches the age of fourteen or fifteen, he comes suddenly into possession of the weapon of logic, and no matter what may have been the teachings and influences of his early years, he will, between the ages of fourteen and twenty, think, doubt, and question for himself. Every human mind, however trustful it may be through childhood, must pass through its period of doubt and mental conflict, and the earlier this period is passed, the better and the safer. Atheists are made out of those minds which receive only the *ipse dixit* of bigoted fathers, after the awakening intellect demands a reason.

When questions begin to present themselves to such minds, questions that insist upon an answer, dissatisfied with the merely dogmatic answer of the father, they naturally appropriate the most logical explanation at hand, which, of course, partakes of the narrowness of their own thought-power, and thus they are often led astray.

There are probably in the world few atheists who would be such had their young logic been answered with logic and not with authority. We believe that a very large per cent. of the world's unbelief is due to a wrong system of Sunday discipline.

But we would not have the children disregard the solemnity and sanctity of the Sabbath. It is natural for children as well as for older people to have their periods of serious thought. But parents should bear in mind that with the child these periods are not naturally quite so serious nor so protracted as their own. We believe the day should be a day of rest, not, however, for the reason usually assigned, viz., that man's physical nature requires it. For to suppose that the natural duties of life constitute a burden so heavy that it cannot be borne without constantly putting it down, is to suppose that God made a mistake in the adaptation of life's powers to its duties.

Man is surely as well adapted to his natural surroundings as the ant or the beaver, and to these, the burden of life's labor is not so great as to require a periodic rest.

We believe that the philosophy of the Sabbath as a day of rest is to be found in Nature's law of *undivided intensity*, the law by which it is impossible for an organized being to act intensely at two or more points at the same time. This law holds with equal force in the physical, intellectual and moral worlds. The physician makes a practical application of its physical phase when he irritates the feet with drafts to cure the headache. The student applies its mental phase when he requires his room to be silent in order that he may put his "whole mind" to his task. And the saint applies its moral phase when he avoids temptation and prays in his closet.

Now the Sabbath is the complement of man's religious nature, and in accordance with the law of "periodicity," of which we have already spoken in our chapter on "Self Culture," this department of his nature must act with special force at certain regular periods. In the light of these facts the whole philosophy of the Sabbath as a day of rest may be seen at a glance by watching a laborer at work. Suddenly a thought seizes him ; one which deeply interests, and vitally concerns him. How instinctively he drops his tool and stands motionless.

Now we have only to regard the world as one man laboring for his daily bread, but, who by a law of his spiritual nature, is called upon once in seven days, to think with special intensity upon the great concerns of the eternal and the unseen. The same instinct that caused the mechanic to drop his tool and stand motionless causes the world to do the same. It is but the instinctive application of this universal law of undivided intensity that closes the furnace door, hushes the roar of the engine, and spreads the mantle of silent thought over the great city.

Is it then a sin to labor on the Sabbath? Yes, a twofold sin, a sin against both our physical and our moral nature. Just as when one eats heartily when engaged in intense mental labor, he sins against both his mind and his stomach. Physicians tell us, we can do nothing more injurious, for the brain having concentrated nearly all the vital energy of the system, the stomach is in consequence left feeble and unable to dispose of its burden without a great strain. Exactly the same principle holds with reference to laboring on the Sabbath. The absorbing occupation of the Sabbath should be the study of ourselves with the one view to symmetrical self culture. Sunday is the day of all others for self culture. It is a day in which we should study our relation to our Maker, and in accordance with the impulses of the moral nature, all our mental energies should be expended in rounding out our characters, and perfecting our whole nature.

But he who attempts this great work on the Sabbath, and at the same time attempts to carry on the ordinary labors of life, is not only thwarting his own efforts at self-improvement, but is doing that which will shorten his life perhaps a score of years.

But he who carries his ordinary labors into the Sabbath does not, of course, observe the day. Then he commits a still worse sin. He not only sins against society, which, however, is a comparatively minor sin, but he refuses to obey a great spiritual law, which is woven into the very constitution of his moral nature.

So that, view the subject as we may, we cannot ignore the Sabbath without sinning against ourselves, and we cannot sin against ourselves without sinning against our God.

"O day to sweet religious thought
So wisely set apart,
Back to the silent strength of life
Help thou my wavering heart.

"Nor let the obtrusive lies of sense
My meditations draw
From the composed, majestic realm
Of everlasting law.

"Break down whatever hindering shapes
I see or seem to see,
And make my soul acquainted with
Celestial company.

"Beyond the wintry waste of death
Shine fields of heavenly light;
Let not this incident of time
Absorb me from their sight.

"I know these outward forms wherein
  So much my hopes I stay,
Are but the shadowy hints of that
  Which cannot pass away.

"That just outside the work-day path
  By man's volition trod,
Lie the resistless issues of
  The things ordained of God."

RESOLUTIONS AND INDIVIDUAL RULES OF LIFE.

SUCCESSFUL culture is never the result of unmethodical effort. The best results are obtained only when due regard is had to a judicious and systematic use of time, when the mind subjects itself to self-government through a code of laws adopted and approved by itself. Mind in all its operations and volitions is under the dominion of law. There is no product of creation's law that in its operations can transcend law. A being, then, develops best and most rapidly when each department of his nature is subjected to the rigid discipline of its own laws. In our chapter on self-culture we have dwelt upon the *general* laws that govern our physical, intellectual, and moral natures; but there are laws of a less general nature, which it is equally important that we should observe, laws pertaining to individuals and growing out of organic or temperamental conditions. These laws each individual must discover and obey for himself; for since they originate in individual peculiarities they cannot be of general significance, and hence cannot be formulated into a code by any but the individual himself. Such are the laws pertaining to the particular time and the amount of sleep required by each person, to the kind and quantity of food desirable for each, and to the processes of thought and mental activity that vary with traits and temperaments.

All these laws should be ascertained by self-examination and by remembering our own experiences. In this connection it is proper to consider the importance of dividing each day into periods for the performance of special duties. Learn from self-observation what part of the day may be with greatest advantage spent in reading and study. Not alone, however, with reference to reading and study, but with reference to each and every function of life. But it is not enough merely to learn these facts. It is far more important, as it is far more difficult, to form and keep the resolutions to which this knowledge should prompt us.

This subject naturally suggests the practice of keeping a journal. And, perhaps, there is no duty of life (and we consider this a duty of all), which, in proportion to the exertion it requires, is capable of yielding such desirable results in the direction of personal culture. Setting aside the advantages of being able, at a moment's notice, to present the written volume of our lives (not the generalities and glowing eulogiums in which biographers and literary executors indulge), such a minute delineation of our daily thoughts and deeds through all our past years, as will enable us at any moment, to tell what function in our life's programme a given day has performed,—setting aside all this, there is probably no one practice more disciplinary in its permanent effects, than that of recording each night the thoughts and deeds of the vanished day. The duty, however, should be conscientiously performed. This disciplinary tendency is in the process itself independent of the record's value. It often happens that the demands of daily life present themselves with such tumultuous rapidity, and in such perplexing confusion, that the great reviewer, Conscience, does not always have time to subject each act to a sufficiently scrutinizing examination. And many of them get a favorable verdict by demanding a haste that conceals their deformities. But when, at the close of day—that hour which seems to offer most leisure for the solution of life's problems—we sit, calmly reviewing our deeds in the order of their occurrence, and in all their inter-relations, then it often happens that Conscience finds occasion to revoke its decision, and to pass a severer verdict. Again, the aid in the cultivation of memory which the practice offers is by no means insignificant, since it especially cultivates that power of memory in which nearly all, particularly Americans, are deficient, viz., the power to reproduce impressions in the order in which they occurred. It is needless to say that this form of memory is the most useful of all. That form of memory which enables one to reproduce a few disjointed links in a chain of thought, although it may reproduce a great many of them, can seldom be of great service to its possessor. The recollection of past events is valuable to us only as it enables us to recognize the relation of the recollected events. Hence the value of that form of memory that can recollect them in their sequential order.

Now the reader will demand no proof of the assertion that there are no means by which this form of memory can be so quickly and thoroughly acquired as by the practice of recalling each night the experiences of the day in their chronological order. The talent for public speaking, so highly prized by all young men, but possessed by few, is almost wholly conferred by this power of consecutive memory. Those who possess it are enabled not only to reproduce the thoughts gathered in the process of preparation, but to reproduce them in their order, one thought suggesting the next, and thus enabling the speaker to dispense with notes.

We cannot too strongly urge the practice of keeping a journal. We have dwelt thus at length upon the subject on account of the importance which we believe it possesses, and because it affords the best possible assistance in carrying out the chief injunction of this chapter, viz., that each individual should govern himself by laws, maxims, and resolutions of his own authorship.

We would recommend, not only the practice of recording, in the evening, the thoughts, deeds, and events of the day, but also of recording, in the morning, that which we intend to accomplish during the day. This practice offers a threefold advantage. First, it enables us to govern ourselves through the day by the laws which we enact in our better moods; second, it leads us to set a high price upon time, and to cultivate a habit of punctuality and method; third, when we have written the record at evening just under the promise of the morning, and the divine conscience within us utters in our spirit's ear the comments that seem fittest, we may be gazing upon one of the most significant lessons of life. For it is a lesson symbolic of the close of many a life; a dark and colorless evening in sad contrast with the brilliant hues and gaudy beauty of youth's morning. The practice can have but one tendency, and that is to make these two records more closely agree.

The journal or diary is the best and most convenient place in which to record those maxims and resolutions, the wisdom and necessity of which we have so strongly urged. As fast as you discover under what particular regulations and circumstances a given function of your life is most advantageously performed, make these regulations and circumstances the theme of a resolution or a maxim, and record it in your diary, to become a law of your life. In this way you will eliminate the evil and conserve the good in your experience. You will grow wiser and better, and in the end, it is possible that your list of resolutions may become a contribution to the world's store of wisdom and virtue. This, however, should not be the object of the resolutions. Your one purpose should be the development in your soul of life's virtues, for it is by these that life is measured.

> "Count life by virtues; these will last
> When life's lame, foiled race is o'er;
> And these, when earthly joys are past,
> Shall cheer us on a brighter shore."

CORRESPONDENCE.

THERE is probably no one accomplishment that reveals so much of human character as that of correspondence. All are familiar with the fact that experts are able from the handwriting alone to give the prominent features of a person's character, and in cases of suspected forgery the uniformity of handwriting is allowed as evidence in the courts.

But much as is revealed by the manner in which we write, still more is revealed by the nature of that which is written,—not only the general merit of the composition, but the thoughts and sentiments expressed, the delicacy and propriety with which they are expressed, the neatness of the written page, the orthography and the grammar. Then there is a certain air that impresses us that comes under none of these heads, too subtile to be reduced to a definition, more ethereal than the perfume of a tropic morning, but which stamps the product unmistakably as the work of a noble soul. This indefinable something transforms all the sharp angles and irregular lines into shapes that please, and covers the ugliness of imperfect chirography with a secondary beauty on which we delight to gaze.

Scholarship, culture, refinement, and inborn nobility nowhere betray themselves so conspicuously as in the act of correspondence. While general culture of the whole mind is necessary to the acquirement of this accomplishment, yet the only specific means to be employed is the study of the best models. Advantage should be taken of the imitative tendency of little children, and accordingly all the best correspondence of the parents should be read repeatedly to the children. They will always be interested in a letter from Aunt —— or Cousin ——, and if the letter is a good model it should be read and re-read in the presence of the child till he begins to catch the phraseology. The best models of the father's business correspondence may be committed to memory by the children. These forms once fixed in their minds will leave their influence long years after the words of the model are forgotten.

The particular examples and problems we solved in our school days are all forgotten, but they have left something in our minds of which we make use every day. So in regard to these models in correspondence. It is not so much the mechanical form of the written page to which we would call the attention of the young reader, as to that intellectual ideal to which the study of the models gives rise, and which embraces not only the mechanical form, but all the qualities that go to make it a finished product of the individual mind.

We have tried to select such models as in themselves convey valuable suggestions and information on the general theme of correspondence.

The one great error into which most young people fall in the matter of correspondence is the idea that to write a letter is to perform a literary feat.

When a child writes his first letter to his cousin or absent friend, he usually makes a day's work of it even with mother's suggestions, while if that cousin or friend were to visit him, he would not only find no difficulty in prattling all day, but would probably much prefer to dispense with his mother's suggestions.

In the following letter from the Hon. Wm. Wirt to his daughter, mark how charmingly natural and simple his language. It seems almost impossible that such should have been written. It seems more like a verbatim report of a fireside conversation.

BALTIMORE, April 18, 1882.

MY DEAR CHILD:—

You wrote me a dutiful letter, equally honorable to your head and heart, for which I thank you, and when I grow to be a light-hearted, light-headed, happy, thoughtless young girl, I will give you a *quid pro quo*. As it is, you must take such a letter as a man of sense can write,.although it has been remarked, that the more sensible the man, the more dull his letter.

Don't ask me by whom remarked, or I shall refer you, with Jenkinson, in the Vicar of Wakefield, to Sanconiathon, Manetho, and Berosus.

This puts me in mind of the card of impressions from the pencil seals, which I intended to enclose last mail, for you to your mother, but forgot. Lo! here they are. These are the best I can find in Baltimore. I have marked them according to my taste; but exercise your own exclusively, and choose for yourself, if either of them please you.

Shall I bring you a Spanish guitar of Giles' choosing? Can you be certain that you will stick to it? And some music for the Spanish guitar? What say you?

There are three necklaces that tempt me—a beautiful mock emerald, a still more beautiful mock ruby with pearls, and a still most beautiful of real topaz,—what say you?

Will you have either of the scarfs described to your mother, and which—the blue or the black? They are very fashionable and beautiful. Any of those wreaths and flowers? Consult your dear mother; always consult her, always respect her. This is the only way to make yourself respectable and lovely. God bless you, and make you happy.

Your affectionate father,

WILLIAM WIRT.

This quality of simplicity is the chief virtue of the family letter and the letter of friendship. In these it is necessary to observe but one principal rule, viz., write just as you would talk if the person to whom you write were by your side. In a letter to mother or father, is no place to display your literary skill by the free use of technical words and high-sounding phrases. When the letters of brothers and sisters become essays, be assured that their heart relations are not what they should be. The vocabularies of affection are not compiled from the glossaries of science and philosophy.

When you write to a friend put yourself into the letter. He does not wish you to instruct him. It isn't what you say, but yourself that he desires. Except that of business, the one object of all correspondence is to serve as a substitute for that interblending of personalities which is the excuse and philosophy of society. It is a miserable substitute at best, and fulfills its office badly enough even when we put all of ourselves into it that we can. It is not egotism to talk about yourself in a letter of friendship, for if your friend is not interested in you, he is not your friend.

The following is from a young man in college to his mother. It does not contain a single allusion to Calculus, nor are there any Latin quotations in it.

——— College, Tuesday evening.

My Dear Mother:—

Though I am now sitting with my back toward you, yet I love you none the less; and what is quite as strange, I can see you just as plainly as if I stood peeping in upon you. I can see you all just as you sit around the table. Tell me if I do not see you?

There is mother on the right of the table with her knitting, and a book open before her; and anon she glances her eye from the work on the paper to that on her needles; now counts the stitches, and then puts her eye on the book and then starts off on another round. There is Mary, looking wise and sewing with all her might; now and then stopping to give Sarah and Louise a lift in their lessons—trying to initiate them in the mysteries of geography. She is on the left side of the table. There, in the background, is silent Joseph, with his slate, now making a mark, and then biting his lip, or scratching his head to see if the algebraic expression may not have hidden in either of those places. George is in the kitchen tinkering his skates, or contriving a trap for that old offender, the rat, whose cunning has so long brought mortification upon all his boastings. I can now hear his hammer and his whistle—that peculiar sucking sort of whistle which indicates a puzzled state of brain. Little William and Henry are in bed, and if you will step to the bedroom door you will barely hear them breathe. And now mother has stopped and is absent and thoughtful, and my heart tells me she is thinking of her only absent child.

You have been even kinder than I expected or you promised. I did not expect to hear from you till to-morrow, at earliest, but as I was walking to-day, one of my classmates cried, "A bundle for you at the stage office!" I was soon in my room with it. Out came my knife, and, forgetting all your good advice about "strings and fragments," the bundle soon opened its very heart to me; and it proved a warm heart, too, for there were the stockings—they are on my feet now, that is, one pair of them,—and there were the flannels, and the bosoms, and the gloves, and the pin-cushion from Louise, and the needle-book from Sarah, and the paper from Mary, and the letters and love from all of you. Thanks to you all for the bundle, letters and love. One corner of my eye is now moistened while I say, "Thanks to ye all, gude folks." I must not forget to mention the apples—"the six apples, one from each,"—and the beautiful little loaf of cake. The apples I have smelled of, and the cake nibbled a little, and pronounced it to be in the finest taste.

Now a word about your letters. I cannot say much, for I have only read mother's three times and Mary's twice. I am glad the spectacles fitted mother's eyes so well. You wonder how I hit it. Why, have I not been told from babyhood that I have my mother's eyes? Now, if I have mother's eyes, what is plainer than that I can pick out glasses that will suit them? I am glad, too, that the new book is a favorite.

I suppose the pond is all frozen over, and the skating good. I know it is foolish; but if mother and Mary had skated as many "moony" nights as I have, they would sigh, not at the thought, but at the fact that my skating days are over.

I am warm, well and comfortable. We all study, and dull fellows, like myself, have to confess that they study hard. We have no genius to help us. My chum is a good fellow. He now sits in yonder corner, his feet poised upon the stove in such a way that the dullness seems to have all run out of his heels into his head, for he is fast asleep.

I have got it framed, and there it hangs—the picture of my father! I never look up without seeing it, and I never see it without thinking that my mother is a widow and that I am her eldest son. What more I think I will not be fool enough to say—you will imagine better than I can say it.

I need not say write, for I know that you will. Love to you all, and much too. Your affectionate son,

HERBERT.

LORD CHESTERFIELD TO HIS SON.

Dear Boy:—

Your letters, except when upon a given subject, are exceedingly laconic, and neither answer my desires nor the purpose of letters; which should be familiar conversations between absent friends. As I desire to live with you upon the footing of an intimate friend, and not of a parent, I could wish that your letters gave me more particular account of yourself, and of your lesser transactions. When you write to me, suppose yourself conversing freely with me, by the fireside. In that case you would naturally mention the incidents of the day, as where you had been, whom you had seen, what you thought of them, etc. Do this in your letters: acquaint me sometimes with your studies, sometimes with your diversions; tell me of any new persons and characters that you meet with in company, and add your own observations upon them; in short, let me see more of you in your letters.

How do you go on with Lord Multeney; and how does he go on at Leipzig? Has he learning, has he parts, has he application? Is he good or ill-natured? In short, what is he? At least, what do you think of him? You may tell me without reserve, for I promise secrecy.

You are now of an age that I am desirous of beginning a confidential correspondence with you, and, as I shall, on my part, write you very freely my opinion upon men and things, which I should often be very unwilling that anybody but you or Mr. Harts should see; so, on your part, if you write me without reserve you may depend upon my inviolable secrecy. If you have ever looked into the letters of Madame De Sevigne to her daughter, Madame De Grignan, you must have observed the ease, freedom, and friendship of that correspondence; and yet I hope, and believe, that they did not love one another better than we do. Tell me what books you are now reading, either by way of study or amusement; how you pass your evenings when at home, and where you pass them when abroad.

* * * * * * * * * * * * * * * * * *

The foregoing letters in themselves contain a whole volume on the subject of correspondence. They leave very little to be said as to what a family letter should be. We will, however, add one more, a genuine love-letter in disguise written by Doctor Franklin. There is nothing in the nature of a love-letter, however, that renders necessary any different suggestions from those we have already given under letters of friendship. We have said there that it is yourself, more that what you say, that your friend desires, and in the case of love-letters the same is especially true, and perhaps in a more literal sense. Some of our sentimental readers may perhaps be a little disappointed after reading the following letter, and may possibly blame us, and accuse us of malicious intent to dash their expectations. But if the letter does not fall under their definition of a love-letter, the fault is doubtless one of age, and not of natural judgment.

DR. FRANKLIN TO HIS WIFE.

MY DEAR CHILD:—

I wrote you, a few days since, by a special messenger, and inclosed letters for all our wives and sweethearts, expecting to hear from you by his return, and to have the northern newspapers and English letters per the packet; but he is just now returned without a scrap for poor us; so I had a good mind not to write to you by this opportunity; but I can never be ill-natured enough, even when there is the most occasion. The messenger says he left the letters at your house, and saw you afterwards at Mr. Duche's, and told you when he would go, and that he lodged at Honey's, next door to you, and yet you did not write; so let Goody Smith give one more just judgment, and say what should be done to you. I think I won't tell you that we are all well, nor that we expect to return about the middle of the week, nor will I send you a word of news—that 's poz.

My duty to mother, love to children, and to Miss Betsey, and Gracey, etc., etc. I am your ~~loving~~ husband,

B. FRANKLIN.

P. S. I have scratched out the loving words, being writ in haste by mistake, when I forgot I was angry.

There is another class of correspondence which requires the observance of a very different class of rules from those already given. We refer to business correspondence. In writing a business letter we should bear in mind that the person addressed cares only for what we have to say, and not for ourselves; being in this respect exactly the reverse of a family letter or a letter of friendship. This is why the chief virtue of a business letter is brevity. The person who is to read it desires to learn what you have to say about your business as quickly as possible, in order that if it be related in any way with his own, he may discharge the obligation arising from that relation, and lose no time. The Anglo Saxon *bisig* is the word from which are derived both business and busy, so that the business man is supposed to be a busy man; hence he has no time to weigh political arguments, nor to consider your peculiar views on the "Trinity."

It is true that business relations may exist between friends, and they may feel like expressing this in their business letters, but if they do so, the letter, to that extent departs from the nature of a business letter and becomes one of friendship. In this case, it is proper, of course, that the letter should be a mixed one, for wherever friendship exists it is the prerogative of the parties concerned alone, to say when and under what circumstances that friendship shall be expressed.

In letters of this kind, it is, as a rule, preferable to devote the first part of the letter to the business, and the latter part to the interests of friendship; but of course circumstances and the relative weight of the two interests must determine this matter in the mind of the writer.

The requirements of a business letter are well met in the following model:—

San Francisco, Cal., Dec. 29, 1882.

Editors Springfield Republican:

Gentlemen:—Enclosed find nine dollars ($9.00), for which please send me, the coming year, your widely known and valuable publication, The Springfield Republican (daily edition), and oblige, Yours respectfully,

P. O. box 1937. Clara M. Sheldon.

It very frequently happens that the members of the family are called upon to write, or to reply to what are called letters of invitation.

The following models will show the form which custom has sanctioned:—

Mr. and Mrs. Cogswell request the favor of Mr. and Mrs. Gile's company at dinner on Thursday, January 21, at 5 o'clock.

THE INVITATION ACCEPTED.

Mr. and Mrs. Gile, with much pleasure, accept Mr. and Mrs. Cogswell's kind invitation for the 21st of January.

THE INVITATION DECLINED.

Mr. and Mrs. Gile regret that the condition of Mrs. Gile's health will not permit them to accept Mr. and Mrs. Cogswell's invitation to dinner for January 21st.

Of course the phraseology need not conform exactly to that of the above models. The only uniform characteristics are a business-like brevity, admitting nothing foreign to the subject, and that they be written in the third person.

Notice that the invitation does not read "we request your company, etc." It may be true, however, that common sense can assign no valid reason why the third person should be used. But since the affectation of fashionable society has established the custom, it is well for us to conform to the same, especially since conformity or non-conformity is not a question of conscience.

It seems proper in this connection to give a few of those forms pertaining to the various kinds of business and commercial transactions which necessarily constitute no insignificant element in the education, not only of the business man, but of all who successfully deal with their fellow men.

And since the home is the school in which children are

supposed to receive in a large degree their education in all that pertains to life and its relations, a work devoted to the home life would hardly seem complete without, at least, a brief consideration of the formulas of business.

The following forms embrace all of importance that the business man, whether farmer, mechanic or merchant, under ordinary circumstances will be called upon to use:—

PROMISSORY NOTE ON DEMAND WITH INTEREST.

SPRINGFIELD, MASS., Feb. 1, 1883.

$225.50.

On demand, I promise to pay H. J. Bennett, or order, two hundred and twenty-five $\frac{50}{100}$ dollars, value received.

O. T. THORNTON.

PROMISSORY NOTE WITHOUT INTEREST.

BARNSTEAD, N. H., Nov. 8, 1883.

$19.80.

Four months after date, I promise to pay Frank C. Cole, or order, nineteen $\frac{80}{100}$ dollars value received.

JOSEPH A. MARSTON.

PROMISSORY NOTE NEGOTIABLE.

LEWISTON, ME., March 3, 1883.

$420.00.

Sixty days after date, for value received, I promise to pay Everett Remick, or order, four hundred and twenty dollars with interest from date.

H. W. COGSWELL.

PROMISSORY NOTE NOT NEGOTIABLE.

BOSTON, MASS., Jan. 5, 1883.

$790.00.

For value received, I promise to pay Toorin H. Harvey, on demand, seven hundred and ninety dollars.

WILLIAM J. MERRILL.

Notice in the above the omission of the phrase "or order."

JOINT NOTE.

CHICOPEE, MASS., Aug. 6, 1882.

$75.00.

Thirty days after date, we promise to pay John Shaw, or order, seventy-five dollars, value received.

TRUE L. PERKINS,
F. H. SARGENT.

JOINT AND SEVERAL NOTE.

ATHOL, MASS., Nov. 22, 1882.

$300.00.

Value received, on demand we, either or both, promise to pay Charles L. Sheldon, or order, three hundred dollars with interest.

O. T. MAXFIELD,
TRUE B. JOHNSON.

The above note might, of course, have any of the characteristics of the others. That is, it might be with or without interest, on demand or after a stated period, negotiable or not negotiable.

There is a modification of the joint and several note, called principal and surety note, like the following:—

CHICHESTER, N. H., July 9, 1882.

$320.00.

Ninety days after date, for value received, I promise to pay Charles J. Carpenter, or order, three hundred and twenty dollars, with interest from date.

F. CABIN LANE, *Principal.*
D. K. FOSTER, *Surety.*

The purpose of this note is more frequently met by the endorsement of the surety. That is, the principal signs his name in the usual manner, and the surety endorses the note by writing his name upon the back of it. In this case he does not sign the note with the principal. The endorser must be notified when the note becomes due, otherwise he cannot be held responsible for its payment.

CHATTEL NOTE.

BANGOR, ME., Jan. 10, 1883.

$900.00.

For value received, I promise to pay F. E. Perhan & Co., or order, nine hundred dollars in ship masts, to be delivered at Portland during the month of March, 1883.

JOSEPH BLY.

DRAFT—TIME FROM SIGHT.

WELLS, ME., Aug. 2, 1882.

$400.00.

At ten days sight, pay to Joshua Hatch, or order, four hundred dollars, value received, and charge to account of

J. G. BLAISDELL.

To D. D. BELCHER,
Wells, Me.

DRAFT—AT SIGHT.

HOLYOKE, MASS., June 2, 1882.

$140.00.

At sight, pay to Eben Clark, or order, one hundred and forty dollars, value received, and charge to account of

H. O. GREENLEAF.

To W. C. KING & Co.,
Springfield, Mass.

DUE BILL—CASH.

AUGUSTA, ME., May 4, 1882.

$25.00.

Due Frank H. Sanborn, on demand, twenty-five dollars with interest from date.

J. W. HODGDON.

DUE BILL—MERCHANDISE.

BOWDOIN, ME., April 30, 1882.

$60.00.

Due H. H. Tucker, or order, sixty dollars, payable in clover seed at the market price on the first day of July, 1882.

W. H. WALKER.

BANK CHECK.

SPRINGFIELD, MASS., Jan. 3, 1883.

$700.40.

CITY NATIONAL BANK.

Pay to the order of J. W. Holton, seven hundred $\frac{40}{100}$ dollars.

No.——

W. C. KING & Co.

RECEIPT IN FULL OF ALL DEMANDS.

SPRINGFIELD, MASS., Feb. 1, 1883.

$48.60.

Received of W. C. King & Co., forty-eight $\frac{60}{100}$ dollars in full of all demands to this date.

W. H. HOLTON.

Perhaps there is no one business form which the common people are so often called upon to use, nor one in which there are so many ludicrous errors committed as the simple form pertaining to indebtedness for ordinary services. How few matrons are able to present in proper form, a simple board bill. The following is the proper form for a bill of indebtedness for rent:—

ALTON, N. H., July 9, 1882.

MRS. MARY N. P. MATHEWS,

To MRS. ALMIRA SARGENT, *Dr.*

To four months rent ending July 11, 1882, @ $11.00, $44.00.

Received payment,

MRS. ALMIRA SARGENT.

The above form is applicable to all kinds of indebtedness for services rendered. In case some article or commodity represented the service, the name of that article or commodity is put in the place of that of the service, and the bill otherwise may be the same.

There are, it is true, many other forms pertaining to business, as deeds, mortgages, bonds, wills, etc., etc., but the occasions which require a knowledge of these are so comparatively rare that we have not thought it expedient to give them. We have given all that are really essential to the business man, and even in those works devoted expressly to business forms, those we have given will be found to be the ones most minutely dwelt upon.

But whatever of importance may be attached to the mere mechanical form of any document, the habit of expressing our thoughts in writing, with naturalness and grace, whether in correspondence, in our private journal, or in the formulas of business, is of far more importance. This most desirable of all accomplishments comes only as the reward for patient and tireless practice.

"To think rightly is of knowledge; to speak fluently is of nature:
To read with profit is with care; but to write aptly is of practice.
No talent among men hath more scholars and fewer masters.

* * * * * * * * * * * * * *

And shouldst thou ask my judgment of that which hath most profit in the world,
For answer take thou this; the prudent penning of a letter.

"Thou hast not lost an hour whereof there is a record,
A written thought at midnight shall redeem the livelong day.
Idea is a shadow that departeth, speech is fleeting as the wind,
Reading is an unremembered pastime; but a writing is eternal."

MANNERS AT HOME.

MANNERS constitute the natural language in which the biography of every man is written. They are the necessary and unconscious expression of our lives and characters.

Politeness in its essence is always the same. The mere rules of etiquette may vary with time and place, but these are only different modes of expressing the principle of politeness within us.

Politeness does not consist in any system of rules, nor in arbitrary forms, but it has a real existence in the instincts of men and women. The ever changing conditions and circumstances of social life may necessitate modifications in the manners and customs of the people, and these modifications may and do extend to the domestic circle. Yet the principle of our nature in which the manners, customs, and rules of etiquette all had their origin, is permanent and unchangeable. All the various rules of etiquette for the government of society are but notes and commentaries on the one great rule, "Love thy neighbor as thyself."

It has truthfully been said: "In politeness, as in everything else connected with the formation of character, we are too apt to begin on the outside, instead of the inside. Instead of beginning with the heart and trusting to that to form the manners, many begin with the manners and leave the heart to chance and influences. The golden rule contains the very life and soul of politeness: 'Do unto others as ye would that they should do unto you.' Unless children and youth are taught, by precept and example, to abhor what is selfish, and prefer another's pleasure and comfort to their own, their politeness will be entirely artificial, and used only when interest and policy dictate. True politeness is perfect freedom and ease—treating othcers just as you love to be treated. Nature is always graceful; fashion, with all her art, can never produce anything half so pleasing. The very perfection of elegance is to imitate nature; how much better to have the reality than the imitation. Anxiety about the opinions of others fetters the freedom of nature and tends to awkwardness; all would appear well if they never tried to assume what they do not possess."

Says the author of "The Illustrated Manners Book," "Every denial of or interference with the personal freedom or absolute rights of another is a violation of good manners. The basis of all true politeness and social enjoyment is the mutual tolerance of personal rights."

La Bruyere says, "Politeness seems to be a certain care,

by the manner of our words and actions, to make others pleased with us and themselves."

Madame Celnart says, "The grand secret of never failing propriety of deportment is to have an intention of always doing right."

There are some persons who possess the instinct of courtesy in so high a degree that they seem to require no instruction or practice in order to be perfectly polite, easy, and graceful. But most people require instruction and rules as to the best and most appropriate manner of expressing that which they may feel. We sometimes find young children with such an aptitude for speech and such a command of language that their grammar is absolutely faultless. They seem to have an instinctive knowledge of the rules of grammar; yet most children without grammatical instruction are prone to errors.

Rules of etiquette are essential, then, but far less so than that cultivation of heart and character, to which all just rules of etiquette must trace their origin.

Personal habits claim the first place in our consideration of home manners; and foremost among these we would place cleanliness. This virtue has been said to be akin to godliness, and surely there is no quality in a human being that more forcibly suggests ungodliness than uncleanliness. An unclean person is an object of disgust to all whom he meets. Foulness of character and moral pollution will not isolate one from the sympathy of his fellow men more effectually than physical uncleanliness. We cannot long retain a love for our best and dearest friend if he is unclean and has a foul breath. We may not despise him, but our love will necessarily lose a little of its ardor, or at best will change to pity. But the disgust of our friends is not by any means the worst result of uncleanliness. It is most destructive to health. It is like sand and mud thrown into the wheels and gearing of a delicate machine. Few persons of unclean habits have died of old age. People may sometimes in their old age come to be uncleanly in consequence of their infirmity, but during their younger days they must have been moderately clean.

We would not advise one to adopt radical views on this subject and take a daily bath through life, although we doubt if such a course would injure most people, yet it would probably be unnecessary, and would be a needless waste of time. A full bath once or twice a week is, perhaps, all that is necessary to escape the charge of being ungodly in consequence of filth.

Most people do not seem to consider the laws of cleanliness as applicable to the head and hair. Even those who are clean in other respects are very apt to neglect the hair. Many ladies who have long and thick hair are, perhaps, unaware how quickly it becomes filthy and emits a disagreeable odor, especially if it be dressed while it is wet. However cleanly the person may be in other respects, the hair will necessarily collect much dust and so become unclean. No father, mother, or child of good breeding will allow the teeth or nails to become unclean. A clean mind cannot dwell in an unclean body.

Perhaps in proportion to the population there are at the present time fewer in the world who are addicted to the disgusting and health-destroying habit of smoking and chewing tobacco than in the days of our grandfathers, yet the number even now is appalling. Although it is a vice too large to be confined within any circle or sphere of life, yet it may, perhaps, appropriately be considered under the head of home manners.

There are few, if any, who will not frankly acknowledge that tobacco in all of its forms is an unalloyed evil, and that they would not desire their children to become addicted to its use. And yet the most effectual way to cause their children to use it certainly is to use it in their presence. After all that has been said and done by moralists and philanthropists, we do not presume to be able to say anything that shall influence the acts of confirmed tobacco users, but if we may be able to give them a few hints by which they shall the better prevent their children from falling into the same habit we shall be satisfied. If fathers will persist in smoking and chewing they should surely try to neutralize, as far as possible, the influence of their example. This is a dangerous influence at best, but it may be rendered more or less so according to the desires and acts of the father. No father should smoke frequently in the presence of his boys, especially if the fumes of tobacco are agreeable to them. But whenever he does so, he should do it with some casual remark as to the folly of the habit. He should aim to convey the impression that he is its slave, and that he would give worlds to be free. It is possible that in this way the very evil may be made a means of good to the child, for thus he may early come to realize the truth that man cannot always trust himself, and that it is dangerous to trifle with any vice lest it bind him with a chain of iron.

He who feels that because he is at home he may act as he chooses and throw off all restraints of politeness and good manners generally finds that when he comes to put on these restraints for special occasions they don't fit, and it becomes evident that the harness wasn't made for him. Even the children can see that his manner is entirely artificial and is not his own. Such men when they are occasionally compelled to go into society experience pain and embarrassment enough to outweigh the cost of being decorous and mannerly at home.

If parents expect their children to be favorites in society, they must teach them good manners. The world's fortress that has stood the bombardment of many a genius has fallen under the more subtle force of good manners. There is no way to teach children good manners except by example. It is an art that cannot be taught to advantage theoretically. The tactics of courtesy can never be mastered without field practice. If husbands are not courteous to their wives, the brothers will not be courteous to their sisters, nor when they in turn become husbands will they be courteous to their wives. Every man owes to his wife and to his daughter at least the same considerations of civility and politeness that he owes to any other women.

From the "Home and Health" we copy the following valuable rules which seem to be so perfectly to the point that we cannot resist the temptation to appropriate them to our purpose:—

HOW TO BE A GOOD HUSBAND.

Honor your wife.
Love your wife.
Show your love.
Suffer for your wife if need be.
Study to keep her young.
Consult her.
Help to bear her burdens.
Be thoughtful of her always.
Don't command, but suggest.
Seek to refine your own nature.
Be a gentleman as well as husband.
Remember the past experience of your wife.
Level up to her character.
Stay at home as much as possible.
Take your wife with you often.

HOW TO BE A GOOD WIFE.

Reverence your husband.

Love him.

Do not conceal your love for him.

Forsake all for him.

Confide in him.

Keep his love.

Cultivate the modesty and delicacy of youth.

Cultivate personal attractiveness.

If you read nothing and make no effort to be intelligent you will soon sink into a dull block of stupidity.

Cultivate physical attractiveness.

Do not forget the power of incidental attentions.

Make your home attractive.

Keep your house clean and in good order.

Preserve sunshine.

Study your husband's character.

Cultivate his better nature.

Study to meet all your duties as a wife.

Seek to secure your husband's happiness.

Study his interest.

Practice frugality.

To toil hard for bread, to fight the wolf from the door, to resist impatient creditors, to struggle against complaining pride at home, is too much to ask of one man.

Another phase of home manners is presented in the attitude of children toward their parents. American children have not, as a rule, that deference and reverence for their parents which they should have. From the author of "How to Behave," we quote the following forcible description of the characteristics of the American child:—

"Young America cannot brook restraint, has no conception of superiority, and reverences nothing. His ideas of equality admit neither limitation nor qualification. He is born with a full comprehension of his own individual rights, but is slow in learning his social duties. Through whose fault comes this state of things? American boys and girls have naturally as much good sense and good nature as those of any other nation, and when well trained no children are more courteous and agreeable. The fault lies in their education. In the days of our grandfathers, children were taught manners at school, a rather rude, backward sort of manners, it is true, but better than the no manners at all of the present day. We must blame parents in this matter, rather than their children. If you would have your children grow up beloved and respected by their elders as well as their contemporaries, teach them good manners in their childhood. The young sovereign should first learn to obey, that he may be the better fitted to command in his turn."

He who does not love, respect, and reverence his mother, is a boor, whatever his pretentions may be. He who can allow any other woman to crowd from his heart the love for his mother does not deserve the affection of any woman.

One of the evil habits exhibited for the most part at

home is that known as "sulking." This not only spoils the comfort of the whole family for the time, but the habit grows stronger with age, until it often ruins the person's disposition and prospect of happiness in life. We have seen cases where this disposition to sulk had produced such effects upon the character that the persons were actually objects of pity. When the sulky child goes out into the world with his vice he will not find a mother who will patiently wait until his sulks have passed away; but society will desert him and leave him alone in his bitterness.

But the opposite condition of perpetual levity is to be avoided as fatal to real earnestness and depth of character. As a rule, the ludicrous is seen on the surface of things, and he who is always finding something to excite laughter is generally of a superficial mind. The deep mind is more apt to overlook this surface coat. It is true there is nothing so good for the health of body or mind as hearty laughter, and he who cannot appreciate a good joke should be pitied. And yet the excess of this good thing does surely indicate, if not positive weakness, a want of habitual action in the more serious faculties of the mind.

We supplement this chapter with the following rules for the government of conduct in society. They should be read and re-read by the members of the family till they are thoroughly mastered, as the student would master the rules of grammar. It is not enough to read them as we would read a novel, from mere curiosity, but they should be studied with a view to being applied.

So much has been written on the subject of etiquette and conduct that it is of course impossible for us to say anything new. The most we have attempted is to recast and adapt to the special needs of the times that which has already been written.

We have consulted the best and most unquestionable authorities, and for each and every phase of life have tried to give a few rules of special importance. So that the list itself is virtually a condensed volume on the subject of etiquette, no vital rule of conduct being omitted.

The golden rule is the embodiment of all true politeness.

Always allow an invalid, an elderly person or a lady to occupy the most comfortable chair in the room, and also to accommodate themselves with reference to light and temperature.

Never make the weakness or misfortunes of another the occasion of mirth or ridicule.

Always respect a social inferior, not in a condescending way, but with the feeling that he is as good as you.

Never answer a serious question in jest, nor a civil question rudely.

The religious opinions of all, even those of infidels, should be respected, for religious tolerance is not only necessary to good manners, but is a cardinal idea in the doctrine of human liberty.

A true gentleman or lady is always quiet and unassuming. The person of real worth can afford to be unassuming, for others will assume for him.

To laugh at one's own jokes will take the temper out of the keenest wit. It is not necessary, however, that he should maintain a serious and pharisaical countenance, he may laugh mildly in sympathy with those who appreciate his wit, provided he is not the first to laugh.

Too great familiarity toward a new acquaintance is not only in bad taste, but is fatal to the continuance of friendship.

The most refined and cultivated always seek to avoid, both in their dress and in their behavior, the appearance of any desire to attract attention. Extremes in fashion and flashy colors are marks of a low degree of cultivation. Savages are never pleased by the finer blendings either in color or sound.

When in company talk as little as possible of yourself or of the business or profession in which you are engaged, at least, do not be the first to introduce these topics.

Every species of affectation is absolutely disgusting. It is also so easily detected that no one but an actor can conceal it.

When it is necessary to call upon a business man in the hours of business, if possible, select that hour in which you have reason to believe he is least engaged. And even then talk only of business unless *he* should introduce other topics. Unless the person sustains some other relation to you than that of business, do not stop a moment after you have completed your business.

If you have wronged any one, not only the rules of etiquette, but the most obvious interpretation of moral obligation requires you to be willing and quick to apologize. And never, under any circumstances, refuse to accept an honest apology for an offense.

Pay whatever attention you choose to your dress and personal appearance before you enter society, but afterwards expel the subject from your mind and do not allow your thoughts to dwell upon it.

Never enter a house, even your own, without removing your hat.

Do not try to be mysterious in company, by alluding in an equivocal manner, to those things which only one or two of the company understand.

Never boast of your own knowledge, and do not, either directly or indirectly, accuse another of a lack of knowledge. Do not even manifest your knowledge of any particular subject in such a way and under such circumstances as will cause another to appear to poor advantage.

Never leave a friend suddenly while engaged in an interesting conversation. Wait till there is a pause or a turn in the conversation.

Do not hesitate to offer any assistance, that the occasion

may seem to demand, to a lady, even though she may be a stranger.

In company mention your husband or wife with the same degree of respect with which you would speak of a stranger, and reserve all pet names for times and places in which they will be better appreciated.

Never violate the confidence of another. Do not seek to avenge a wrong by revealing the secrets of an enemy, which were told to you while he was a friend.

Always dispose of your time as if your watch were too fast, you will then have a few moments' margin in the fulfillment of all engagements. To break an engagement almost always injures you more than the other party.

Treat a woman, whatever may be her social or moral rank, as though she were a princess.

Always show a willingness to converse with a lady on any topic that she may select.

Do not ask questions concerning the private affairs of your friends, nor be curious in regard to the business relations of any one.

Wrangling and contradictions are not only violations of etiquette, but they also violate the requirements of tact, since they defeat the very purpose of respectful discussion, viz., to convince.

Return a borrowed book, when you have finished reading it, without delay. A library made up of borrowed books is a disgraceful possession.

When entering a room bow slightly to the whole company, but to no one in particular.

Make the comfort and welfare of others a prime object of your life, and you will thereby fulfill all the requirements of etiquette.

In addition to the foregoing, we present another list of rules which ought to be of special interest to every American citizen, not only on account of their intrinsic worth, but also on account of their origin, for their author was George Washington. He called them his "Rules of Civility and Decent Behavior in Company." They were written at the age of thirteen, and have been termed "Washington's Maxims."

1. Every action in company ought to be with some sign of respect to those present.

2. In the presence of others sing not to yourself with a humming voice, nor drum with your fingers or feet.

3. Speak not when others speak, sit not when others stand, and walk not when others stop.

4. Turn not your back to others, especially in speaking ; jog not the table or desk on which another reads or writes ; lean not on any one.

5. Be no flatterer, neither play with any one that delights not to be played with.

6. Read no letters, books or papers in company; but when there is a necessity for doing it, you must not leave. Come not near the books or writings of any one so as to read them unasked ; also look not nigh when another is writing a letter.

7. Let your countenance be pleasant, but in serious matters somewhat grave.

8. Show not yourself glad at the misfortune of another, though he were your enemy.

9. They that are in dignity or office have in all places precedency, but whilst they are young, they ought to respect those that are their equals in birth or other qualities, though they have no public charge.

10. It is good manners to prefer them to whom we speak before ourselves, especially if they be above us.

11. Let your discourse with men of business be short and comprehensive.

12. In visiting the sick do not presently play the physician if you be not knowing therein.

13. In writing or speaking, give to every person his due title according to his degree and the custom of the place.

14. Strive not with your superiors in argument, but always submit your judgment to others with modesty.

15. Undertake not to teach your equal in the art he himself professes ; it savors arrogancy.

16. When a man does all he can though it succeeds not well, blame not him that did it.

17. Being to advise or reprehend any one, consider whether it ought to be in public or in private, presently or at some other time, also in what terms to do it ; and in reproving show no signs of choler, but do it with sweetness and mildness.

18. Mock not nor jest at anything of importance ; break no jests that are sharp or biting, and if you deliver anything witty or pleasant, abstain from laughing thereat yourself.

19. Wherein you reprove another be unblamable yourself, for example is more prevalent than precept.

20. Use no reproachful language against any one, neither curses or revilings.

21. Be not hasty to believe flying reports to the disparagement of any one.

22. In your apparel be modest, and endeavor to accommodate nature rather than procure admiration. Keep to the fashion of your equals, such as are civil and orderly with respect to time and place.

23. Play not the peacock, looking everywhere about you to see if you be well decked, if your shoes fit well, if your stockings set neatly and clothes handsomely.

24. Associate yourself with men of good quality if you esteem your reputation, for it is better to be alone than in bad company.

25. Let your conversation be without malice or envy, for it is a sign of a tractable and commendable nature ; and in all cases of passion admit reason to govern.

26. Be not immodest in urging your friend to discover a secret.

27. Utter not base and frivolous things amongst grown and learned men, nor very difficult questions or subjects amongst the ignorant, nor things hard to be believed.

28. Speak not of doleful things in time of mirth nor at the table; speak not of melancholy things, as death and wounds; and if others mention them, change, if you can, the discourse. Tell not your dreams but to your intimate friends.

29. Break not a jest when none take pleasure in mirth.

Laugh not aloud, nor at all without occasion. Deride no man's misfortunes, though there seem to be some cause.

30. Speak not injurious words, neither in jest nor earnest. Scoff at none, although they give occasion.

31. Be not forward, but friendly and courteous, the first to salute, hear and answer, and be not pensive when it is time to converse.

32. Detract not from others, but neither be excessive in commending.

33. Go not thither where you know not whether you shall be welcome or not. Give not advice without being asked; and when desired, do it briefly.

34. If two contend together, take not the part of either unconstrained, and be not obstinate in your opinions; in things indifferent be of the major side.

35. Reprehend not the imperfection of others, for that belongs to parents, masters and superiors.

36. Gaze not on the marks or blemishes of others, and ask not how they came. What you may speak in secret to your friend deliver not before others.

37. Speak not in an unknown tongue in company, but in your own language; and that as those of quality do, and not as the vulgar. Sublime matters treat seriously.

38. Think before you speak; pronounce not imperfectly, nor bring out your words too heartily, but orderly and distinctly.

39. When another speaks, be attentive yourself, and disturb not the audience. If any hesitate in his words, help him not, nor prompt him without being desired; interrupt him not, nor answer him till his speech be ended.

40. Treat with men at fit times about business, and whisper not in the company of others.

41. Make no comparisons; and if any of the company be commended for any brave act of virtue, commend not another for the same.

42. Be not apt to relate news if you know not the truth thereof. In discoursing of things that you have heard, name not your author always. A secret discover not.

43. Be not curious to know the affairs of others, neither approach to those who speak in private.

44. Undertake not what you cannot perform; but be careful to keep your promise.

45. When you deliver a matter, do it without passion and indiscretion, however mean the person may be you do it to.

46. When your superiors talk to anybody, hear them; neither speak nor laugh.

47. In disputes be not so desirous to overcome as not to give liberty to each one to deliver his opinion, and submit to the judgment of the major part, especially if they are judges of the dispute.

48. Be not tedious in discourse, make not many digressions, nor repeat often the same matter of discourse.

49. Speak no evil of the absent, for it is unjust.

50. Be not angry at table, whatever happens; and if you have reason to be so show it not; put on a cheerful countenance, especially if there be strangers, for good humor makes one dish a feast.

51. Set not yourself at the upper end of the table; but if it

be your due, or the master of the house will have it so, contend not, lest you should trouble the company.

52. When you speak of God or his attributes, let it be seriously, in reverence and honor, and obey your natural parents.

53. Let your recreations be manful, not sinful.

54. Labor to keep alive in your breast that little spark of celestial fire called conscience.

> " Few to good breeding make a just pretense;
> Good breeding is the blossom of good sense;
> The last result of an accomplish'd mind,
> With outward grace, the body's virtue, join'd."

BY

C. E. SARGENT, A. B.

WITH LETTER OF INTRODUCTION

BY

MRS. LUCRETIA R. GARFIELD.

ILLUSTRATED.

Volume II

KING, RICHARDSON & CO., PUBLISHERS,
SPRINGFIELD, MASS.
1888.

May peace be in thy home
And joy within thy heart.

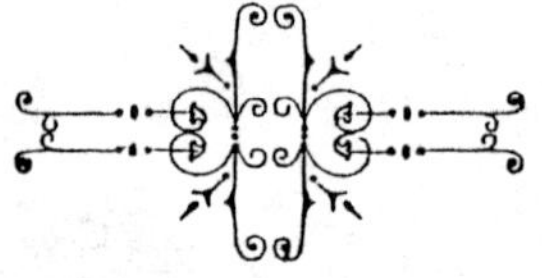

Archive Publishers, Heber City, UT 84032
www.archivepublishers.com

FAMILY SECRETS.

NATURE'S most beneficent operations are hidden from our sight beneath the surface of things. The germination of all life is under a veil. She will not let a seed sprout till she has buried it. All Nature is one great hall of free-masonry where every movement is at the gesture of a spectral hand. In secrecy and even deception, she is an adept. Not only does she hide her operations from our sight, but she actually gives false signals. She is an accomplished ventriloquist, and we cannot tell whence come her most characteristic sounds. The cry of the new born infant comes to us from the thicket, and at the birthday party of a child the irresponsible parrot becomes the orator of the day. The mocking-bird, in droll mimicry, utters the wail of sorrow and the laugh of joy. The spider touched, feigns death. The earthquake is prone to imitate the thunder. The voices of the night are interchangeable. The stupid owl steals the voice of sorrow, and the breeze whispers every sentiment. The sky presents the delusion of a blue tent cover, while every tree that looks into the mirror of the stream sees itself a broken staff. We look upon the flat stretched canvas, and through the cunning jugglery of light and shade it becomes a living, breathing reality.

Yet who shall dare prove Nature a liar and face the corollary? A work is never better than its author, and if we regard Nature as the work of God, the awfulness of that corollary should surely cause us to review our thoughts.

Nature is not a liar. No act of hers falls under any possible definition of a lie. She simply possesses the instinct of secrecy.

Honesty compels no man to stop on the highway to explain his errand, and if curious idlers inquire of him, there is no phrase in honesty's law that bids him divulge a rightful secret. And if the man perceives that he is watched by these idlers, he may, with truth's approval, take the first cross road that leads him in the opposite direction from the object of his errand. Perhaps the idler's highest good demands that the secret be withheld from him.

Now let us see if these limitations do not cover every license of Nature.

For some wise purpose most of Nature's secrets are withheld from us. We may believe that to know them would harm us. Perhaps our pride demands that they be withheld, or perhaps again the scheme of development and spirit growth demands it. However this may be, we know that most of the secrets are withheld. We are idle questioners, and often compel her to take cross roads, or to walk in brooks to destroy the scent of her trail. In every case she but withholds a rightful secret. The purpose of the mocking-bird is simply to defeat our pride when we claim to know what Nature is about by the intonations of her voice. She hides the knowledge of disease from us while she attempts to cure it without frightening us. To gaze forever on a ghastly skeleton would sicken us of life. Hence Nature with cunning and deceptive fingers has buried deep beneath her broidery of flesh the awful suggestion of death.

Thus, while we have freed Nature from our own implied charge of falsehood, we have yet learned from her a grand lesson. We have learned that she is the great advocate of family secrets.

Secrecy is one of the first duties that the domestic relation imposes. It is one of the cardinal necessities to the existence of the family. Every family has its secrets and must have them while it is a family. To publish the secrets of any family would be to dissipate that family.

The sacred right to secrecy transcends all etiquette. No rule of manners can compel one to divulge one secret of his domestic relations. Without confidence the marriage bond would be a rope of sand. But secrecy is the only condition that can maintain confidence.

It is the custom of many married people to make no secret of their love, and on all public occasions they seek, in a most sickening manner, to display their affection. This is not only a violation of good taste, but it is a violation of the instincts of human nature as well. The sentiment of love in all its phases seeks instinctively the haunts of privacy. Whether in its first pure awakening in the breast of youth and maiden, or, in its maturer and grander form, when crowned with fruits immortal, it alike retreats from the gaze of those who cannot sympathize.

Love is poetical until we see it manifested in others. It then becomes disgusting, and those who indulge in public demonstrations are always the objects of ridicule.

Not that a man should feign coldness or indifference toward his wife in public. This is not at all the import of what we have said. Husbands and wives should appear tender and considerate of each other in public places. It is perfectly proper that their manner should proclaim their relation. But true love between husband and wife demands a more engrossing attention, the tenderer endearments and caresses which society in the aggregate cannot understand. They constitute a language that only love can understand. Hence Nature has kindly given to us a disposition to conceal them.

The fact that the heart shrinks from the public manifestation of affection is the highest compliment to its innocence and purity, a proof that it is above the comprehension of the world's common moods. And in this fact is based the philosophy of family secrets.

The family is the outgrowth of love, and love's eternal condition is secrecy. Hence the family relation in all its phases is more or less intimately connected with the instinct of secrecy. It is a native impulse of every high-minded person to keep those facts a secret which pertain to the history of his family—even those facts which in their nature do not demand secrecy.

Nature hides the embryo of every seed, and carries on in the dark the process by which she rears and trains the little plant, and the mother should follow Nature's example in rearing and training her child. Children punished, or in any way disciplined in the presence of others, are almost always made worse thereby, instead of better. That intuitive confidence and mutual knowledge that exists between mother and child is so delicate in its nature that the presence of a third party, even if it be a brother or a sister, is sometimes fatal to its proper action.

Parents should never censure their children, nor even speak disparagingly of them, in the presence of strangers or visitors.

There are certain private rights which belong to each member of a family, and should not be violated, and yet their rights are too often disregarded.

Every one naturally holds back the expression of the greater parts of his thoughts. For every thought that we express we have a thousand that never pass the limits of our own consciousness. This, of course, we feel to be a natural right, and when it is encroached upon, we instinctively act upon the defensive. When one's sphere of privacy is trespassed upon by another, there is a spontaneous and joint action of the inventive and secretive functions, which results in an attempt to deceive. Hence the habit of falsehood may be produced in a child by not conceding to him the natural right of privacy. We quote the following from the author of "The Illustrated Manners Book":—

"One of the rights commonly trespassed upon, constituting a violent breach of good manners, is the right of privacy, or of the control of one's own person and affairs. There are places in this country where there exists scarcely the slightest recognition of this right. A man or woman bolts into your house without knocking. No room is sacred unless you lock the door, and an exclusion would be an insult. Parents intrude upon children and children upon parents! The husband thinks he has a right to enter his wife's room, and the wife would feel injured if excluded by night or day from her husband's. It is said that they even open each other's letters, and claim as a right that neither should have any secrets from the other.

"It is difficult to conceive of such a state of intense barbarism in a civilized country, such a denial of the simplest and most primitive rights, such an utter absence of delicacy and good manners; and had we not been assured on good authority that such things exist, we should consider any suggestion respecting them needless and impertinent.

"Every person in a dwelling should, if possible, have a room as sacred from intrusion as the house is to the family. No child grown to the years of discretion should be outraged by intrusion. No relation, however intimate, can justify it. So the trunks, boxes, papers and letters of every individual, locked or unlocked, sealed or unsealed, are sacred."

This matter of privacy can, no doubt, be carried to excess, and whether we endorse all of the foregoing or not, it certainly contains much truth. The tendency of civilization has always been toward the development of individuality and private interest. In the rude civilization of frontier life, one room serves as parlor, kitchen, and sleeping room for the whole family, and all private interests within the family are ignored. This principle is still more forcibly illustrated by comparing savage with civilized life. Although civilization tends to the multiplication and development of social institutions, yet it tends still more to the development of the individual. It brings the aggregate interest into harmony with that of the individual. This it does not so much by curtailing and modifying the rights of the mass, as by recognizing and increasing the rights of the individual.

We do not mean by individual rights, individual isolation in the sense in which we find it on the first pages of human history. The individual and the family were then sufficiently isolated. Every family was a nation in itself, but it had no rights which it could not sustain with rock and club. The family and society could not then exist together, but civilization finds its one great problem in the proposition of their union. While society is still developing, the isolation of the family and of the individual is retained, and family secrets are rendered more necessary by every advance of civilization.

But family secrets does not mean family reserve or estrangement. Better a thousand times that every individual right should be ignored than that husbands and wives and brothers and sisters should become cold and distant and indifferent. This is the most fatal catastrophe that can befall a family. Indeed, it is the death blow to home, and what remains is but the ghastly skeleton from which the spirit has forever flown. The family whose members do not mutually consult and advise and work together for each other's good have virtually surrendered the charter of home, and are living as strangers whom circumstances have compelled to live in close proximity. History affords hardly an example of a man who has proved a grand success, who did not make his wife a partner in his schemes. Behind every brilliant career there will be found a Martha or a Josephine. The very fact of legitimate family secrets renders more beautiful the intercourse of home, and sweetens the very associations and heart-bleedings that are legitimate nowhere else but in the heart of home.

"From the outward world about us,
  From the hurry and the din,
Oh, how little do we gather
  Of the other world within!

* * * * * *

But when the hearth is kindled,
  And the house is hushed at night—
Ah, then the secret writing
  Of the spirit comes to light!
Through the mother's light caressing
  Of the baby on her knee,
We see the mystic writing
  That she does not know we see—
By the love-light as it flashes
  In her tender-lidded eyes,
We know if that her vision rest
  On earth, or in the skies;
And by the song she chooses,
  By the very tune she sings,
We know if that her heart be set
  On seen, or unseen things."

DUTIES OF HOME.

THE word home seems to be inseparably connected with certain specific duties. One cannot dwell within the circle of home without being morally responsible for the discharge of special duties that owe their origin to the home relations.

The first duty of home in the order of development, since it is developed as soon as the home is established, is the duty of husband and wife to each other. Men too often forget that they owe any special duties to their wives, and yet there is no man who has a worthy wife but owes her a debt he can never pay. She has given him what fortune cannot purchase, a human heart. She has paid him the highest compliment that one human being can pay to another. She has told him by actions that cannot lie, that he is more to her than all the associations of her life; more than the sweet playmates of her girlhood; more than her sister's caress and brother's pride; more than the love and tenderness of parents; more than her dear old home. She leaves all these for him, although her heart strings cannot be unwound from any of them, but must be broken and torn away. Does human life present a more touching spectacle than that of a young bride suppressing her tears and forcing a smile while she kisses her mother and father and sister and brother farewell? How hard hearted, how unworthy of her, how even beastly, must be the man, if we may give him that title, who does not under those circumstances feel his knees bend a little with the instinctive impulse of adoration.

The husband can discharge the duties which he owes to his wife only by keeping perpetually in his mind that he owes her a debt to pay which, it will be necessary to take advantage of every passing opportunity.

But the obligations and duties are not all on the part of the husband. If the wife is the woman that she ought to be, and esteems herself accordingly, and at the same time considers the man whom she has accepted as worthy of her, she ought certainly to feel under the deepest obligation to him.

The first duty that a wife owes to her husband is to appear attractive to him. She should dress with almost exclusive reference to his tastes. This subject, idle as it may seem, is fraught with deep consequences to the race. We cannot tell the reader all about it without discussing at length the broad question of "natural selection," which would be out of place in a work like this. Suffice it to say, that great law demands that the wife should continually appeal as strongly as possible, to the sense of beauty in her husband. No man ever yet loved a woman who was not to him beautiful. It is beauty that man loves in woman, and when other things are equal his love for his wife is just proportionate to her beauty.

There have been, doubtless, many women so ill-formed and so unsymmetrical in their features that they could not possibly present to any man a single trace of physical beauty, and yet they have been the objects of the tenderest love.

But in every such case there will be found either an intellectual or a moral beauty that has charmed the lover.

George Eliot and the wife of Carlyle could not lay claim to very much of the "dimpled beauty," yet was there not a higher beauty in their souls, that even found expression in their faces when closely observed, and for which the giddy girl might well desire to exchange her dimples.

And yet physical beauty has its high office. Every face of beauty is from the chisel of the Eternal Sculptor. Every dimple is the finger print of the Divine. Woman's highest and grandest endowment is her beauty, physical, intellectual and spiritual.

Thrice happy is that woman who possesses all these. She is a star of the first magnitude in the firmament of human society. God never endowed a woman with this threefold beauty without reserving a claim upon her power. Such a woman belongs to humanity, She is ministrant to human need.

Of these three forms of beauty, the spiritual is of the first importance, intellectual of the second, and physical of the third. Although no amount of physical beauty can fully compensate for the slightest deficiency of the spiritual, yet it must be acknowledged that the lack of physical beauty is never so painfully obvious as when accompanied by a like spiritual deficiency.

It is a law established by observations made on the entire animal kingdom, that the worth of offspring, other things being equal, is in the ratio of the mother's beauty. It may not be a beauty that would stand before the criticism of the world, but it must be a beauty that charms the husband.

In view of these facts is it not the highest duty of woman, a duty which she owes to God and to humanity, to make herself at all times as beautiful in her husband's eyes as possible? It is a diviner art to maintain affection than to awaken it. It cannot long be maintained, if the advantages under which it was awakened are withdrawn. Your husband wooed and won you in your best attire, in an atmosphere surcharged with the bewilderment of roses, perfume and of song, amid the sweet intoxication of woodland rambles and moonlight poetry. You come to his house, take off the myrtle from your hair and cast the rosebud from your throat, and exchange the rustling perfumed robes of love for soiled calico. Can you expect anything but a chilling shock to the affections of him who before had stood gazing upon you in the moveless trance of love?

Ladies need but little advice of this kind concerning their personal appearance when they go into society. Indeed, it would be far better for them and for the world if they would appear a little less attractive in the presence of other husbands, and a little more so in the presence of their own. Is it any wonder that the husband grows cold and indifferent towards his wife when he sees her exhausting every resource of invention to enhance her attractiveness in the presence of other men, while she appears continually in his presence with soiled dress and disheveled hair? How often we hear ladies making an almost ludicrous attempt to revive the forgotten lore of their early seminary culture, in the hope of winning the admiration of some brilliant society man, when their conversation with their husbands never rises to higher themes than the last month's rent and a new dress to wear to church.

This is an almost universal vice. No creed or social position is free from it. It is daily committed alike by the rich and the poor, in ignorance of one of the great laws that govern human love.

We have told the secret of many a conjugal tragedy. It costs but little to dress becomingly, to put a rose-bud in the hair, and she who cannot find time to do this may, perhaps, by and by find time to mourn over blighted hopes and buried love.

Important as are the duties that husband and wife owe to each other, no less important are those which they owe to their children. It is the duty of parents to make the home of childhood pleasant and attractive, for children develop more perfectly in pleasant than in unpleasant homes. We do not mean, however, mere outward attractiveness. It is not essential that the home should overlook some rich and beautiful landscape; but that the associations of home should be pleasant and agreeable to the children; so that they may not become restless and desirous of leaving it.

It is the duty of parents to make their children love them. Not that they should compel love with the authority of the rod, for that would be impossible; but by the wise application of the law that "love begets love." No person has any right to be the parent of a child that doesn't love him. Thoughtlessness and narrow views of life's relations are often fatal to filial love. Parents too often forget that they themselves were once children with children's tastes, desires, and whims.

It is natural for children to love their parents, not only during the years of childhood, but through life. And yet we often see very little filial love among grown up children. This is chiefly because the parents failed to make a proper concession to the demands of childhood. A child cannot love one, be it parent or teacher, who suppresses his child nature. When once the tender bond of sympathy between parent and child has thus been broken it can never be fully reunited; and when the child becomes a man he is very apt to dislike his parents for the needless pain they have caused him, in not governing him in accordance with the laws of his nature.

By sympathy we do not mean love. It is possible for love to exist without sympathy, or at least without that intimate, almost mesmeric sympathy that ought to exist between parent and child. Such parents usually love their children with much tenderness, but they somehow manage to place a great gulf between themselves and the objects of their affection. They do not understand that the art of rearing children is the art of becoming "a child again," of going back where the children are, and so growing up again with them. Yes, the way to bring up a child is to go back and get him and take him along with you up to manhood. You should not stand on the height and call him up, for he would be very apt to lose his way. He is not acquainted with the path. You know it is a narrow path, only wide enough for one, and that all who would climb that height must go "single file."

But the obligations of parents and children are reciprocal, and corresponding to the duties that parents owe to their children are those that children owe to their parents. That children owe to their parents a debt of gratitude, that they owe them the duty of obedience, love and respect, is a proposition that requires no demonstration, for it meets the approval of every true child.

Less recognized than the above are the duties that children owe to each other. The older children owe to the younger ones the duty of tenderness and consideration for their age, and should not in their dealings with them apply the ethics of society, "Do to others as others do to you." They should rather apply the golden rule as it reads, and patiently trust to a more mature age to develop in their thoughtless little brothers and sisters a deeper sense of obligation and moral responsibility. The older children are very apt to take advantage of the younger ones, and often use their superior tact in pleading their own case to the parents. Now everything of this sort is a violation of the duties that older children owe to the younger.

But the younger children owe certain duties to the older ones. Children should always be taught to respect superior knowledge and experience, whether found in parent, teacher, or older brothers and sisters. Hence the younger children owe to the older ones the duty of respect and, to a certain extent, obedience.

Brothers owe to their sisters precisely the same respect and gallantry that they owe to women everywhere. They will be rewarded for this in the ease with which when they become older they can enter the society of ladies, and sisters will receive the same reward for properly discharging at home the duties that they owe to every man.

The duties of home then are simply the aggregate of all the obligations that grow out of the family relation, and on the discharge of these depends the success or failure of the home life. Home may be made happy or wretched, according to the discharge of these obligations. It is not, however, the great questions of moral obligation that most vitally affect the happiness of the home, but the aggregate of all those little obligations that love always imposes. The crowning glory of the home life is that it draws its supremest joy from the little events.

"Our daily paths, with thorns or flowers
We can at will bestrew them;
What bliss would gild the passing hours,
If we but rightly knew them!
The way of life is rough at best,
But briers yield the roses;
So that which leads to joy and rest
The hardest path discloses.

"The weeds that oft we cast away,
Their simple beauty scorning,
Would form a wreath of purest ray,
And prove the best adorning.
So in our daily paths, 'twere well
To call each gift a treasure,
However slight, where love can dwell
With life-renewing pleasure."

CONTENTMENT AT HOME.

THE men who are discontented at home, are, as a rule, discontented everywhere. There are, indeed, exceptions to this rule, for there are those who are better than their homes, great souls that have sprung up out of vicious homes where intemperance and still darker vices have shrouded their early years in painful memories. In such homes those noble souls who, from some favorable combination of circumstances, have risen above their surroundings, may well feel discontented. But even in these cases we may believe that there is still that which justifies something of the spirit of content. They are discontented not necessarily with the identity of the home itself, but with its condition, and if they were to surround themselves with the influences of an ideal home they would in most cases retain the identity of the old. The new house would rise on the foundation of the old. Like the boy's jack knife that required a new blade and a new handle, and that when these were supplied was to him the old knife still; so many objects seem to have a subtle spirit independent of their material structure, but depending solely on associations that constitute to us their identity. With this spiritual identity of our home we may be, and ought to be, content. If the influence of our home be evil, if its atmosphere be injurious, then we should spend our lives in making it better, and in purifying its atmosphere. In this noblest of all forms of human labor we should find contentment. Contentment is simply a willingness to be happy. Almost any sphere or condition of life furnishes the necessary material for happiness if we will only appropriate it in the spirit of contentment. It is questionable if there is any outward condition of human life in which it does not lie within one's power to be content. Our desires feed upon their own gratification. One is always and necessarily contented at the moment of the first gratification. It is only when a desire has been unlawfully gratified that the gratification fails to bring satisfaction and content. Hence discontent is subjective rather than objective. Now there are no pain and sorrow like subjective pains and sorrows; those which the mind experiences within its own dominion, and to which it can assign no adequate cause. In such cases the mind itself cannot see why it should feel discontent. Such suffering of the mind is analogous to nervousness in the body. How often we hear it said of sensitive and complaining women, "nothing ails her, she 's only nervous." We do not stop to consider that nervousness is the most absolutely real of all diseases; it is the reality of the unreal, and the unreality of the real. With healthy nerve and an unvitiated imagination we may render real, or divest of reality, whatever we choose. But can the victim of delirium tremens—can the nervous patient render unreal the disease which he fancies is preying at his vitals? or can he render real the fact that his imagination is disordered? "nothing ails him!" There is nothing so absolutely real as a delusion. Nervousness is the only real disease. In like manner the only real sorrow is subjective sorrow, that sorrow which the suffering mind itself cannot account for. The great sorrows of human experience arise from this inner source.

They consist in a brooding discontent, a stubborn refusal of the mind to respond in a satisfactory manner to any external stimulant. The world holds up to our vision many illustrious examples of human sorrow and suffering,—suffering from outward conditions and circumstances, and, perhaps, the most noted of these is that almost typical character, Job. But the illustrious examples of that other sorrow, the world can never see, for it is the sorrow of midnight and silence. It is a sorrow which cannot be shared, and one which the world will not recognize. We can, however, see its fruits, for it sometimes bears the divinest fruit, but, as with the tree of evil everywhere, the tree which bore it must first be cut and burned. 'Tis from the ashes of the tree of evil that fruit divine appears. He who conquers this subjective sorrow and comes triumphantly out of the dark forest of inward discontent into the sweet light of peace and contentment, is a conqueror in the grandest and sublimest sense of the word, and on his brow there rests forevermore a crown of victory.

Discontent, then, is in almost every case the result of this subjective mental action, a continual yearning for something more than the present experience. That is the most awful form of human disease in which the cognizable objects and the cognizing faculties are out of gear. What then is the remedy for discontent? We have said that desires feed upon their own gratification, and the kind of food determines the kind of desires. An unlawful gratification produces in its turn another unlawful desire. Now, since there is no natural object or circumstance that can respond to an unlawful desire, it follows that in the home where objects and circumstances are natural, the unlawful desire must remain ungratified, and hence the source of yearning and discontent must also remain, till unlawful gratification has been obtained elsewhere.

A pertinent illustration of this view of the subject may be seen in the behavior of a slightly depraved appetite, and among a civilized people this is the condition of almost every one's appetite. Every one knows that when he is hungry a simple piece of dry bread tastes good and satisfies the hunger; but let him cover it with highly seasoned sauce, and after partaking of it attempt to go back to the dry bread, he will find that it tastes insipid and does not satisfy him. If, however, he had taken a juicy pear instead of the spicy sauce, he could have returned to the dry bread with satisfaction. Here then lies a principle. The dry bread and the pear both sustain a normal relation to our appetites, and gratify a lawful desire, but not so with the sauce; for spices and artificial flavors were never meant to satisfy a healthy appetite. There is nothing in a healthy appetite that corresponds to them. The dry bread and the pear, feeding nothing but a healthy and lawful desire, in their turn give rise to a healthy and lawful desire; and this, dry bread can satisfy. But the sauce satisfying an unnatural, and hence unlawful, appetite, gives rise to nothing but unhealthy and unlawful desires, and these the dry bread cannot satisfy. Apply the principle involved in this illustration, and the solution which it suggests to the higher faculties of the mind, and you have the whole philosophy of discontent. But, says one, shall we follow out this doctrine to its full extent, and seek to awaken no desire which our surrounding circumstances cannot gratify? If discontent consists simply in ungratified desires, then it would be reasonable to suppress all desires that we cannot gratify. But would not this be fatal to all progress? Would it not tend to keep us forever on the dead level of the present? There is an infinite difference between the absolute inability to gratify a desire, and the mere inability to gratify it immediately. The lion cannot gratify at once his desire for food, but the suspension of the gratification does not result in discontent. He, perhaps, knows that his diligent search will make the gratification still keener when it comes. So the young man who desires to be great and useful need not crush that desire simply because he is unable to gratify it at once. His highest delight may spring from his contemplation of its final gratification. There is a continual gratification simply in the prospect of ultimate gratification.

But if one has a desire that it is absolutely impossible for him to gratify, then the quicker it is crushed, the better. If a cripple should become ambitious to be an acrobat, then the harboring of that ambition could lead to nothing but discontent. Then crush all desires that cannot, in the nature of things, be satisfied. Crush all unlawful desires, and seek to gratify all lawful ones, and contentment will be the necessary result.

"Sweet are the thoughts that savor of content—
  The quiet mind is richer than a crown.
Sweet are the nights in careless slumber spent,
  The poor estate scorns fortune's angry frown;
Such sweet content, such minds, such sleep, such bliss,
  Beggars enjoy, when princes oft do miss.

"The homely house that harbors quiet rest,
  The cottage that affords no pride or care,
The mien that 'grees with country music best,
  The sweet consort of mirth and music's fare,
Obscured life sets down a type of bliss:—
  A mind content both crown and kingdom is."

VISITING.

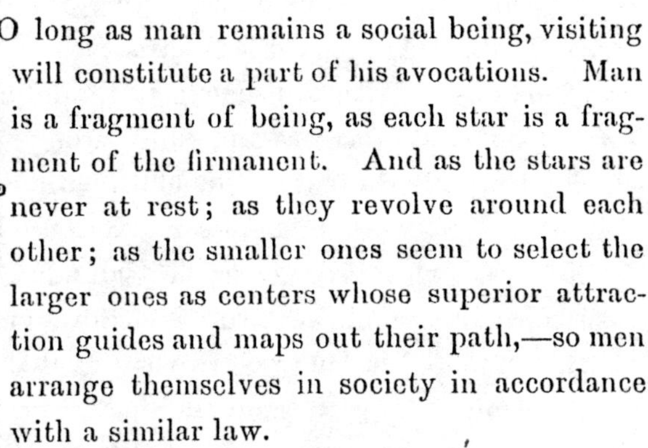

SO long as man remains a social being, visiting will constitute a part of his avocations. Man is a fragment of being, as each star is a fragment of the firmament. And as the stars are never at rest; as they revolve around each other; as the smaller ones seem to select the larger ones as centers whose superior attraction guides and maps out their path,—so men arrange themselves in society in accordance with a similar law.

There are suns and planets and asteroids in human society, and these take their proper places by an eternal law of human affinity.

Man is, in his individuality, an imperfectly adapted being. The divine declaration, "It is not good for man to be alone," long before it was written by human pen was written in the nature of man by virtue of this law, that man is but fragmentary.

Hence the necessity and philosophy of society and of the custom of visiting. A home without visitors is not a perfect home, inasmuch as the members of that home cannot become perfect, but must forever remain undeveloped unless they come in contact with the great world. We have all seen such homes, where the frozen pride of wealth congeals the fountains of worth and usefulness. There are certain families that never visit; but the vital instincts of society soon eliminate them, as a sliver or any foreign substance is eliminated from the flesh.

In such cases Nature disconnects the foreign substance from all the vital processes and builds around it a hard case, which effectually shuts it off from all relation with the vital organism, as it were in a prison. Society has the same instincts, and when it discovers in itself a foreign substance in the form of a family destitute of fellow sympathy, a family who do not visit nor receive visitors, it rapidly cuts off all vital connection with them and encloses them within the prison walls of their own reserve. With what pitying contempt society looks upon such a family! How even the children point to the home as the dwelling of some monstrosity, and learn to taunt the inmates as the parrot learns to taunt the barn fowl. We pity the members of such a family. We have often wondered what the source of their enjoyment can be. That same coldness and lack of sympathy which makes them shun the world, most certainly will make them cold and distant in one another's society.

Such homes are usually the abodes of gilded misery. It is a curious fact that these families soon become extinct. They live but a few generations at best, become sickly and vicious, and finally die out, and leave the world no better and, perhaps, no worse.

There is a lesson in this fact, not only a moral lesson, but a lesson in science as well. There is no subject that men have studied so little as the science of human nature, although it is the grandest subject that can engross the human intellect. They have, however, developed a few grand results, and one of them is the law that governs the phenomenon we have just referred to. The discovery was made, however, not by a direct study of human nature, but chiefly by observation on the lower octaves in life's scale. This law is known as the law of the "survival of the fittest." It teaches that when a being or a faculty ceases to act in a manner consistent with the general good it is destroyed by a power of natural selection.

Nature does this in self defense. When a being violates the laws of his nature he is destroyed if he persists in the violation. When he persists in the violation of his moral nature he dies as a moral being, although he may still survive as a physical and intellectual being. If he violates his intellectual nature he dies as an intellectual being. If his social nature, then he dies as a social being. But these calamities are not confined to the individual alone. The organic weakness resulting from his violation is transmitted to his children, who transmit to their offspring in still greater degree the iniquity of the fathers, till finally the family becomes too weak to perpetuate itself.

Now the ability to perpetuate the species is more vitally related to the social nature than to the intellectual or the moral; and families that violate their social nature, as do those we are considering, are striking at the tap root of their family life.

Such families seldom do the world much injury, because society, with the aid of nature, rids itself of the pest with the greatest economy of effort and the least expenditure of its forces. Since man is but a fragment he requires the presence of his supplementary fragments to develop his possibilities.

As woman is essential to man and man to woman in order to call out and develop the latent possibilities in each, so every human being, in order to call forth his highest possibilities, must first be wedded to his supplement humanity. He must lose his identity in the great current of human want before he can find it again in a larger and grander sense.

The muscle grows strong most rapidly when it wastes most rapidly. The magnet grows powerful by imparting its magnetic properties to iron and steel. The teacher grows wise by imparting wisdom. The rose fills all the air with its sweet gift of incense, and through the little railway tunnels fly the trains that bear from nature's laboratory the precious freight that still replenishes the ever wasting stream.

Now social intercourse is simply a process of imparting

to others a portion of ourselves. When the rose begins to hoard its fragrance, it dies. So when man would hoard his influence and wrap around him the mantle of solitude, he is fading away in the noblest attributes of his being.

There is a possible interpretation of the above that we would not wish to submit to the test of history. It is that the love of solitude is an illegitimate love. This interpretation meets its rebuke in the lives of poets and philosophers. The world's grandest characters have been lovers of solitude. There is something pathetically beautiful in the yearning which poets have always felt for the sweet breath of nature untainted by the smoke and noxious vapors of the city. There is both a legitimate and an illegitimate love of solitude.

Jesus loved solitude as probably no other being ever did. The honey bee loves solitude, and loves it for the same reason that Jesus and the poets love it, because guided by a heavenly instinct they know that solitude alone can minister to the throng, and they are its ministers divinely elect. The bee must leave the merry swarm and seek the silent solitude where blush in unconscious beauty the wild rose and the lily. So Jesus, although his heart was with the dying throng, still sought the lonely heights, because it was there alone from the divine flower of solitude that he could extract the honey for the "healing of the nations." Poets love solitude, not from selfishness. They desire it as a sick man desires medicine. It ministers to the highest necessities of their being. They love to go into solitude, not because their hearts do not beat with the great multitude, but because they can get nearer to nature's heart when removed from the roaring factory and the rushing train, and with purer soul receive her gracious benediction. All then should love solitude, but as the bee loves it, because they can find something there fresh from God to bring to the hive of humanity.

The poet and the philosopher can minister to the world while they remain in solitude; but not so with the "common people"; the toiling men and women without genius must find their field of labor in the social world. Then let the gates of cottage and palace be flung open to the tides of humanity. Let us entertertain and be entertained. Let us make it a part of our life work to give ourselves to others, and in our turn derive from society what must come from that source, if it ever comes to us at all.

Society does not consist in physical proximity. It does not consist in vying with one another in the display of fine dwellings and costly tables. Social intercourse, to be right and profitable, must contain its own excuse. It must be the outgrowth of an instinctive impulse to mingle within the sphere of mutual interest, in spiritual as well as physical proximity.

We do not wish to recommend that practice so prevalent among certain classes, of gadding from house to house for the purpose of retailing the morning news. This is not what we mean by social intercourse. Nor would we recommend the "formal call," where each family keeps a record and returns a call as it would pay for a barrel of flour. We have no faith in the book-keeping of calls. Perhaps there is no other relation of life that fosters so much of deception and falsehood as the system of fashionable calling.

Mrs. A. calls upon Mrs. B., who has just settled in the neighborhood, because if she were not to do so, Mrs. B. would think that Mrs. A. was not acquainted with the ways of society. Mrs. B. is, of course, delighted to see Mrs. A., notwithstanding she threw up her hands in horror when the door bell rang. When Mrs. A. departs amid the mournful protests of Mrs. B., Mrs. B. has too much confidence in Mrs. A.'s "society education" to have any fears that she will heed the earnest and heartfelt (?) entreaty to "call again" and not to be "so formal."

Such calls involve the commercial instincts of our nature, for they are regarded as merchandise and subject to the laws of debit and credit. They do not appeal to the social faculty at all, and hence have no tendency in the direction of its cultivation, but on the other hand they weaken it, for they are in almost every case regarded as painful duties, and it is a law of our being that the painful or disagreeable action of any function, whether physical or mental, has a direct tendency to weaken the function involved.

Then, as the first and essential condition to the cultitivation of the social faculty, let the call be divested of all its formalty. Neighboring parents should learn a lesson from their own children, who play in adjoining yards and seek each other's presence often for the sake of that presence alone. Not in their "beauty's best attire" nor at the feast where pride sits queen, but in the mood and dress of every day. Let them meet and spend the evening around each other's hearthstone, nor recognize any hour as fashionable or unfashionable, but "drop in" with that simplicity and informality that calls forth the exclamation of surprise which no actor's skill can feign.

We cannot better close this chapter than by quoting the words of that almost marvelous student of human nature, Harriet Beecher Stowe.

"There would be a great deal more obedience to the apostolic injunction, 'be not forgetful to entertain strangers,' if it once could be clearly got into the heads of well intending people what it is that strangers want. What do you want when away from home in a strange city? Is it not the warmth of the home fireside and the sight of people that you know care for you? Is it not the blessed privilege of speaking and acting yourself out unconstrainedly among those who you know understand you? And had you not rather dine with an old friend on simple cold mutton offered with a warm heart, than go to a splendid ceremonious dinner party among people who don't care a rush for you? Well, then, set it down in your book that other people are like you, and that the art of entertaining is the art of really caring for people. If you have a warm heart, congenial tastes, and a real interest in your stranger, don't fear to invite him though you have no best dinner set and your existing plates are sadly chipped at the edges, and even though there be a handle broken off from the side of your vegetable dish. Set it down in your belief that you can give something better than a dinner, however good,—you can give a part of yourself. You can give love, good will, and sympathy, of which there has perhaps been quite as much over cracked plates and restricted table furniture as over Sèvres china and silver."

"Blest be that spot where cheerful guests retire
To pause from toil, and trim their evening fire;
Blest that abode, where want and pain repair,
And every stranger finds a ready chair:
Blest be those feasts with simple plenty crown'd,
Where all the ruddy family around
Laugh at the jest or pranks, that never fail,
Or sigh with pity at some mournful tale,
Or press the bashful stranger to his food,
And learn the luxury of doing good."

UNSELFISHNESS AT HOME.

IN accordance with an eternal law, selfishness defeats its own ends. The selfish man, from the very nature of selfishness, declares war against the universe, and in that unequal fight is sure to fall. The only way we can get God on our side is to enlist in his army.

The conditions of our own happiness are so blended and interwoven with the conditions of other's happiness, that we cannot successfully seek our own highest interest while we are unmindful of the welfare of others. There is but one rational and successful way in which a man may work for himself, and that is by forgetting self in his desire for the well-being of others. Human society is a vast machine in which every man is a wheel, but the wheels of a machine never move independently. No matter how small and apparently insignificant they may be, they each perform an essential office, and their value is represented in the product of the great machine.

Man is a compound of function or faculties, and is so constituted that the action of each produces pleasure and only pleasure. The sum total of man's happiness, then, depends on the number of faculties that he brings into healthy and normal exercise.

One of these faculties is conscience, that voice in the soul which bids us do right, and do unto others as we would have them do unto us, a duty that cannot be performed from selfish motives. But unless this duty be performed, we are deprived of that exquisite pleasure which comes from the approval of conscience.

Another of our faculties is benevolence, whose legitimate function is to prompt us to love our neighbor as ourselves, the very essence of unselfishness. But if we through selfishness refuse to fulfill this function, we must forego that pure and exalted pleasure of which it has been declared "it is more blessed to give than to receive." Man is a social being, and from his several social faculties derives by far the greatest portion of his happiness; but only as he observes the golden rule. For society will not be cheated. Its system of book-keeping is perfect, and he who expects to receive from society more than he is willing to give in return, will be sadly disappointed.

And so it is that all those faculties which relate men to their fellow men can yield us no pleasure so long as we are selfish. By selfishness we are cut off from the pleasures arising from the action of a large number of the most important faculties of the mind. To use a paradox, the only rational and consistent selfishness is that of unselfishness.

If we desire our own highest pleasure we cannot obtain it till we forget our object.

If this be true with reference to the great world, how much truer is it with reference to the little world, the home. Perhaps the truest picture of total depravity which the mind can paint is that of a home where selfishness reigns.

Selfishness is fatal to the very existence of home. Home may be defined as an isolated portion of society, bound together by a stronger degree of love than exists between the different members of the human family in general. Home and selfishness are nearly opposite in their meaning, and cannot exist together any more than love and hate.

Selfishness, then, is fatal to love; and since love is the basis of home, it follows that selfishness is the great destroyer of home.

As in the outward world, he who falls in love with himself always has the field clear, no rivals ever molesting him; so in the home, he who makes his own happiness paramount, to that same extent severs his connection with the family, and becomes, in a certain sense, an outcast. The sister, perceiving the brother's selfishness, will seek other companions, and thus a coldness and indifference springs up between brother and sister.

There are many arguments in favor of unselfishness, but we have made prominent the least and lowest. We have, however, had a purpose in this. It is to the selfish we would speak. The unselfish require no advice or exhortation, and from the very nature of selfishness it cannot be moved by any but a selfish argument.

Why is that little street boy so dwarfed in his mental and moral nature? Why is it usually so difficult to develop one of that class and make him a noble and powerful man? Simply because the selfishness in that wretched home whence he came has arrested his development, so that he can never be anything but a child. He can seldom be trusted, because the early selfishness at home, engendered by misery and want, it may be, has left its demon cunning in his mind.

It is a fact with which all are familiar, that the character is written in the face. If we cannot read it, it is not because it is not written there, but because of our obtuseness. Yet there are few so obtuse that they cannot distinguish between selfishness and generosity. Who has not noticed the narrow, pinched, and indescribably repulsive countenance of the miser? Who has not contrasted it with the open, frank, and attractive countenance of the philanthropist?

It seems as if the very selfishness of the world should make us unselfish at home. Think of the pain and suffering that is born of selfishness! As you gather round the board of plenty for the evening repast, or round the roaring fire while the storm sends its fitful but harmless gusts against the windows, think of the pale, sad faces that are pressing against the panes of dingy hovels, gazing into the starless night in the imploring anguish of hunger and cold and want. How, with this sad thought in mind, can little brothers and sisters be selfish at home? How can they quarrel, as they sometimes do, over an apple or a pear, when they remember that there are thousands who would gladly gather up the leavings that they trample under their feet, and devour them with the eagerness of a starving dog?

The young man who is selfish at home, who is eager to get the largest and fairest apple, and does not seek to share it with sister or brother, surely will not share it with wife and children, when he becomes the owner of a home. Let young ladies beware of those young men who are selfish at home; for if they do not manifest their selfishness in the society of ladies, it is only from policy, or lack of opportunity.

It is a fact which mathematics alone cannot explain, that the more affection we leave at home the more we carry with us.

There is something in the nature of selfishness, whether at home or in society, that makes it peculiarly repugnant to us, and leads us instinctively to brand it as among the most ignoble of vices. There is hardly another vice that has not some shadow of a redeeming feature. We pity the drunkard, perhaps because his almost proverbial generosity appeals to our sympathies. He cannot, from the very nature of his sin, be a narrow, miserly soul. Even robbers and murderers may have some attractive qualities. It costs us an effort not to admire such characters as Lightfoot and Thunderbolt, who spent their lives in robbing the rich that they might give to the poor. Of course all such crimes are heinous in the sight of God, and should be in the sight of man, but they almost always are accompanied by some virtues, and as we do not always stop to separate the crimes from the attending virtues, we sometimes do not hate them as we ought.

But this difficulty does not exist in the case of selfishness, for it has no redeeming features. It stands alone in its ignominy, a black picture on a background of infinite hatefulness.

> "Oh, if the selfish knew how much they lost,
> What would they not endeavor and endure
> To imitate, as far as in them lay,
> Him who his wisdom and his power employs
> In making others happy."

PATIENCE.

PATIENCE has been defined as "the courage of virtue," and the definition seems to us peculiarly appropriate, for it is that quality of the soul that bids it stand firm at the post of duty where God has placed it, undaunted by the assaults of vice. It is that which closes the lips against all complaining, and folds its wings over a wounded heart and waits.

It is a noble thing to act, but it is a nobler thing to wait, for to act is the soul's most natural tendency. It is its first and simplest desire. The child takes no account of time or indirect motion in the gratification of its wish.

Place a brute within a few feet of food, but make the only possible means of reaching it indirect; make it necessary that he should first go back from the food, perhaps out of sight of it, for a moment, and then by a circuitous route come around to it. Under these conditions the brute will starve in sight of the food. This would not be merely an experiment upon the brute's intellect; it would involve this principle of patience. The impatience of the brute in this case would be due to the fact that he had not passed that stage in which all gratification is sought by direct and uninterrupted action. This brute impatience cannot go *from* the object of its desire, even when intellect declares such an act necessary. It is quite essential in this experiment, however, that we select the right kind of brute, for there are brutes which are endowed with a wonderful degree of patience. We may forcibly illustrate from the brute kingdom both patience and impatience. Those which are endowed with patience are not usually those which are most intelligent. This shows that the phenomenon in the foregoing experiment is not an intellectual one. An ox, which possesses considerable intelligence, would stand and fret for hours before it would go back *from* the food, while the rat, which possesses far less intelligence, would set itself to work at once, and dig, if need be, for a whole night through solid earth. He would go back, or round, or over, or under; in short, he would labor *patiently* till his efforts were crowned with success. This quality of patience in brutes does not seem to bear any relation to their rank in the scale of intelligence, and yet it must be regarded as one of the noblest attributes, either of man or brute; for the fact that a quality is possessed by a brute does not prevent it from being among the noblest human attributes.

Even the great mass of mankind have not yet passed that stage in which they cannot bide the lapse of time between a desire and its gratification. It is a characteristic of the highest souls to feel that they may be approaching the object of their desire while they see it receding.

It is true that it requires but little intellectual power to see that in many cases this may be so; and yet there is a wide difference between a mere intellectual conception and that attribute of the soul which converts the conception into a living truth. The wide gulf that stretches between the mere intellectual assent to the highest spiritual fact, and that element in the soul which takes hold of it as a part of its own living self, is just that which stretches between faith and reason, patience and impatience.

In this view of the subject patience is allied to faith. Patience is that which makes us willing to wait, and faith is that which makes us feel that the waiting will bear us a sweet fruition.

Patience is a higher and grander virtue than the world has yet acknowledged. It is that noble element which appreciates time and indirect motion in the gratification of desires. It is allied to the divine instinct of the tree that waits for the flower and the fruit.

Trials, sorrow, and death await us all. It is useless to attempt to escape them, for they are inevitable. They are the frosts that open the hard burrs of human hearts. But it is only as instruments in the hands of patience that they become ministrant to our development.

God imposes upon man the obligation to no virtue which he has not first woven into the constitution of nature. Every cardinal virtue is first a cosmical law. Thus the grand virtue of patience is eternally mated with nature's law of constancy. It is the patience of nature that rears and completes the proud temple of the oak. It is her patience through which the never-wearying rootlet embraces the rocky ribs of the moveless boulder. Through what long and weary ages has nature pounded on the granite doors of giant mountains, pleading for the crumbs that fall from the rocky tables, that she may bear them down to the vales, to feed the hungry guests that wait in her halls below. Through uncounted eras she has stood with patient hand and sifted into river beds and ocean depths the fine alluvial morsels that she begged from miser mountains. Thus does patience bear the credentials of its own divinity. 'T is the same patience, divinely born, that we trace through all the instinctive movements and laborious life of bee, and spider, and architectonic beaver. The great law of patience bears the same divine approval, whether we find it in the silent consecutiveness of natural law, in the tireless movements of the laboring ant, in the sweet innocence of childhood building its play-house, in the stern bread-battle of human life, in the pale, wasting vigilance of the brain-toiling, star-reading scientist, or in divine simplicity, thorn-crowned and bleeding, on the quaking brow of Calvary. Thus patience is divine, and to be patient is to be God-like.

Patience is the grandest representative of God. It has been the captain of the divine forces; out from the fiery halls of chaos it has led, in shining battalions, the helmeted stars. On earth it has produced the highest results that mark the career of man. There is no shining goal of human glory too bright or too remote for patience. No height can tire its wing. Strike from the firmament of human greatness every star that has been placed there by the hand of patience, and you cover that firmament with the veil of midnight darkness. It is patience that has crushed mighty evils and wrought sublime reforms in human history; patience, that dared to stand up and meet the taunts of ignorance and bigotry; patience, that has calmly walked back into the shadow of defeat, with "Thy will be done" upon its lips; patience, that has breathed the fiery smoke of torment with upturned brow.

Truly has it been said, "Patience comforts the poor and moderates the rich; she makes us humble in prosperity, cheerful in adversity, unmoved by calumny, and above reproach; she teaches us to forgive those who have injured us, and to be the first in asking the forgiveness of those whom we have injured; she delights the faithful, and invites the unbelieving; she adorns the woman and approves the man; she is beautiful in either sex and every age."

It is the sin of this high-pressure age, that it cannot

wait; and here again the accusation must rest with peculiar emphasis on Young America. We have yet to learn from orchard and garden that the best in nature ripens slowest. The American child has much to learn in this respect, from English and German children, especially the latter; the Germans are the world's models of patience.

The American boy reads the life of some eminent man, and immediately he is fired with a desire to be like him. He ignores the elements of time and indirect action. He sets aside the factor of life's developing hardships, and entertains the insane idea that he can be like his ideal in a short time. He buys advanced works on his special theme. He cannot stop to master the elementary works. His theory is that the greater includes the less. He sits up late at night, vainly trying to comprehend his ponderous books, until he becomes discouraged and abandons all further attempts to be a great man.

Now the fact of his wild enthusiasm proves that he had in him the elements of greatness, a greatness that would have justified his aspirations, had not the American vice of impatience crushed it in the bud. The world is full of such defeated greatness. Genius with patience is invincible and divine, but without patience it is a blind Ulysses groping in the darkness.

"Full many a flower is born to blush unseen,"

only because it insists on being seen before it has blossomed, and the world will not look at it.

Young men are apt to be in too much of a hurry to reach the goal of their aspiration. Now and then we find one, who, in his youth, is willing to study with patience, and

"Learn to labor and to wait."

But the great majority of young men seem to feel that the highest triumph of life is to complete their education in their teens. And such ones are apt to accomplish that exceedingly lofty object, from the very fact that those who commence an education with such foolish views of life are pretty sure to halt in their pursuit of knowledge at about that time. They are not likely to add much to the stock of forced knowledge which they bring away from college. And, in such cases, even this is not usually a great amount, from the fact of their having gone to college too early to make it of much use to them.

It is true that many great and useful men have completed their college education while very young, but it was because they were by nature able to do this without impatient haste. Their genius had, perhaps, a slight tinge of precocity, an element, however, which constitutes no part of genius. It is entirely foreign to it, and may exist, and far oftener does, in connection with talents that are below mediocrity. Genius consists in a special aptitude for labor, patient labor.

Our common schools are a living monument of the impatience of America, and it is not impossible that the monument may yet crumble with its own weight, They may yet thwart the very object of that intense and headlong desire, of which the impatience both of parents and educators is the expression. Neither Greece nor Rome attained her glory through such impatient culture.

But there is another reason why we should cultivate patience. It is conducive to health and longevity. No impatient man ever died of old age. Impatience is a friction in the wheels of life. Intemperance will not wear out the machinery of life sooner than impatience. And not only does the patient man live longer than the impatient man, when length of life is computed in years and months, but he also lives longer in another and important sense. In computing the duration of a human life in the actual sense of life, if we wish to obtain the result in minutes and seconds, we must strike out from the calculation all those minutes and seconds in which he does not live in the proper sense of the word. This would include all periods of unconsciousness, of intoxication, and of mental alienation. In short, all moments which when past leave in our nature no rational record of their passage.

Now the patient man has a calm and rational appreciation of each moment of his conscious life, and his moments of unconsciousness are fewer than those of the impatient man. The patient man, as a general rule, requires less sleep than one who is impatient, for the brain and all the physical powers require time for recuperation in sleep just in proportion to the amount of waste during wakefulness. But nothing so wastes the vital and mental power as the spasmodic, fitful, ineffectual and half unconscious movements, thoughts and feelings of the impatient man. "Well I'm tired, but I haven't done anything," is the habitual expression of the impatient, while the patient accomplish a great deal but are seldom tired. The reason is plain. The impatient man cannot stop to see where to take hold, and so takes hold several times, and makes as many useless movements, all of which weary and exhaust. But the patient man takes hold in the right place the first time, and thus not only saves time, but physical and mental energy. And so while the patient man calmly and without friction accomplishes life's mission, the impatient man wears out his powers and dies of exhaustion before he gets ready to begin the work.

"'Tis mine to work, and not to win;
The soul must wait to have her wings;
Even time is but a landmark in
The great eternity of things.

"Is it so much that thou below,
O heart, shouldst fail of thy desire,
When death, as we believe and know,
Is but a call to come up higher?"

TEMPERANCE.

THE word temperance, from the Latin *temperantia*, meant simply moderation, and when it came to be first applied with special emphasis to the use of alcoholic beverages it meant only a moderate use of them, and did not convey the remotest idea of total abstinence.

If the fate of the temperance reform rested upon the primitive significance of dead words, then, indeed, were its advocates hopeless.

But no, the temperance reform and the words that designate its glorious sentiment were born together, born amid the thunder storm of oppression, born of the heartless parentage of hisses and of scorn, parents who tried to strangle their own offspring, but could not do it, for it bore upon its forehead the birth-mark of immortality. Its birth was an event that lay along the inevitable path of human development.

We will not contend with those who would prostitute their scholarship to rear a feeble argument upon the dusty lexicons of Greece and Rome, claiming that the world has never before found occasion for a word to designate the total abstinence from intoxicating beverages. We have no wish to dispute the significance of those old roots that lie dead and brittle in the soil of the ages.

These definitions were assigned by an infant world, but it has outgrown them now. We well remember when the word "star" signified to us only a shining speck, only a "gimlet hole to let the light of heaven through." But to our ampler vision they are the chariots of God that glide across the longitudes of night. Words are the products of human thought. They are born amid the agonizing throes that accompany the aggressions of intellect. Every conquest, every victory, is marked by the birth of a new word and the death of an old one. Like the corpuscles of the blood, they are springing into being and dying with every pulsation of the world's brain. The "dead languages" are but the moss-covered monuments that mark the cemeteries of the world's perished ideals.

We do not mean, of course, that there literally comes into use a new word with every new idea. Much less do we mean that a word actually becomes obsolete. We mean that language is a thing of growth, that it is modified to meet the ever changing conditions of human unfolding, and that words pass out of use or change their meanings with every outgrown idea.

He who does not dare advocate the temperance cause today in its boldest and most radical form is a coward, and in a certain sense a dead weight upon society. But those who steal the livery of science and clothe themselves in the cunning drapery of sophistry and become the hired pleaders for passion and for vice, deserve the everlasting execration of humanity. If we summon the saddest meaning that "doom" possesses it is but mild beside their crime. To misinterpret the divine message of science, and thus place in the hands of vice the devil's magic wand, is the crowning sin of man.

And yet there are hundreds that incur this guilt. Men whose names ensure their recognition seek to defend their own vices with the awe inspiring weapons of high sounding technicalities and scientific phrases. Such are those who tell us that alcohol is transformed into nervous tissue, that it is a respiratory food, etc. They tell us that it is nerve food, because its use occasions a greater manifestation of strength and nervous energy. A conflagration in a city is usually attended with considerable activity on the part of its citizens, but fires are not generally regarded as desirable stimulants to industry. War is always the occasion of a nation's highest energy, but shall we, therefore, say that war is a source of strength, and that it feeds a nation with the elements of energy? Is it not rather a wasting process, and is not the strength manifested in its expenditure rather than in its accumulation? We see the energy as it goes out from the nation in a wasting stream, and not as it goes in.

Just so with the nervous energy, it manifests itself in its

outward passage. The alcohol simply worries and frets the nervous system, and causes it to act in self-defense to cast out the intruder, just as war worries and frets a nation. When a sliver is lodged in the flesh the vital instincts are at once summoned to the spot, and, with might and main, strive to cast out the foreign substance, the intruder which has no right to be there. Every one knows how this is accomplished. There is first a redness, an increased vital action in the part and a swelling. This is because the vital forces are aroused and rush to the spot to see what is the matter. Just as the forces of the city, at the cry of fire, rush to the spot. There is a swelling of the city, in the part affected, an increase of its vital action attended with symptoms of morbid inflammation, almost exactly what happens in the vital system. The analogy is striking, and indicates beyond a doubt that a common principle is involved in both cases. When these vital instincts have ascertained what is the matter, they set themselves to work to cast the sliver out. They throw up around it a secretion which cuts it off from all connection with the system, and isolates it, and after a short time it falls out of its own accord.

Exactly in the same way these vital instincts drive the alcohol to the surface, through the skin, and lungs, and kidneys, and brain. This is why long after alcohol has been drunk, its odor may be detected in the breath. With every breath it is thrown out from the lungs. The odor may also be detected in the perspiration. As it is borne along the circulation to the brain, it excites that organ to an unnatural degree of activity, or if the dose is too great, the vital instincts give up the attempt for a time, the brain sinks into a torpid state, and the person is said to be dead-drunk.

But alcohol is said to be a respiratory food, meaning that it is burnt in the body like the carbon of our food, that it unites with the oxygen in the lungs and thus in many cases prevents the tissues from consuming themselves.

There is but one solitary fact that by any method of manipulation can be made to take the semblance of an argument in support of this theory, and that one fact is that alcohol warms the system. But cayenne pepper warms the system, so does quinine, so does sulphuric acid, so does pain, so does intense joy, so does laughter, so does love, so does hate, so do spasms and convulsions, so does rheumatism, so does a fever, so does the cramp colic.

All these, of course, are respiratory food, since they "warm the system." It is true that our scientists (?) have not yet succeeded in demonstrating that the cramp colic is oxidized in the lungs, but we can't tell what the future may develop.

When one is suddenly awakened from sleep to find that he must engage in a hand to hand fight with a midnight assassin, we have a striking illustration of what takes place when the assassin alcohol enters the dwelling of the hu. man soul. That vital instinct which allows no foreign substance within its domain at once grapples the intruder, a sharp contest ensues, in which the alcohol is beaten and driven out through the open door of the skin, the kidneys, the lungs, or the brain. And just here is the origin of the heat which alcohol occasions. It is due to the overaction of the vital forces in their attempt to rid themselves of a deadly foe. The midnight fight, just referred to, would naturally be a warming process, but we have never known physicians to prescribe midnight assassins as respiratory food. We presume, however, that they might take the place of most of the nostrums of the *materia medica* with little disadvantage to the suffering part of the community.

We must look beyond the Sons of Temperance or the Good Templars for the secret of success in the temperance reform.

Organization is essential to the success of any great reform, but it is simply the machinery that is driven by an unseen principle. It never yet of itself wrought a revolution. The solution of the great problem lies deeper than the mystery of the "pass word." It lies in the knowledge of natural law, in the thorough education of the people. When the people learn that alcohol is a poison in all quantities and under all circumstances, when they learn that it is never necessary either in health or disease, then we may look for gratifying results in the temperance reform.

The world has too little faith in nature and too much in medicine. Disease itself is a curative effort of nature, and is not a thing to be conquered by a poison, but an action to be regulated by favorable conditions. So long as people possess that insane faith in the efficacy of medicine, so long will they believe anything that unprincipled physicians (?) may choose to tell them about alcohol. The contest is between true philosophy and the lingering superstition of the nineteenth century.

Perhaps the most conspicuous mental feature of the savage man is his superstitious fear of medicine and the "medicine man." The world has always advanced just as fast as it has lost faith in medicine.

There is one fact with which the temperance reform has to contend, more formidable than all others combined. It is the fact that people so readily yield to the argument of their feelings. It requires much intellectual courage not to believe what our feelings tell us.

It is a fact that alcohol often makes people feel better. It elevates their spirits and makes them feel strong, buoyant and hopeful. Under such circumstances it requires almost a divine argument to convince them that they are not being benefited.

Temperance will triumph when the argument of reason becomes stronger than that of feeling with the masses. We are so constituted that our feelings are generally final in their authority. Hence the necessity of distinguishing between the significance of the natural and the artificial. People must be taught to do this before we can expect them to abandon the use of alcohol.

How then shall this be brought about? Surely not by legislation, not by seizures and fines, but by the slow and laborious process of education. This education must be specific, and must be directed for the most part to the rising generation. The pathetic stories of reformed drunkards may have their influence in shaping public sentiment, but at best they can be only subsidiary to a more substantial and abiding force. Legal measures may serve their purpose, but the reformatory efforts should be directed mainly to the securing of that condition which shall render legal measures unnecessary. This condition must be sought in the education of the children, who not only must be taught to distinguish the significance of natural and normal appetites from the unnatural and abnormal, but their training and education must be such that they shall have no unnatural and abnormal appetites. Unnatural appetites are the product of wrong physical training, and intemperance is the product of unnatural appetites. Hence wrong training is the origin of intemperance.

In our chapter on home training we have spoken of the process by which wrong physical training produces drunkards. We repeat its substance, however, for the sake of special emphasis. All that is necessary to make a drunkard is, first, a good healthy boy as material; and second, plenty of candy, pastry, pickles, and medicine as tools. Any mother with such an outfit can manufacture a drunkard. The process is extremely simple. Drunkenness, as we have said, is the product of a diseased or unnatural appetite, and the appetite may be diseased or rendered unnatural by taking advantage of the slight caprice which all appetites possess, especially in the civilized world, thus causing it to accept at times that which it otherwise would not, and which it does not naturally crave.

Unnatural appetites crave unnatural food, and accordingly unnatural food will in its turn induce an unnatural appetite; so that all a mother who desires to experiment in this direction has to do is to give her boy unnatural food, and every mother knows what we mean by unnatural food. It is not necessary for us to enumerate the many articles to which this adjective is applicable. The phrase at once suggests to the ordinary mind the abominations of spice, pickle, pork, and pastry, that fill the dining-halls of civilization with their sickly odors, that would nauseate the healthier appetites of the South Sea Island cannibals.

The mother who desires to make a drunkard must tamper with her boy's appetite by offering him that which he does not crave; by compelling him to go without a meal as a punishment for some offense, and thus become very hungry, so that he will be sure to overeat at the next meal; by compelling him always to eat all that he happens to have in his plate whether he desires it or not, instead of teaching him to drop his knife and fork at the first suggestion of sated appetite. Of course we take it for granted that she believes root beer, etc., etc., to be "very wholesome." She should use a great deal of spice in her cooking. She should aim to take away as completely as possible, the natural flavor of fruits and vegetables, and substitute an artificial one. She should always manifest great anxiety lest her boy should not eat enough to "keep up his strength." She should, of course, give him plenty of candy—it is good for the teeth, that is, for false teeth. But what is of more importance than everything else, she should dose him freely with medicine whenever he is slightly indisposed. By the way, we came near forgetting to advise a free use of tea and coffee.

We have said but little about intemperance in the ordinary way. We have told no stories of neglected wives and broken-hearted mothers. We leave that phase of the subject to the sentimental lecturer. But we have given in language somewhat ironical, that which we believe the people need, and that which every mother ought to reflect upon.

The one fact which we have tried to make prominent is that the appetite for alcoholic beverages is not necessarily induced by the use of these beverages themselves, but may be created by the use of whatever inflames the system, or vitiates the taste.

It is sufficient simply to state that the predisposition to alcoholic intemperance may be, and often is, transmitted from parent to child. This is a fact which is very generally known, but it is not, perhaps, so generally known, that it is often transmitted from grandparent to grandchild, thus passing over one and sometimes two generations of temperate parents. The fact that intemperance, or a tendency to intemperance, is thus hereditary, should render all parents doubly vigilant in the training of their children.

We have aimed in this chapter at a deeper consideration of the subject of temperance in its relation to the home life than a mere enumeration of those superficial evils of which society is chiefly cognizant. The following poem with sufficient accuracy portrays this class of evils:—

> "Now horrid frays
> Commence, the brimming glasses now are hurled
> With dire intent; bottles with bottles clash
> In rude encounter, round their temples fly
> The sharp-edged fragments, down their battered cheeks
> Mixed gore and cider flow; what shall we say
> Of rash Elpenor, who in evil hour
> Dried an immeasurable bowl and thought
> To exhale his surfeit by irriguous sleep,
> Imprudent? him death's iron sleep oppressed,
> Descending from his couch; the fall
> Luxed his neck-joint and spinal marrow bruised.
> Nor need we tell what anxious cares attend
> The turbulent mirth of wine; nor all the kinds
> Of maladies that lead to death's grim care,
> Wrought by intemperance, joint racking gout,
> Intestine stone, and pining atrophy,
> Chill, even when the sun with July heats
> Fires the scorched soil, and dropsy all afloat,
> Yet craving liquids: nor the Centaurs' tale
> Be here repeated: how, with lust and wine
> Inflamed, they fought, and spilt their drunken souls
> At feasting hour."

ECONOMY OF HOME.

THE institution of home is in itself a divine application of the law of economy. It contains the first suggestion of the "division of labor."

It is a fact within the observation of society in general, and has almost become an adage, that man and woman can live at less expense together than separately. This is certainly a benevolent provision, offering as it does another inducement to the only legitimate life, the home life.

Nature is the model economist. She never wastes a leaf, and yet she is the most benevolent of all givers. She will give you without stint of her golden cheeked and luscious flavored fruits, and yet she never throws away even her decayed products, but turns them into her laboratory and makes them over into good fruit, a subtle reproof to the unfrugal housewife who throws away the remains of the supper, that might be warmed over for breakfast. Nature knows the secret of being both economical and generous, she knows how to be frugal without being penurious. She is not lazy, and yet she always takes the shortest path. Of two equally good conductors the electric charge always takes the shorter. It will even choose the poorer conductor rather than take the longer one. The principle of "least action" in mechanics is of the same nature. These facts show that economy is a law of nature, and pervades the very soul of the universe.

But not only is it a law of the outward universe, it is an innate sentiment or instinct of hūman nature,—and not only of human nature, but of all conscious existence. We see it manifested in the squirrel, when he gathers during the autumn his store of nuts and corn for his sustenance during the coming winter.

The same instinct that prompts the squirrel to do this is the moving impulse of the great commercial world. In both instances it is simply an instinct, a faculty that brings its possessor into sympathy with the economic law that governs the movements of nature. It is the instinct of economy that tells the worm, the bee, the cat, the dog, and, in short, all animals, that a straight line is the shortest distance between two points, and that makes it to the human intellect an axiom.

The law of economy, then, is simply that by which all necessary results in nature are brought about with the least possible expenditure of force, and what we call economy in man is an instinctive appreciation and application of this law.

To the low and mean the word economy signifies dishonest acquisition and theft. To the honest but hard working man it means industry and frugality. To the moralist and philosopher it means social science, civilizing tendencies, and universal culture. So it is that one's definition of economy to a certain extent defines his character also. But he who takes his definition from nature's lips cannot err.

Nature will not allow an idle atom in her realm. She compels every rain-drop to become her minister, to bear her proffered treaty between the warring clouds and earth, and thus disarm them of their wrath, and with its subtle diplomacy to reconcile them to the pledge of peace. And with an eye to the economy of travel she bids her messengers pause upon the mountain summit, as they pass from cloud to earth, and take down with them from decaying rocks and mountain gorges a load of timber from which to form her fertile soil.

She makes the birds and zephyrs her husbandmen to garner and sow the seeds of myriad plants. She bends the neck of the proud lightning, and makes it her scavenger to purify the atmosphere. She lays her shaggy mountains on the toiling backs of earthquakes, and bids them lift the burden to the sky. She makes the omnipresent oxygen her domestic servant, and tasks his eyesight and skillful fingers to unravel her snarled and complicated skeins of chemical elements; or, if she will, exalts him to the higher office of attorney, and pleads through him for the divorce of unhappily wedded constituents.

The home is the reproduction of nature on a small scale, and not the least so in this matter of economy.

Nature is the pattern for the home, and every man and woman who in any capacity represent a home should take advantage of her example, and learn a lesson from the way in which she scrapes up her "odds and ends," and utilizes them. To all of us she says, "Accumulate all you can; employ every moment; let no opportunity pass without grasping its hand to see if there is not hidden in its palm a golden coin."

But nature is no miser. Her economy does not consist in meanness. She accumulates that she may give. She is honest and will do as she agrees. We need not take her note, her word is good. It is a law founded in the eternal beneficence of things, written on every tree whose friendly foliage shields us from the scorching sun; on every sparkling rivulet that weeps soft tears of rain upon the thirsty land, which in its turn gives back the gracious tribute of its shrubs and flowers, and with an answering compliment flings its rich gift of roses to deck the river banks; on every circling satellite, upon the moon's sweet face, who in her modesty sends down to us the flood of kisses which the sun, her gallant lover, showers upon her blushing brow,—on all of these is written the great law, that to give is to receive, and whoever would receive must give.

The prudent farmer, while he is generous and free, will still allow no stream of fertility to run to waste. While he is industrious and ever active, he will still compel the wind and water to saw his wood and thresh his grain and grind his corn. He will make the forest mold fertilize his corn field. There is no dishonesty in turning our labor over to nature. She expects to do all of our work before long, but not, however, till she is requested to do so. She never forces her services on us. We must first tell her just what we wish her to do, and how we wish her to do it. We must furnish the tools for her to work with. And even then, if they do not suit her, she will not work. She will not draw a train of cars, unless she can have a delicately constructed engine expressly for her.

The reason why men employed nature so little in the past ages is because she was so particular about her tools that they could not suit her.

Now the highest economy is the highest invention. That is, he is the most economical man, other things being equal, who is the most skillful in devising tools for nature to work with.

Home is a broad field for the exercise of invention. It is chiefly in the home, or in some way connected with domestic life, that we find that large class of inventions which minister directly to human comfort.

It is not necessary, however, that every great and useful invention should be the product of an inventive genius. On every farm and in every home there are thousands of opportunities for the exercise of this faculty. The inventive farmer will make his horses load his logs, while the uninventive one must load them himself. The inventive man can repair his broken implements, while the uninventive must take them to the blacksmith's or the carpenter's, and there pay so much out of the profits of his daily labor. There is no good reason why every farmer should not be a blacksmith, a carpenter, and a wheelwright. He could then repair his own buildings, shoe his own horses and oxen, and make his own carriages. Few, perhaps, have ever stopped to estimate how much might be saved in this way. Nearly all that sort of work may be done during days in which nothing profitable could be accomplished on the farm. Since the farmer's work is so varied he requires but little absolute rest. Hence, if he were familiar with these trades, the rainy days might be made the most profitable ones of the year. While nature is irrigating his farm, he might be devising tools for her to perform some other service with.

Again, the recreation, the discipline, and the exercise of mechanical ingenuity thus afforded would have a developing influence on mind and body. It is a fact worth remembering that the men who have made farming pay in rocky New England have nearly all been of this sort.

Every wife and mother should be a tailoress, a milliner, and a dress-maker. She should know something about every article needed in the household. There is no reason why she should be obliged to take the sewing machine to the shop, or call her husband to repair it; she should have inventive talent enough, and might have it if she would cultivate it, to take the machine to pieces and put it together again. She should be able to repair the churn and solder the milk pans. Even if she cannot find time to make use of these accomplishments, they will enable her more readily to tell others what she wishes them to do for her. She can make better selections of clothing for herself and family. She can make wiser bargains in whatever she purchases. Numberless are the ways in which knowledge and inventive skill will enable one to save money.

The highest economy, however, does not consist merely in saving. Much has been said, and very prettily and poetically too, about the saving of pennies. But the pennies must first be earned. That economy which exercises itself wholly in saving and does not stimulate the inventive and intellectual powers in the direction of acquisition is almost sure to degenerate into meanness and penuriousness. It is very frequently the case that the saving propensity is carried so far as to be a positive obstruction to the earning. As when the farmer refuses to hire help because it must be paid for, and thus allows his crops to deteriorate on account of a too late harvesting, or when the wife refuses to employ a domestic servant and becomes sick on account of overwork. It is not economy to mow all summer with a scythe, when a few days' use of a machine would accomplish the same result. True economy consists in that broad and comprehensive knowledge of affairs, that clear foresight and calculation, that willingness to spend money lavishly in the procuring of the proper means, which in the moving of circumstances gives us the long arm of the lever.

There is no more disgusting spectacle than that of a penurious farmer whose prosperity is crippled by his own avarice. Such a man is likely to be found using a wooden plow which his father left him. He goes barefooted week days in order to make his boots last two years of Sundays. If he buys a new coat he must pay for it with beans or some product of the farm. He must change directly too. He could not think of selling the beans for money and buying the coat, for that would be paying money for the coat. Indeed, he has well nigh dispensed with that instrument of civilization—money. He has gone back so far toward barbarism that he desires to barter instead of buy and sell with money. Not because he has no love of money, but because he does have that irrational love which becomes the "root of all evil."

But some may ask how that can be the root of all evil which owes its existence to a God-given instinct, and finds its guarantee in an eternal law of nature.

The irrational love of money finds its guarantee in no law or instinct. It is not the moderate and normal love of money which is the root of all evil, nor is such love an evil at all, but a great blessing.

The sentiment of economy is one of those which manifest themselves within very narrow limits. It seems to be always leaning to the one side or the other, and getting oüt of its path. It is apt to become prodigality or penuriousness. It requires much skill in navigation on life's sea to sail safely between these two rocks. When we first embark we are very apt to run against the rock of prodigality, but after we have had more experience, unless we profit well by that experience, and learn the golden mean, we are prone to the opposite extreme and run against the rock of penuriousness. It is the inordinate love of money for its own sake that is the root of all evil; while true economy is the trusty helm that guides us safely between two dark and threatening rocks.

This disposition to hoard money for its own sake, independent of its proper function, is not, however, to be wholly condemned. There is a ministry of good in the very consciousness of possession. It is usually easy to distinguish the men of wealth in a crowd of people, by their bearing of conscious power. It is the natural and legitimate condition of man to feel that he is in a certain sense the conqueror and possessor of nature.

The lion is called the king of beasts, not because he is the largest or the strongest, but because he calls himself the king of beasts. He does this by his noble bearing, and the consciousness of power. Now man, like the lion, should feel and manifest a sense of power, only in a far higher degree. It is this conscious power manifesting itself in the human eye which accounts for the fact that no wild beast can withstand the human gaze.

All that is necessary to cause the lion to skulk away to the den like a whipped cur, is to gaze full in his eye while you calmly maintain a consciousness of victory and superiority over all that moves upon the earth.

This feeling in man is the strongest safeguard against low and mean acts. It places one above meanness. The lion is the most magnanimous of beasts. He never does a mean act. This is because of his consciousness of power which makes him feel too noble to be mean.

This, then, is our plea for wealth, that its moderate possession makes men noble and magnanimous. One noble, generous, wealthy man in a community is sometimes a source of inspiration for hundreds of young men.

Let it be remarked, however, that the kind of wealth which produces this desirable result is that which is born of toil and economy. No man can become suddenly wealthy without being injured thereby, for the mode of thought and the whole character must change to meet the conditions of wealth. Whole new lines of thought, new schemes, new plans of life must be originated, and this change cannot take place suddenly without too great a shock to the character.

We claim that no man has any moral right to extreme wealth. No man can possibly have any moral right to anything in this life which he does not earn, for otherwise he must trespass on the rights of his fellows.

Men are born destitute of all possessions. No one brings anything into the world. What right, then, has one to gather riches through another's toil and misfortune? The man who has the ability to begin with nothing and accumulate ten thousand dollars by his own industry and economy, has just ability enough to take care of ten thousand dollars and be made better and nobler thereby.

But the accumulation of wealth, grand as is its possible ministry, is not, by any means, the only object that concerns the instinct and spirit of economy.

It is not the chief object of the economy of home. The object of home is to mold character, and the object of home economy is, or should be, the accumulation of all those means and instrumentalities that minister to that end.

Those things which minister to the intellectual and æsthetic nature are as properly the objects of the economical faculty as dollars and cents.

Let children be taught to believe that good books are among the most desirable of earthly possessions. Let them begin to accumulate books even before they can read. It would be infinitely better than to give them a little bank and teach them that the accumulation of coppers is all that is desirable. They may be allowed to vie with each other in the accumulation of good books and works of art, and when they become old enough to appreciate them, they will, perhaps, have a respectable library. They will also have what is far better, a true idea of life and its significance.

If all parents would follow this course with their children, the world's mad scramble for money would be transferred to books, facts, principles, thoughts, beauty, art, education, culture, righteousness, and all that can lift the soul, and bring the spirit and genius of humanity nearer to its God.

In all cases the children should be made to earn these books with their own hands, that they may early learn that labor is the price of thought as well as of bread. They cannot too early be taught that labor is necessarily the price of all honest possessions.

> "Thus is it over all the earth,
> That which we call the fairest,
> And prize for its surpassing worth,
> Is always rarest.
>
> "Iron is heaped in mountain piles
> And gluts the laggard forges,
> But gold-flakes gleam in dim defiles
> And lonely gorges.
>
> "The snowy marble flecks the land
> With heaped and rounded ledges,
> But diamonds hide within the sand
> Their starry edges.
>
> "The finny armies clog the twine
> That sweeps the lazy river,
> But pearls come singly from the brine
> With the pale diver.
>
> "God gives no value unto men
> Unmatched by meed of labor;
> And cost of worth has ever been
> The closest neighbor.

* * * * * * *

"Were every hill a precious mine,
  And golden all the mountains;
Were all the rivers fed with wine
  By tireless fountains;

"Life would be ravished of its zest,
  And shorn of its ambition,
And sink into the dreamless rest
  Of inanition.

"Up the broad stairs that value rears,
  Stand motives beck'ning earthward,
To summon men to nobler spheres,
  And lead them worthward."

HOME ADORNMENTS.

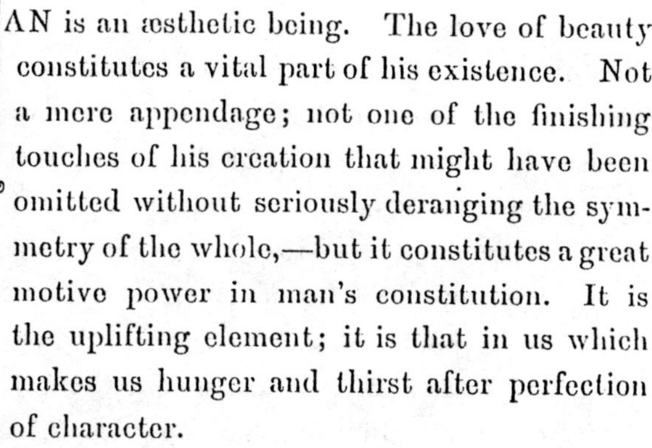

MAN is an æsthetic being. The love of beauty constitutes a vital part of his existence. Not a mere appendage; not one of the finishing touches of his creation that might have been omitted without seriously deranging the symmetry of the whole,—but it constitutes a great motive power in man's constitution. It is the uplifting element; it is that in us which makes us hunger and thirst after perfection of character.

The law of beauty is the law of completeness, and that law in the soul gives the desire for spiritual completeness and perfection.

The law of material beauty is, doubtless, that by which matter tends to assume the form of completeness, which is that of the circle. The circle everywhere prevails. Nature always makes a perfect circle when she can; and when she cannot she usually makes a compromise with the opposing forces and together they make an ellipse, or some form of the curve. The stars are spheres; atoms are by common consent regarded as spheres. The paths of all the heavenly bodies are ellipses. The transverse sections of trees and almost all forms of vegetables are circular. Most of the animal tissues are circular, or are made up of circular parts.

But it is not alone in the geometrical figure that we see the spirit of the circle. We see it in the repetitions of history, in the ceaseless round of the seasons, in the death and resurrection of the roses, in the successive pulses of music, in colors that suggest their complements, in the bud that suggests the completion of the flower, in the unutterable emotions that come to us while gazing upon the "breathing canvas and speaking marble," in the soul-lifting suggestion of the poet's metaphor, which is always the segment that completes a circle of consistent thought.

It is our imagination that supplies these missing segments, and accordingly imagination and fancy are found to be essential faculties in the production or appreciation of beauty. Imagination is that faculty which gives us a desire to complete all our mental operations, and thus give to them something of the spirit of the circle. The law of beauty is nature's imagination, which tends to complete all her operations and give to everything a circular tendency.

Since, then, the principle of beauty is so far-reaching in nature, and since it forms so large and vital a part of man's nature, is not its cultivation of the utmost importance? We cannot do violence to this part of our nature without violating the whole. To withhold the influences that tend to develop a love of beauty is as sure to cause a one-sided and unsymmetrical growth, as to withhold a needed element of food. Beauty is one of the elements of the soul's food. The cultivation of beauty in the soul requires no costly tutorage. Beauty's lessons may be learned without a teacher. The universe is one vast cabinet open to our inspection. Every gate of nature turns upon golden hinges. The sky each morning is broidered by the rosy fingers of the dawn, and every evening the sun, amid beauty that awes the soul to silence, like a gallant knight rides down the perilous cataract of molten gold. The beauty of the clouds, the sweet simplicity of nature's drab dress, is past all description of novelist or poet. A spirit may grow divine by gazing on the clouds, and it costs us nothing to appropriate this beauty except the trouble of taking our nooning in the open air. There is a flower in every nook and corner of nature's domain, which it costs us nothing to look at.

But it is not alone in nature that beauty may minister to our souls. It is the chief object of this chapter to show, in a general way, how art may serve this purpose.

Nature hangs no landscapes on our parlor walls, nor does she set bouquets in our windows. She will cause the bouquets to grow and blossom, however, if we will but take the trouble to plant them.

Flowers are the soul's best friends. There is the breath

of the angels on their petals. It is needless to contend that there is no deep meaning in the tribute which the universal heart of man in all ages has paid to flowers.

A flower garden is within the reach of every family that has the control of a house; for the beds may be made close about the house, and there are few tenements even in the denser parts of cities where there is not a sufficient quantity of land for a flower-bed.

Notwithstanding the fact that there has been much discussion concerning the wholesomeness of house plants, it is nevertheless the opinion of the most eminent scientists that they are positively beneficial to health. Indeed, to suppose otherwise would be a violation of the logic of analogy, for the whole vegetable kingdom constantly consumes carbonic acid, an invisible gas which is poisonous to us, but which constitutes the food of plants. They also exhale oxygen, which is the all-sustaining element of animal life, and which in civilized homes is usually deficient, owing to the lack of proper ventilation. Thus house plants in part neutralize the bad effects of imperfect ventilation. One of the most striking provisions of nature is seen in the mutual adaptation of plants and animals. Plants give to us just what we require, while we give to them just what they require. How admirably then are men and plants adapted to live together.

The beauty of art is not alone for the mansion of wealth. Artistic and tasteful adornments are the products of ingenuity and not of wealth. Trees may be planted about the house, also vines and roses. Arbors and shady nooks may be made to render home attractive, and to give an added charm in after years to its memories. It is true that "be it ever so humble there's no place like home," but that home would be sweeter and would touch a tenderer chord in the spirit's harp if we could look back to a cottage vine-wreathed and rosy-decked. There is something in the nature of beauty when it surrounds our early home, that never loses its power, and never ceases to exert a molding influence over us.

There is no end to the tasty and pleasing devices by which an intelligent wife or daughter may adorn a home, and that with little expense beyond the time it requires, and this is usually mere pastime. The plot about the house may be either a sand desert covered with barrel hoops, broken cart wheels, and decaying rubbish, or it may be clean, wholesome, and beautiful. One cannot live in a wretched hovel where there is no beauty, where the lawn suggests a lumber yard, a cattle yard, and a slaughter yard combined, without sharing in the degradation of the surroundings.

It is as much the duty of parents, then, to adorn and beautify their home as it is to keep the moral atmosphere of that home pure.

Indeed, the latter cannot exist without the former. The best characters and the noblest men come from the modest homes which taste, refinement, and labor have adorned and beautified.

Beauty is a positive force, a developing potency in the universe. The language of beauty everywhere is the language of aspiration. If our dull ears could be quickened till we could hear and understand the divine dialect of the opening flowers, we should hear them say :—

"All things have their mission, and God gives us ours,
And this is a part of the mission of flowers:
To give life to the weary and hope to the sad,
Fresh faith to the faithless, new joys to the glad;
To cheer the desponding, give strength to the weak;
To bring health's bright bloom to the invalid's cheek;
To blush on the brow of the beautiful bride;
To cheer homes of mourning where sorrows betide;
To rob dreaded death of a part of his gloom,
By decking the dear one arrayed for the tomb;
To furnish the home with a lasting delight,
With our perfumes so lovely, our blossoms so bright;
To hallow the homestead, embellish the lawn,
Reflecting the tints of the roseate dawn."

DIGNITY AT HOME.

DIGNITY is self-respect, or rather the manifestation of self-respect. It is the involuntary and unconscious expression of one's appraisal of himself. Hence dignity may be called a secondary or dependent virtue. It is not in itself a cardinal virtue, but the language of one. Politeness is not absolutely necessary to a noble character, but that virtue of which politeness is the expression is one of the grandest in the world. It is that of benevolence.

In exhorting one to be polite, it is more philosophical to exhort him to cultivate the Christian grace of benevolence than merely to study etiquette. So with dignity. There is no use in studying the postures, gestures, and bearing of dignity, if there be not behind it the true source of dignity, self-respect. It is dishonest to appear to be what we are not; and if we have not the true spirit of dignity, it is better for us to appear undignified. Then the world will know better how to measure our worth. Artificial dignity and artificial politeness are to be condemned as dishonest and hypocritical. Let young men and women be dignified, but let it be a true expression of their self-respect. Self-confidence is a trait of character whose worth is usually underestimated, especially in the young. At some stage of their mental growth, young men are almost always considered conceited; but in the majority of cases the conduct that gives rise to this belief originates in other sentiments than that of self-esteem. Most people have this element of their character too feebly developed. The more self-esteem one possesses, if he be not haughty and overbearing, the better. This function of the mind gives us noble thoughts, and makes us hate anything that is low or mean. It makes the possessor feel that he is better than any mean act; hence it is one of the strongest fortifications of virtue.

The dignified man always receives more respect than the undignified. Society is inclined to take a man at his own appraisal. The world, while it may question a man's claims to its homage, always believes all the accusations which he brings against himself, and if a man by his downcast head, his low and mean associates, his vulgar thoughts and profane words, in short, by his lack of dignity, proclaims to the world that he is unworthy of its esteem, it will surely take him at his word.

To the dignified man everything that he does becomes dignified. If he is a wood-chopper, then wood-chopping becomes as dignified and honorable as statesmanship.

Wherever the dignified man or woman goes, there goes before a sense of honor and respect. He seems to be a kind of balance wheel to the society in which he moves. The laugh is never too long or loud; mirth and hilarity never go too far when he is present. At the same time he is not a burden or a painful restraint upon the natural flow of sentiment, and the play of social forces.

Nations and individuals usually attain a height corresponding to their own ideals. The beautiful, *ideal* life of the Greek was the necessary prelude to the glorious reality, and those individuals who have climbed the rugged heights and poised themselves on glory's giddy summit, have been those who with bleeding feet, calloused hands, and toiling brains have worked out a cherished ideal. The dignity of a being measures the worth of his life's ideal. So that, other things being equal, he who is most dignified is most rapidly advancing along the path of his own possibilities.

These facts are as applicable to the little world of home as to the great world of human society. The boy who is dignified at home receives the confidence of his sisters, brothers, and parents. Just as the world takes the man at his own price, and grants its confidence only as his dignity shows him worthy of it, so the parent takes the child at his own price. In proportion as children are dignified will parents grant them liberties, and place them in positions of honor and trust in the family economy. The dignified girl need not be a premature woman. She may romp and play with her brothers, as she should do, and still be dignified. Dignity, as we have intimated, does not consist of outward acts; it has no necessary ritual; it is not "studied gestures or well-practiced smiles."

The father who gets down on the floor to please his little child is not undignified. The mother who joins in the happy sports of her children, even with all the mirth and merriment of her early girlhood, is not undignified so long as she has a noble purpose in life, and sees a grand object in being.

Indeed, we believe that those who walk with measured step, and whose faces suggest a lengthened cloud, are not the finest embodiments of true dignity. Everything which is counterfeit betrays its spuriousness, whatever may be the skill of the counterfeiter. The sly, giggling, and simpering false modesty need never be mistaken for the open frankness and fearlessness of true modesty. So there is always something about the bearing of a false dignity that betrays it. It is false dignity that cannot afford to smile, but true dignity can afford to be light hearted. We find it enthroned upon the mother's brow as she shakes the rattle, and smiles and creeps upon the floor to please her baby. But how grandly, when suddenly called upon to perform a higher duty, does she step out of the enchanted atmosphere of her baby's life, unwreathe the nursery smiles from her face, and stand forth in the glory of her womanhood. It is then that she displays a dignity that awes us, a dignity before which the vile insulter slinks back like the hyena at the gaze of day.

This is what we mean by dignity. It is something which the little girl may cultivate as much as she chooses. It will not hurt her. It will not make her prematurely old. It will not cause her to ripen too quickly like a shriveled fall apple, but it will help to develop her and make her a true and noble woman.

There is always a certain degree of reserve that accompanies true dignity, so that its possessor is never quite transparent. He may be, and in fact must be, free, open and social, but there is always a reserved force of individuality. He may be translucent, but not transparent. And there is always a charm in that which we have almost but not quite seen. Hence the mind of the dignified man is an inexhaustible fountain of pleasure to his friends. He is always courted and never shunned. The boy who is dignified will be a central figure among his brothers and sisters and schoolmates.

There are certain virtues that have corresponding vices, resulting not from the absence but from the excess or wrong direction of the virtue. Dignity is one of those peculiar virtues, separated from the vice of conceit only by a thin veil. Economy is a virtue that all boys and girls are exhorted to cultivate, but how thin is the partition that separates this virtue from the hateful vice of penuriousness, that vice which has shriveled the soul of many a miser like the foliage of a girdled tree. Even the worship of God may be but a hair's breadth from idolatry. The flower of every virtue grows close to the precipice of a vice.

It is a law without exception that the lower the plane the more stable the virtue, while the higher the plane, the more unstable.

The heavenly gift of love trembles over the abyss of sensuality, while the crowning sentiment of divine worship is easily tumbled from its lofty pedestal into the mire of idolatry.

Hence dignity finds its highest complement in the fact that it is separated by a thin partition from the vice of pride and haughtiness. Let us then cultivate dignity, but weed the flower with a careful hand.

"A man of haughty spirit is daily adding to his enemies;
He standeth as an Arab in the desert, and the hands of all men are against him.
A man of a base mind daily subtracteth from his friends,
For he holdeth himself so cheaply, that others learn to despise him.
But where the meekness of self-knowledge veileth the front of self-respect,
There look thou for the man whom none can know but they will honor.
Humility is the softening shadow before the statue of Excellence,
And lieth lowly on the ground, beloved and lovely as the violet."

SUCCESS OR FAILURE FORESHADOWED AT HOME.

SUCCESS and failure are relative terms. What would be success to one might be failure to another. Success is simply the best possible results under existing circumstances. He who was born without the use of his arms and hands, and also without artistic ability, and yet who, by patient effort, has learned to write with his toes, even though his writing be but a miserable scrawl, if it be legible, has surely achieved a wonderful success in the art of penmanship. But for him who possesses the free use of his hands, and has in addition the taste of an artist, such a result would certainly be but moderate success. The pious rural maiden, who spends her life in ministering to the sick, the poor, and the ignorant in her little neighborhood, even though her name is never heard beyond a radius of ten miles, has achieved a success of which the record is in heaven, but had she been endowed with the ten talents that God gave to Florence Nightingale, she surely would have shuddered to offer so meager a return to her master.

When one asks himself the question, "Can I succeed?" he must have before his mind a definite standard of success, or his words become meaningless. Circumstances and native ability must determine the scope of the question. The first stage in all success is a preparation for success, and the number of stages is limited only by natural capacity and length of life. He who has prepared for success, even though it has required his lifetime, has succeeded better than he who has passed over a thousand stages, but has missed one stage that he might have passed.

According to this definition of success, which is the only proper one, all may succeed, and failure is never necessary. All can certainly do their best, and the result will be success. Failure, as the word implies, is simply the failure to act according to our highest possibilities. The world is full of the brilliant failures of fortune's sons—those who seemingly possessed every advantage that fate could bestow. On the other hand, the poor-house has been the theater of many a sublime success.

He has succeeded well who has met and conquered the dark hosts of evil passions that assail so many unfortunate souls. If he has subdued self, that mightiest enemy of humanity, he may count his life a grand success, even though the victory came but with the death angel's reinforcement. Success is his if he can greet his stern ally thus:—

> "Were the whole world to come before me now,—
> Wealth with its treasures; pleasure with its cup;
> Power robed in purple; beauty in its pride;
> And with love's sweetest blossoms garlanded;
> Fame with its bays, and glory with its crown,—
> To tempt me lifeward, I would turn away,
> And stretch my hands with utter eagerness
> Toward the pale angel waiting for me now,
> And give myself to him, to be led out
> Serenely singing to the land of shade."

We are glad, however, that the world contains but few who must buy success at such an awful price.

Success or failure is the natural fruit of character. The apple tree cannot bear anything but apples, neither can a good character bear anything but success. Failure is the only fruit we can reasonably expect to reap from a bad character.

But some may object to this, and point us to the frequent and brilliant success of bad men; but what they would call success would not probably fall within our definition. If dishonest acquisition is success, then is the highway robber the most successful of men; and on that roll of honor the brute-hearted pirate must be allowed to write his name. Hence the word success loses all significance unless we restrict it at least to honest acquisition. This must be done even by those who claim that dollars and cents are its only standard. Yes, it is character that determines our success or failure. Our deeds, both the good and the bad, are the visible herd which the unseen shepherd, character, drives across the desert of our lives.

If he be a good shepherd, the herd also will be good, and, fearless of the prowling wolf, will move in orderly procession straight to the fold of success; but if he is a bad shepherd, the flock will not obey him, but will scatter in wild confusion, and hide themselves in the dark and noisome caves of failure.

Since, then, it is the character that brings us success or failure, we must go where characters are formed, to the home, in order to speak our words of warning and advice.

The chief cause of all failures is a lack of persistency. He who begins life as a fruit vender, with nothing but a persistent mind, has a better chance of success in life, than he who begins with a million dollars and a vacillating mind.

In America, financial success is possible to every young man of ordinary ability. It is certainly important that he should choose the vocation for which nature has best fitted him, but it is far more important that he persist in the one which he does choose.

There are certain excesses and deficiencies which are national peculiarities, and this lack of persistency is surely a deficiency in Americans. With the Germans the reverse is true, thoroughness with them is almost an excess. Failures are very rare in Germany, because every man is so thoroughly taught in his one special subject that he has the advantage both of a perfect knowledge of his business, and a natural tendency to be contented for life with one occupation.

By failures we do not mean what is generally called a "financial failure." But rather the failure to do justice to one's native powers, failure to attain to what most men regard as success.

Perhaps there are more failures of this kind among Americans in proportion to the population, than among any other people in the world, and the fact accords well with their known fickleness.

The young American has much difficulty in deciding what occupation he shall follow. He is usually undecided whether he shall be a shoe-maker or statesman. He generally thinks quite favorably of all the intermediate trades and professions. As a rule, he tries as many of these as time and circumstances will permit. He enters a store as a clerk, and while the novelty lasts his mind is fully made up that he will be a merchant, and have a store on Broadway, but after a time his work becomes prose instead of poetry. His hasty decision was based on no abiding relation between himself and trade. He leaves the store and obtains a position in a bank, and immediately he decides that he will be a great banker. He reads and studies about the mysteries of Wall Street. But in a few weeks or months it occurs to him that he didn't stop to measure the distance between a chore boy in a country bank and a great stock operator on Wall Street, so he thinks he won't be a banker or a broker, but perhaps decides to be a printer, and goes into a printing office fully determined that he has at last found out what nature intended to do with him. He is well satisfied for a time. He reads the life of Benjamin Franklin. His ambition is awakened. He begins to see, too, that the printer is only the servant of the writer. This touches his pride, and he conceives the idea of going to college, and becoming a great writer and speaker. So his father's little farm is mortgaged and he starts for college, carrying with him that same indecision, and after four years of aimless study comes home to choose his life work, having forgotten all about his last resolution to be a great writer. So habituated has he become to frequent change of occupation, that it is now absolutely impossible for him to be satisfied in any sphere of life.

There is no objection to a mere change of occupation if circumstances render it desirable. The evil is in the mental condition that prompts a change. A young man may be a clerk, a banker and a printer if he chooses, and be the better for it, provided these occupations are used simply as means for the accomplishment of some definite and specific purpose. If a boy chooses to be a printer, let him be a printer, and if circumstances render it necessary or desirable that he should for a time engage in some other occupation, let him do it feeling that he is simply for a time working out of his element. It is the mental change, the change of motive and desire, and not the mere physical change which produces the best result.

Now, since success and failure are products of the character, and since character is formed by the influences of *home*, it is easy to determine with approximate certainty from an inspection of the home, what are the prospects of success or failure in life.

Moreover, one derives a feeling of fortunate relief from the thought that all evils which can be foreseen, and which owe their origin to human volition, can be prevented.

Children should be taught the importance of persistency. It is not necessary that they should early choose their vocation; yet it is necessary that when they do choose it, they should choose it for life. An occupation once chosen should be entered upon with a feeling that there is no other occupation. The ships should be burned behind. So long as there is in the mind a lingering thought that after all some other occupation will constitute the life work, failure is almost certain, for the mind is not concentrated, and its acts are like the acts of those who are half in jest.

Young men who contemplate a profession are sometimes advised to learn some trade first, then, they are told, if they fail in the profession they will have something to "fall back on." This is a first rate way to make certain their failure in the profession. If you wish to ensure the defeat of an army make elaborate preparations for an easy retreat, but if you wish to make them invincible, tear up the roads and burn the bridges behind them. So if you would ensure success in your boy's career don't foster nor tolerate the feeling that it isn't absolutely necessary that he should succeed in that particular trade or profession.

But what if the man has made a mistake? Suppose he has entered the medical profession, and then discovers that he was doubtless intended for the law? In that case it is a matter to be settled by his own judgment and the advice of his friends whether he shall continue in the medical profession or change to the law. If he is young and circumstances are favorable, perhaps it would be advisable to make the change. It would not as a rule be advisable.

We have said that it is less important that a young man should choose just the occupation for which he is best adapted, than that he persist in the one which he does choose. There may be exceptions to this, but it is true as a rule, from the very fact that without persistency failure is certain, even in the occupation for which he is best adapted. With persistency he is sure of a moderate success at least, even in the vocation to which he is poorly adapted; but without this quality he is sure of failure in any vocation.

We would not convey the impression that we attach but little importance to the right choice of pursuits. There are few things in human life more important than a right matrimonial selection, and yet it is far less important than a firm determination to live through life peacefully and lovingly with the one who has been chosen; so it is very questionable whether one should attempt to correct any mistake that may have been made in choosing his calling.

It is not to be presumed that the young man has made any mistake in the choice of his occupation. If he has been advised and counseled by wise and cautious parents, there is but little probability that he has made a wrong choice. Nature has so kindly and wisely blended our tastes and talents that what we desire to do most, that, as a rule, we can do best.

But unmingled success is not always the best thing for a young man. There are few who would not be spoiled by it. There is hardly a great orator whose biography does not contain some story of an early failure. He who has never failed is necessarily a weak man. Temporary failure is the best cure for egotism. It reduces our standard of self measurement to the denominations of the world's system.

Temporary failure sustains the same relation to the character that sorrow does; if not administered in overdoses, it strengthens and develops.

> "What most men covet, wealth, distinction, power,
> Are bawbles nothing worth; they only serve
> To rouse us up, as children at the school
> Are roused up to exertion; our reward
> Is in the race we run, not in the prize.
> Those few, to whom is given what they ne'er earned,
> Having by favor or inheritance
> The dangerous gifts placed in their hands,
> Know not, nor ever can, the generous pride
> That glows in him who on himself relies.
> Entering the lists of life, he speeds beyond
> Them all, and foremost in the race succeeds.
> His joy is not that he has got his crown,
> But that the power to win the crown is his."

FALLACIES ABOUT GENIUS.

GENIUS may be defined as an irrepressible impulse to work for work's sake. He whose whole soul does not quiver in response to the very name of work is not a genius and never can be.

There is, perhaps, nothing that more forcibly betrays the weakness and folly of human nature than the tendency in almost every young man, to fancy himself a genius and hence beyond the necessity of *labor*. The object of this chapter is to expose that folly, and to show the wide-spread misconception concerning the nature of genius.

If work costs you effort, you may be talented but you are not a genius. If it is easy for you to work, and costs but little self-denial, you are on the border-land of genius: but if you cannot help working, if work is your spirit's breath, if when the spell is upon you the very spheres must hush their music to give you sleep, if the insanity of ceaseless impulse lays its frenzied fingers on your brain at midnight, you may pitch your tent upon the star-lit heights, and your mission is to reach up to God and down to man.

Great achievements, although they always accompany

genius, do not constitute it, they only indicate it, they are the natural language, the gestures of genius.

We are told that intense application, and concentration of effort and purpose will accomplish the results of genius. And why should they not, for they are genius itself. It is wonderful that men who are so remarkable for common sense in the every-day affairs of life should show to such poor advantage when they attempt to elucidate the principles of mental science and human nature. There are no subjects on which the popular writers become so hopelessly confused as on those pertaining to psychology. Let it be understood once and forever by the world, that there can be no act of being that is not the outgrowth of an organic function, and this pernicious indefiniteness which makes ludicrous and insignificant distinctions between synonymous words, will vanish from our literature. Concentration of purpose and intense application are as truly elements of genius as the imagination of the poet. From these writers we should gather that there may be one or two faculties essential to greatness, which may be native and individual, but that all the other elements, such as will, concentration, perseverance, self-reliance, etc., etc., are possessed in equal quantities by all, and those who do not use them as extensively as the greatest men, are to be censured.

Now it is as reasonable to censure a boy because he cannot compose music like Beethoven as to censure him because he "does not want to." The elements that give the desire are the same that give the ability. You may as well exhort him to write poetry like Shakespeare as to exhort him to have the concentration, the perseverance, or the self reliance of Shakespeare, for all these qualities are as much parts of genius, and are just as dependent on hereditary and organic influences as those which are recognized as the prime factors of genius.

Genius has many and unmistakable characteristics, and among them the earliest, if not the most marked, is intellectual boldness. The first symptom of genius is a scorn for the opinions of men. Genius sees through the clouds that intercept the world's vision, and hence the world never sympathizes with genius. Hisses are the highest compliment the world can pay to genius. He who does not sometimes enrage his fellow men may well question his claim to genius.

This rule, however, applies with less force in certain spheres of genius, as music, painting, sculpture, etc. Yet even here the grandest efforts have been scorned by the critics, the interpreters of genius. But in that highest sphere, in which it rough-hews the timbers of the world's new thought, it cannot receive the sympathy of men. "Loose unto us Barabbas" is the world's cry. It is genius they would crucify, for it is genius that moves them to wrath. For it reveals itself not in soft words and "pretty thoughts," but in discordant words and ugly thoughts; tumultuous thoughts; thoughts that burn into the tablet of the centuries with a hiss. It is the honied words of talent that please the ears of mankind.

Another distinguishing characteristic of genius is that it always tells the world something that it did not know before. Genius stands nearest to the source of all wisdom, and catches whispers that never reach the common ear. It is God's interpreter. It reveals and interprets the unwritten language of nature's pantomime; hence the world, in spite of its antipathy for genius, instinctively recognizes its power. For in all ages men have made the words of genius canonical. Homer was the world's first Bible.

Genius works without regard to the value of the product. It works, as we have said, because it cannot help it. And herein seems to consist the divinity of genius, for it appears to be guided by a divine influence. It forgets that it is hungry and works all night. Tested by the received canons, it is radical and fanatical. It recognizes no formulated law of thought or logic. It both walks upon the earth, and flies in the air. It knows that which talent doubts, and believes that which talent laughs at.

It is not our purpose to discourage young men, yet we do not hesitate to do so, if thereby we may dispel from their minds the foolish fancy that they are geniuses. Nor need this discourage them. Every mind is satisfied with its own sphere. Talent does not suffer from disappointment because it cannot be genius, any more than the child suffers because it cannot be a man. The child is ambitious only to be noted among his playmates as possessing, in a remarkable degree, the qualities of a child. So talent, unless there be a want of harmony in the mental constitution, is satisfied with its own sphere, and does not seek to rise in its aspirations into the cloud heights of genius. We do not mean that a person without genius does not frequently wish that he might occupy the highest place in the estimation of his fellows. There are few to whom this wish is a stranger, yet it causes no suffering and does not touch the question of disappointed aspirations. In its relation to genius we have used the word aspiration with its strongest meaning, that in which it signifies not merely a wish to be great, but a burning, sleepless impulse, which suffers all things, forgets the weak pleadings of sense, and labors unceasingly for the accomplishment of its purpose.

So we are not actuated by a malicious desire to dash the cherished hopes of college boys who mistake that indefinite desire for greatness which every one has felt, for that divine uplifting which not only seeks the goal of greatness, but actually rejoices that the path to glory is so rough and steep. It is a characteristic of genius that it loves to tread stony paths, for the sake of crushing the stones.

No! no! young man, don't wait any longer for genius to blossom, for the fact that you are waiting proves that there is no bud to blossom.

We have paid this exalted and possibly extravagant

tribute to genius solely for the purpose of placing in the hands of that class of young men who fancy themselves geniuses, a means of detecting their own folly. These young men are proverbially the lazy young men; they are those who from some strange cause have conceived the idea that to work would be to surrender their claim to genius. Hence they abandon themselves to idleness. They have been told that Poe and Byron were idlers. But if the truth were known it would, doubtless, be found that these unhappy geniuses through sleepless nights of wasting toil worked themselves into untimely graves.

Since genius consists solely in spontaneous and involuntary labor in contradistinction to the irksome effort of mediocrity, it follows that these young men are barred, at the outset, from all claim to genius.

Probably more talented young men have been rendered useless by the delusion that genius is a compound of wine and laziness than by any other one cause. But let no young man entertain the foolish idea that by getting drunk and being lazy he can be a Poe.

In the first place, Poe was not lazy. Genius, it is true, often works somewhat irregularly, because the moving power in genius is impulse, whereas in talent it is usually motives of economy or duty. And in the second place, Poe would probably have been a much greater poet had he been temperate. But there seems to be in perverted human nature a propensity to copy after the incidental weakness of greatness. Let a man of genius display one trait of the idiot and hundreds of young men will appropriate it and complacently consider themselves possessed of at least one characteristic of genius.

So long as the young man of talent can readily find a field for the full exercise of his powers, and one in which the rewards of toil are worthy of his highest effort, he need not feel discouraged because he cannot be a genius. As well might he lament because he was not born into a more refined and beautiful world than this. So long as he fulfills the duties which his talent imposes, he should be content and happy in his sphere, and never stop to consider whether he be a genius or a mediocre. The semi-idiot, if he employs to the best possible advantage the weak talents that he possesses, may be as deserving of praise as Plato, Paul, or Newton.

It is the function of genius to go in advance of the world's march, and "set the stakes" to guide the advancing column. But one genius can do this for an army of ten thousand, while the lieutenants and corporals of talent must be scattered all along the line. Genius in every relation of life is more or less independent of experience. It knows things without learning them. It exemplifies the doctrine of "innate ideas." Talent knows only what it sees, but genius does not see what it knows. In its loftiest moods the beams of truth flash into its inmost chambers, and it cannot tell from whence comes the light. It is awed at its own achievements, and looks with wonder upon its own offspring. It sees, as mere talent can never learn to see, the infinite significance of *wholeness*.

Genius is creative rather than executive. It may exist, however, in the line of any one of the several faculties of the mind, and hence may find its expression in the executive faculties themselves. Yet even in this case genius finds its chief function in marking out the lines of action and in telling others what to do and how to do it, thus leaving the ultimate execution in the hands of talent. So it may be true that genius is *always* creative and not executive. The girl may surpass Beethoven in the mere execution at the piano-forte, yet it is the fiat of Beethoven's genius that directs every quiver of her flying fingers. The inventive genius is proverbial for its lack of executive ability. This quality, together with intuitiveness, to which it is closely related, and upon which it chiefly depends, is, doubtless, the most distinguishing characteristic of genius.

But talent and genius may and often do exist together. There is nothing in the nature of the one that necessarily precludes the other. Those in whom they exist together will exhibit that same irrepressible impulse to labor, but there will be, in their labor, the method and regularity and moderation which characterizes that of talent. It is doubtful if pure genius is ever of the highest order. Poe was perhaps one of the best illustrations of pure genius in all history, and yet we cannot regard him as worthy of the highest honor. Pure genius is fitful and irregular. It is only when it is mixed with talent that it becomes grand, imposing and effective. The genius of Cæsar, Napoleon or Shakespeare would not have produced the grand results that it did, had it not been mixed with talent, whereby it was tempered and made self-regulating. Goethe, perhaps, furnishes the best illustration of the combination of genius and talent.

We have indicated a very sharp contrast between genius and talent, or rather between the results of genius and talent. But the question, what is genius, remains unanswered.

There are all degrees of genius, as there are all degrees of talent, and the line where the highest degree of talent meets the lowest degree of genius is a question that can be determined only by the arbitration of mankind. There is no natural law by which we can say with certainty that one mind is on this side and another on the other side of that line. There are doubtless thousands far below the line who have passed for geniuses, while thousands more, as far above the line, have hardly received the rank to which mediocrity should entitle them. Yet notwithstanding such injustice, resulting from weakness and prejudice, the fact of genius still remains. The distinction of kitten and cat, of cub and lion, of child and adult, are genuine and natural distinctions, yet who shall designate the moment when a boy becomes a man? This moment cannot be ascertained with certainty within several years. A margin of at least five years must be allowed for variation of opinion concerning definitions.

Genius, then, is but developed talent, and the lowest degree of talent holds in potentiality the highest degree of genius.

Talent in man corresponds to strength of material in the engine, which is approximately indicated by the figures on the steam gauge. It is the steady power of resistance. But there is another quality of the engine of a subtiler nature. It may be called sensitiveness. This quality depends not upon the size and strength of material, but upon the "finish" and the nice adjustment of parts, whereby friction is diminished. It enables us to determine the per cent. of discount that must be made, on the indications of the steam gauge, in estimating the efficiency or working power of the engine.

Now genius is that in the organization which corresponds to this quality in the engine. It may be termed organic quality. It is the finish of the brain, and by it the mental powers are made responsive. It is great just in proportion to the per cent. of organic power utilized. Hence spontaneity is the one word that approaches nearest to a synonym of genius.

Since genius results from a quality of the organism, we see why it often seems to defy the organic law that size measures power. Emerson is a puzzle to the phrenologists, even with all the qualifications implied in their "cæteris paribus." This fact, however, is no disparagement to the science. Even astronomy, the oldest of sciences, must recognize its insolvable problems. It cannot trace the comet through its hyperbolic and parabolic orbits. So mental science cannot solve the "mystery of genius." For genius lies beyond the reach of science. It is a comet whose orbit is the infinite parabola.

There are degrees of organic quality far above that which the phrenologist marks "seven," and in these rarefied realms dwells genius. Nay, genius is the reigning spirit of the realm itself.

It should be a pleasing thought to the great mass of mankind, that the most glorious achievements of the race, the aggregate of which constitutes most that we prize in history, have not been the products of what men term genius. But talent, with toiling brain and sweating brow, has wrought the revolutions whose issues are the landmarks of history. But this does not debase the glorious mission of genius. Had it not been for genius, the great problems that talent has solved, would never have been formulated.

Let the young man, whether he has talent or genius, be content to labor in his own sphere, and let his motto be—

"Seize this very minute,
What you can do, or dream you can, begin it.
Boldness has genius, power, and magic in it.
Only engage, and then the mind grows heated,—
Begin, and then the work will be completed."

COURAGE
TO MEET LIFE'S DUTIES.

HUMAN life is fraught with duties. The fact of existence imposes them upon every one. There is no hour of our lives that does not hold a note against us. Every moment is a creditor. Our lives and what they signify are so woven into the web of universal being that there is never a moment of release.

But by far the larger portion of life's duties lie along the soul's path of aggressive movement, and require something of courage to meet them.

Courage is that quality of the soul which makes it fearless of consequences in the presence of opposition. With this definition, courage becomes an element in the performance of every duty of life, for the human soul is confronted by no duty which is not armed. Every duty demands an aggressive act, and hence courage—and he who shrinks from a duty is a coward. The duties of life consist in the aggregate of all the acts toward which the sense of right, of honor, and of self respect impel us.

Life is the arena of many forms of courage, as many as there are possible lines of human action. There is physical courage, which dares to meet and overcome physical opposition. It is that which makes us willing to take the possible consequences of the physical danger, in the accomplishment of an effort. This form of courage is by no means low. It is true that it is the form of courage which defends the cub of the wild beast, and which belongs to that department of man's nature which he possesses in common with the brute creation, yet without it all the higher powers of man would be helpless prisoners in the hands of circumstances. We would not exalt physical courage to that position which we would assign to reason, and yet we must regard it as one of the noble attributes of man. Washington's integrity and honor and patriotism might have existed in vain, for without physical courage they could never have made a nation grand. The early Christians might have died from the very excess of their joy, but without the physical courage that scorns the flame there would never have been a martyr.

But there are higher forms of courage. To be a martyr one must have something more than the courage to meet a high degree of temperature. He must have the courage to think the unthought and speak the unspoken, and not only to think and speak thus, but to do it amid the jeers of hatred and the hisses of calumny. Without this form of courage no triumphant vessel would to-day move upon the waters, no engine would jar the earth with its iron hoofs, no magic wires would belt the globe with zones of love.

History would be unstained with blood, and the simple record would read as sweetly as the story of a maiden's life; and yet out of the rayless midnight of that history would rise no star. The darkness of the past has been illumed by the fagot fires kindled at the feet of courage. No grand libraries would adorn our cities, had not moral courage dared to pen its own doom.

Every great book in history was born amid the death throes of its heroic author.

The steps of the world's progress have been over the red altars of human sacrifice.

Physical, intellectual, and moral courage have been the grand leaders in the ceaseless conquest of thought. God bless the martyrs to science and religion! bless those whose pale, thoughtful brows have pressed through weary days and lingering nights against the bars of prison windows!

It is often said that the age of heroism is past, since, as it is claimed, there is no longer any demand for great displays of courage. The inventor is no longer pointed at with scorn, nor accused of too intimate association with the devil.

The authors of new thought are not now doomed to starvation. But notwithstanding all this there never was a period in the history of the world when life demanded so much of courage as to-day. The most dastardly form of cowardice is that which makes us afraid to be ourselves.

The highest need of human society to-day is a bold and fearless spirit of individuality. A thousand years ago one could be conservative and not fall behind the race. But now, while humanity rides on steam and lightning, one cannot afford to imitate the clumsy gait of those who went through life on foot.

With the momentum of six thousand years behind him, man is now rushing with terrific speed toward the goal of his destiny. He started as a long train starts from its station, with snail pace and amid the tolling bells of dying martyrs. One did not need then to have a high degree of individuality. He could keep with the race while he remained almost at rest. There was little demand then for this form of courage, for every one was like every other, and individuality was an attribute of the nation rather than of the man. Then the individual man was a part of the mass with no visible line of demarcation between, but now he is a detached fragment, and must maintain his own identity and assert his own individuality by a ceaseless act of courage, or be hurled as refuse into the world's intellectual and moral sewer.

No age of human history has offered such a grand reward to courage as the present. In politics and religion we see the disgusting cowardice that makes men slaves to base schemes and cunning tyranny.

There are few men who dare to think for themselves; they must see what the political paper or the minister says before they have the courage to say what they believe. Few ever consider what a powerful factor in life's programme is moral courage. Let the young man learn to think for himself. The feeblest thought that was ever born of a human brain, if it be the unrestricted product of that brain and comes forth unfettered by fear of nonconformity, is a grander thing than the proudest creation of genius, if that creation be shaped in trusting subservience to man.

One courageous thought is worth more than volumes of prostituted genius. Originality is not a peculiarity of great minds. The smallest minds may become wonderfully original simply through courage, by daring to question that which they read and hear. Of course the disagreeable habit of egotism is not to be encouraged. One should presume himself ignorant of all things and then dare to question all things.

Authority should not be disregarded, and yet it should be taken as affording merely a presumption, and not a demonstration. The truths that fall within the ken of human vision are few. All truths cannot be seen even by the most gifted. The spider sees many things that the eagle overlooks. As much depends upon the attitude of the eye as upon its power, and there are little truths and certain aspects of great truths which must, from their nature, be discerned by little minds alone. It is cowardice to believe or disbelieve because Plato says so. The first symptom of genius is the bold daring with which it disputes the fables of the nursery. We would not, however, have it understood by young men that the disagreeable and unmannerly habit of disputing for the sake of disputing is in any way a symptom of greatness.

We have used the word dispute in a broader sense, that in which it means to question why, to weigh the probabilities, to demand consistency, and to doubt, if need be. The civilization of the nineteenth century was born of doubts and questions, whose answers have been hisses. Emerson says: "Have courage not to adopt another's courage."

That certainly means much. It means that we should stand upon our own individuality, and dare to respond to our own name in the roll call of life.

Courage gives a man a kind of magic control over everything in nature. It actually strengthens the muscles of the body.

The courageous man can lift a heavier weight, other things being equal, than the timid man; he can do more work in the same time and with less exhaustion.

Courage adds to one's peace of mind. The timid man is never at peace. To him life's duties assume the form of living, malicious intelligence, whose only desire seems to be to defeat his efforts and cause him pain.

Fear weakens every fiber of our being, physical, intellectual, and moral; which, in effect, is the same as strengthening the obstacles and resistances of life. Whatever strengthens the muscles virtually lightens the weight. Thus does courage give to man a control over inanimate nature.

But not alone over inanimate nature, for he who possesses courage holds the wand that rules the world. He sets the world a thought-copy which it gladly follows. There is something in the glance of courage, born of conscious power, before which man and beast alike quail. Under the gaze of the wild beast, man is safe till he loses his courage.

"Ah! from your bosom banish, if you can,
Those fatal guests: and first the demon fear,
That trembles at impossible events;
Lest aged Atlas should resign his load,
And heaven's eternal battlements rush down.
Is there an evil worse than fear itself?
And what avails it that indulgent heaven
From mortal eyes has wrapt the woes to come,
If we, ingenious to torment ourselves,
Grow pale at hideous fictions of our own!
Enjoy the present; nor with needless cares,
Of what may spring from blind misfortune's womb
Appall the surest hour that life bestows.
Serene, and master of yourself, prepare
For what may come; and leave the rest to heaven."

THE IMPORTANT STEP.

IN the history of every one there comes a time when an important step must be taken and a momentous question decided. The period in which this step is taken is a most critical one, one fraught with the mightiest consequences for weal or woe. It holds the destiny of human life. An error here cannot be corrected.

A happy decision is a fortune to which nothing on earth can be compared.

It is the custom to speak lightly on this subject, and to consider the most awful issue of life as a fit occasion for mirth and idle jest. There can be no doubt that this custom lies at the root of a large percentage of the miseries that mar the happiness of the race.

So long as young boys and girls are allowed to trifle with each other's affections, as if that were their highest use, the world will be the theater of untold sorrow. It is true that the love element will not bear to be reduced to the standard of a commercial transaction. It must have the liberty to spread its wings in the atmosphere of its own divine romance. We must not take away the poetry which is its vital breath.

And yet there are certain phases of it that may and should be submitted to the tribunal of reason. We do not believe that reason can in any sense furnish the motive power of love. We even doubt if nature intended it to play any part whatever in the programme.

We belong to that school which teaches that each and every part of man's nature contains a principle of wisdom in itself, and holds the elements of its own regulation. It is not the natural office of reason to dictate the amount or quality of food that we should take, and yet in the case of dyspepsia it often becomes necessary that reason should perform this function, for the natural instinct is then dethroned and there is no longer any trustworthy guide, and reason may in this case serve as a poor substitute.

The foregoing illustration contains the whole truth concerning the relation of reason to the love principle. If the delicate sentiments have not been outraged, and the tastes are unvitiated, they will invariably lead to desirable results, when the proper conditions are supplied. But in most cases this subtile instinct is but an imperfect guide, because it has been perverted by improper action.

Under these circumstances it becomes necessary to submit the dyspeptic caprice of the unregulated love to the sound judgment of reason.

It is said that "love is blind," but this fancy originated in the observed phenomena of its perversion, and not of its normal action. There is nothing that can see so well as pure love. It is all eyes. No nicely adjusted lenses of science can detect the motes which its naked eye discerns.

The young man or woman whose love intuitions are unclouded will seldom make a mistake in the disposal of the affections.

There is, however, a danger from one other source, which we will presently mention. It is the theory of most parents that girls and young ladies should never be permitted to associate freely with gentlemen until they contemplate matrimony. There seems to be a sickly sentiment prevalent on this subject. The young lady must feel that there was a kind of special providence in her love affair, and that it would have been absolutely impossible for her to love any one else. This diseased sentiment is common to both sexes, but it exists for the most part in those who have been excluded from the society of the other sex. The fact that girls who have brothers and boys who have sisters always make the wisest matrimonial selections, is one that bears significantly on this subject. The lady who has never been permitted to associate with gentlemen, and who has no brothers, is very likely to make a mistake in the bestowal of her affections. The conjugal choice is made through an instinct that is attracted by the congenial, and repelled by the uncongenial. But there is, however, a faint attraction between the sexes even when the parties are not conjugally adapted, and if the young lady has never had an opportunity to compare this faint attraction, which she may have felt, with stronger ones, she will be very apt to misinterpret its significance, and regard this slight attraction as a positive impulse of her nature. This, then, is the source of danger. It is the fact that nature seldom permits an absolute repulsion between ladies and gentlemen, even between those who are ill adapted as conjugal partners, but simply a weakening of the attraction.

Hence it becomes necessary in order to rightly interpret our impulses that we should have the opportunity to compare them.

If nature had sharply drawn the lines of attraction and repulsion between the compatible and the incompatible, there could be no such thing as a matrimonial mistake. But since she prefers to suggest, by a weakened attraction, rather than to command by a positive repulsion, it requires a little acuteness to understand her suggestions.

It is a fact proved from every realm of natural history that it is the female's rightful function to make the matrimonial selection. The lioness accepts her mate only after ample opportunities for comparison and choice. In this, as in many other respects, the higher intelligence may learn a lesson from the lower. The young lady should have the opportunity of making her selection from a wide circle of gentlemen friends, otherwise she cannot so easily distinguish the false from the true.

The highest possible compliment that can be paid to a young man is to be "singled out" by the divine instinct of a pure maiden who has been the idol of her brothers, and who through her early years played with the little boys of her acquaintance.

We are not by any means advocating that fatal vice known as flirting. A flirt is one who purposely wins, or tries to win, the affections of the other sex with no serious intention, or simply for sport, and the wicked pleasure that some experience in being able to pain another's heart. Perhaps more hearts are won by cunning coquettes for the ruthless purpose of seeing them bleed when cast aside than for any other purpose.

We do not hesitate to express our firm belief that the evils of flirtation are more widespread and disastrous in their consequences than those of intemperance. They blight the tenderest sentiments as the frost blights the buds. They freeze the holiest emotions of the soul, and leave the heart a barren waste. Like the cornfield whose fences have been burned away, they leave the heart open to the devouring herds of vice.

But young ladies and gentlemen may associate without flirtation. There is nothing better for a young man than to associate as a friend with a pure-minded young lady, and the benefit is equally great to the young lady.

When love begins in friendship it rarely makes a mistake. Love should never be contemplated between parties who cannot first be firm friends. But such exclusive association is not at all necessary. It is, perhaps, as well that the young man or woman should have a circle of friends and acquaintances made up of both sexes. In this case, if the early training has been what it should have been, and the natural and pure impulses of the child have not been interfered with, there will seldom be a need of any other form of association.

One of the worst things a parent can do is to shame a little girl because she is inclined to play with little boys. She should be taught to feel that there is nothing wrong or unladylike in such conduct. So the boy should not be teased by his parents or older brothers and sisters because he smiles upon a little girl, or manifests a preference for her society. Such preferences, of course, should not be strong, since they would then be unnatural and would indicate precocity, which should be dreaded as among the worst calamities to which childhood is subject.

Young ladies may allow themselves to be frequently escorted by gentlemen, but should not permit the exclusive attention of any particular one unless from the divine motive of pure affection, which alone can sanctify such association.

The best girls, the best sweethearts, the best wives, and the best mothers are those who have been the intimate but innocent associates of young men.

But so long as so many, especially of young ladies, have not been permitted to associate with the other sex, and still more have, by flirtations, so vitiated their intuitive perceptions of congeniality that these are no longer safe guides, it is, perhaps, as well to give some advice in regard to those cases in which it becomes necessary to substitute reason in place of instinct.

In the first place, it is necessary to ascertain what direction, under the given circumstances, instinct would take if it were in a healthy state, or if it were to act under more favorable conditions.

Its action is as strictly subject to law as that of gravitation and may be studied with the most satisfactory results. Love's preferences are not unreasonable. The tall, spare dark-eyed, young man does not single out the plump, blonde, blue-eyed maiden without a cause.

The rosy cheeked brunette, with face and shoulders shaped like her father's, does not toss her raven locks invitingly to the blue-eyed, fair-skinned, short, stout and sanguine young man, from any mere whim of lawless caprice. The hand that guides the stars is not more unswerving than the law of sexual preferences. Nor is this law hidden and inscrutable. It lies upon the surface and may be easily discovered and formulated.

Briefly stated, it is simply the law by which individual eccentricities are prevented from coming under the law of entailment, or more properly, by which the law of entailment is made to neutralize them. Without this provision, eccentricities would perpetually accumulate and reinforce themselves until all the affinities of the race would be lost in unapproachable differences.

Just in so far as one departs from symmetry in his own physical or mental make up, this law causes him to prefer in the other sex, those opposite peculiarities which will counterbalance his own, and which, when blended, and subjected to the law of heredity, re-establishes the lost symmetry. Each sex desires in the other the complement of its own eccentricities. There is a neutral point where each desires its own likeness. This point is absolute symmetry and perfection. It corresponds to the neutral point of a magnet. On either side of this point like eccentricities repel, and unlike attract.

If a human being could be found perfect and symmetrical in all respects, that person would be drawn toward one of the other sex exactly like himself. This law of sexual preference would in his case be entirely suspended, as there would be nothing for it to do.

He would be left to act in accordance with another law, which is antagonistic to that of sexual preferences. It is that by which we are drawn toward those possessing the same peculiarities as ourselves.

These two tendencies, though antagonistic, are not inconsistent. The one acts between the sexes, the other between those of the same sex. In the case of perfect symmetry which we have supposed, the latter law would act even between persons of opposite sexes.

Human eccentricities may be conceived as arcs of circles circumscribed about the point of absolute perfection. The field of this sexual law lies within these circles, and the strongest affinity is that between corresponding arcs which would be joined by a line passing through the center.

Having discovered the law then, all that is necessary in order to make application of it when our instinctive perception of conjugal adaptation becomes untrustworthy, is simply to ascertain our own peculiarities, excesses and deficiencies, and match them with opposite ones in the other sex.

There is a limit, however, to the degree of difference that is permissible. It should never be so great that each cannot sympathize with the other, and take an interest in those things which interest the other. The lady who is unusually refined will naturally be attracted by a man not over refined, but somewhat gruff, and she will often be proud of his deep voice and uncombed hair. Yet coarseness and vulgarity she cannot sympathize with, and should never seek that degree of difference. One who is musical need not select one who cannot distinguish one tune from another; but the one should be sufficiently endowed, at least, to appreciate the superiority of the other.

It is not so necessary that there should be a diversity in respect to talent, as in respect to character and disposition. The talents, tastes and proficiencies may be in the same general line in both parties, but all physical peculiarities and all eccentricities of disposition should be conscientiously submitted to the law of sexual preference.

But a right matrimonial selection is not all that is necessary. The preservation of love is the finest of the fine arts. To win a heart is within the capacity of most men, but to keep it lies within the power of few. He who shall discover the magic secret of preserving love, and shall induce the world to adopt it, shall confer the grandest blessing ever yet conferred by mortal. He shall deserve a prouder fame than ever draped a funeral car, or marched beneath a nation's drooping banners. Humanity shall write his name close beside that which is written upon the universal heart.

This tribute will not seem overwrought to those who understand and realize how much of human sin is traceable to the absence of love in parentage. The world can never know how large a part of its idiotic, its intellectually and morally deformed, were the unwelcome offspring of unloved and unloving mothers.

It cannot be that love was intended only for life's rosy dawn, that its first thrill is its death throe. Could God so mock the brightest and sweetest hopes of earth as to ordain that love should grow cold and vanish like a summer dream while yet the fragrance of the orange blossoms lingers, and the bridal vow still trembles on the unkissed lips? Is it true that love is but the brilliant rainbow that spans the storm wrapt arch of life, and trembles for a moment through the silver mist of human tears, then fades forever while we gaze?

We cannot, will not, believe that God has made the human heart to single out this one gay hour from all the hours of life, as the brightest star in all the firmament of human joys, while yet that star is but a meteor which darts a moment, flame-winged and glorious, then sinks and falls, consumed by its own breath, leaving behind its brilliant train a darkened path forever. Ah no! the very law of heredity demands the preservation of love. Nature punishes its withdrawal with intellectual and moral idiocy.

The magic secret of which we spoke lies not in the means of preserving love, but in securing the world's consent to use the means that lie within its reach. There is no secret in the means.

They are contained in the formulated expression of a well known law that love cannot live unless its physical phase is entirely and completely subjected to its spiritual.

Spiritual love lives by its own right, but the physical lives only by lease of the spiritual. They can live together only on one changeless and eternal condition, and that condition is the perfect supremacy of the spiritual over the physical. This then is all that is necessary to the preservation of wedded love. When this condition is reversed the spiritual phase soon dies altogether, and at last even the physical itself, and two hearts that once beat together are severed past reuniting.

'Tis passing strange that the world so stubbornly refuses to profit by its own experience. Every untried ship that sails so proudly from the port with its "freight of spirits twain" passes on every side a shivering wreck; yet they heed not the wailing cries from the perishing, but sail straight onward to the fatal rock on which nature has set the seal of her deepest damnation.

We have pointed out the divine means by which alone love can live. Try it, O man! O woman! and be blessed. Try it by all the holy visions of your hopeful youth. Try it by all the divine significance of heredity, by all that being signifies, by all the prayers and tender yearnings at the cradle side, by your hopes of heaven, try it.

Let woman remember that this doctrine appeals to her with doubled force. It is through you, O woman, that the world must heed it. Whatever other wrongs you may submit to, whatever rights may be denied you in the social world, remember that in this matter you should proclaim yourself the sovereign ruler, nor brook a question why. Your voice may be silenced in the roaring mart, you may be pushed aside by the mad crowd, but behind the silken folds that hide the sanctity of wedded joy you are the sovereign divinely ordained. By the necessities and consistencies of your being, by every argument from the exhaustless realm of natural history, by every law of nature and of God, you bear the badge of rightful sovereignty.

"Fair youth, too timid to lift your eyes
To the maiden with downcast look,
As you mingle the gold and brown of your curls
Together over a book;

A fluttering hope that she dare not name
Her trembling bosom heaves;
And your heart is thrilled, when your fingers meet,
As you softly turn the leaves.

"Perchance you two will walk alone
Next year at some sweet day's close,
And your talk will fall to a tenderer tone,
As you liken her cheek to a rose;
And then her face will flush and glow,
With a hopeful, happy red;
Outblushing all the flowers that grow
Anear in the garden-bed.

"If you plead for hope, she may bashful drop
Her head on your shoulder, low;
And you will be lovers and sweethearts then
As youths and maidens go:
Lovers and sweethearts, dreaming dreams,
And seeing visions that please,
With never a thought that life is made
Of great realities;

"That the cords of love must be strong as death
Which hold and keep a heart,
Not daisy-chains, that snap in the breeze,
Or break with their weight apart;
For the pretty colors of youth's fair morn
Fade out from the noonday sky;
And blushing loves in the roses born
Alas! with the roses die!

"But the love, that when youth's morn is past,
Still sweet and true survives,
Is the faith we need to lean upon
In the crises of our lives:
The love that shines in the eyes grown dim,
In the voice that trembles, speaks;
And sees the roses that a year ago
Withered and died in our cheeks;

"That sheds a halo round us still,
Of soft immortal light,
When we change youth's golden coronal
For a crown of silver white;

A love for sickness and for health,
For rapture and for tears;
That will live for us, and bear with us
Through all our mortal years.

"And such there is; there are lovers here,
On the brink of the grave that stand,
Who shall cross to the hills beyond, and walk
Forever hand in hand!
Pray, youth and maid, that your end be theirs.
Who are joined no more to part;
For death comes not to the living soul,
Nor age to the loving heart!"

LEAVING HOME.

EVERY one must leave his home. The young eaglet cannot forever nestle beneath the protecting wing of its mother. It is a law of life itself that we cannot always stay at home. If the children were to remain at home through life, if this were the natural order of things, the institution of home would be impossible, for each home would grow with the accumulating generations, till at length it would outgrow the boundaries that must define a home, and the institution would be lost in general society. To avert this disaster nature has arranged that the child shall leave his home when he has become competent to care for himself, and should organize another home. Thus each generation repeats the programme of the preceding.

The proper function of the home is to serve as the nursery of the race, to protect the young germs of manhood and womanhood till they have become sufficiently strong to compel society and the world to yield them the required physical and mental sustenance. And yet this metaphor hardly serves our purpose, since the child does not leave his home to enter into the great tide of the world and become a floating speck on the turbulent surface of society, but, like the young tree, he is simply transplanted from the nursery to become the fruitful source of another nursery. There is no natural requirement of life that is not preceded by a desire and impulse in that direction. Accordingly the young man, as he approaches the age of maturity, begins to feel the gentle stimulus of a curious enterprise urging him to look beyond the walls of the old home out into the great world. He hears the distant hum of the great city, he feels the electric throb of the rushing train, and longs to mingle in the ceaseless tumult of life,—

> In the strife of brain and pen,
> 'Mid the rumble of the presses
> Where they measure men with men.

Under the impulse of this feeling, he leaves the old home, but not forever. No young man or woman ever leaves home with the intention of abandoning it forever. The dutiful child carries away the home with him. He is himself a product of the home. Every feature of his character reflects the character of the home. As the tree records the character of the soil and climate, so the young man carries ever with him the old home. Every mother is carried into the city on the brow of her son. Her care, her love, her examples, her prayers, are all written there. The city knows the country in this way. It reads the history of the country on the brows of the farmer boys. How careful, then, should parents be in regard to these reports which they are sending into the cities. The little home that nestles among the hills shall be published to the world, and the silent influence of its daily life shall blend with the surging passions that drive the tide of human life along the crowded streets.

Mother! your life is not insignificant. It is not and cannot be isolated from universal significance, for your boy shall bear it into the great tide that never ebbs. The story of the fireside is written upon the altars of great cathedrals, in senate chambers, and in the busy mart. It is inscribed in invisible characters upon the sides of steamboats and railway trains, and on the marble fronts of the brilliant temples of trade. The great outward world of commercial storm and sunshine, of laughter and weeping, of honor and dishonor, draws its life from the home. It is linked to the hearthstone by a thousand ties that run far under the surface of society. The leaving of home is an experience in one's life freighted with momentous consequences. It is a fact in botany that the critical period in the life of a plant is when it has consumed all the albumen stored up in the seed for its support, and is just beginning to put forth its tender little rootlets into the outer soil, to draw henceforth in independence its life from the earth's great storehouse. So the critical and dangerous period of a child's life is when he has burst the environments of home, and steps out from the little quiet circle to earn his first morsel of bread with his own hands, and to negotiate independently with the great crafty world. This is the period that tries the character and tests its genuineness. If the young man withstands the shock that comes with the first wild consciousness that he is in a city, and that the currents and counter currents of life are dashing in bewildering torrents at his feet, if amid the surges and the clinging spray, he stands firmly anchored to the rock of home-born principle, if he does not grow dizzy and mad with the ceaseless roar and rumble, if he, in safety, passes for the first time the brilliant fronts of illuminated hells, and with mother's benediction on his lips, turns coldly from the first alluring invitation of the tempter, he has passed the fearful crisis of his life. We would not, of course, contend that the only danger to this young man from city influences comes with his first actual entrance into the city, that he is never in danger after he has once passed by a brilliantly lighted den of iniquity.

We simply mean that if the young man succeeds in resisting the temptations that beset him during that period in which he feels the elation of his independence, he has passed the most critical period. This is the period in which the young man's character is particularly susceptible to evil influences, and if he succeeds in establishing his social relations in the city on the proper basis, and becomes himself established as a permanent member of society, he is comparatively safe. There is always a feeling of romance which accompanies the young man on his first entrance into the city. There is a poetry in the rhythmic vibrations of the living mass. He feels himself a part of this mass, and in a certain sense he feels that he is the mechanical equivalent of its never ceasing motion. Under such circumstances one is peculiarly susceptible to social influences.

Those things which awaken the sense of the poetical and the romantic are the most powerful in their influences over one who is trying to veil the rural and take on the airs of city life. Unfortunately for the race, the most poetical and romantic in life is often that which is in some way associated with profligacy and vice. Thousands of young men of literary aspirations and brilliant talents, through the glittering but deadly romance of Poe's life, and the poetry of Byron's gilded vice, have gone out like stars which the veil of the storm has hidden.

Hence the evil influences of the city which appeal most strongly to the young country lad, suddenly transformed into a poet through the inspiration of the great city, are those which clothe themselves with the livery of beauty, which sparkle with the gems of wit, and lull to sleep on enticing couches with the drowsy strains of tinkling music.

Were it not for that perverted principle in human nature that sees poetry in vice, the leaving of home would not be such a catastrophe to the young man. Parents should be careful not to allow their children, except in cases of necessity, to leave home until their characters are so far established as to be comparatively safe from the evil influences that must surround them elsewhere. *Young* children are never safe away from home.

There is no age in which a person can enter for the first time into general society away from home with absolute safety, yet the danger is particularly great to the young. If a child is of a romantic turn of mind and enjoys the reading of novels, his parents should be particularly solicitous concerning his welfare when he goes for the first time into society.

Even a fondness for poetry, which would seem to be the purest and most innocent affection of the mind, indicates the presence of those characteristics which render one peculiarly susceptible to the temptations of the great city. The wisest precaution that a parent can take when his child is about to leave home, is to arrange his social relations in advance for him. Arrangements can almost always be made for his introduction into those circles of society where he may find desirable amusements, and at the same time be surrounded by good and wholesome influences.

Probably the most frequent cause for which children leave home earlier than they ought, is for the purpose of attending school. The practice of sending young children away to boarding schools is, however, not so common as formerly, from the fact that the common schools are becoming more efficient. Boys can now be fitted for college in many of the free public schools, while they still remain at home and under the supervision of their parents.

This is certainly better than sending them away. Indeed, except in rare cases, the latter practice should be abandoned altogether. There are several circumstances that combine to render children at boarding school peculiarly liable to danger. In the first place, they are usually at that age when they would be most easily led astray; and, second, the occupation at school being of course wholly mental, the body is left without sufficient exercise, and, in consequence, the whole physical being feels a buoyancy which is very dangerous unless under the guidance and oversight of parents. Again, the stringent rules of conduct at most boarding schools always have a tendency to awaken the mischievous in boys and girls.

It is a fact which has been proved by the experience of every educational institution in which such rules exist, that the tendency to violation is almost in direct ratio to the stringency of the rules. Consider, for example, the ordinary boarding school rules relative to the association of the sexes. In many cases the young man might call upon a lady school-mate with profit to both parties, if there were no rules prohibiting such an association, but when a young man calls clandestinely upon a young lady, the secret sense of having violated rules whose authority they are supposed to recognize often has a disastrous effect upon their whole moral nature. But whatever we may believe concerning the propriety or impropriety of such rules, it cannot alter the fact of their existence in almost every seminary and boarding school. The rules may be the choice of the smaller evil. On this subject, however, we have our doubts, and yet we do not deny that there might be danger without them.

Under the circumstances we think the wisest course for parents is to secure the education of their children where they can exercise a personal supervision over them. Whatever may be the occasion for leaving home, whatever may have been the character of the home, there comes to every soul at that moment a pang of regret which scorns the finest ministries of language. Earth has no more pathetic scene than that divine tableau of youth's departure from the old home where mother and child, beneath the changing colors of joy and sorrow, stand folded in the final embrace amid the silence of tears and kisses. That gush of holy emotion serves a purpose in the economy of our nature; it is to bind the soul with cords of everlasting remembrances to that firm anchor in the great deep of life, the home of childhood.

"I never knew how well I loved
The little cot where I was born,
Until I stood beside the gate
One pleasant, early summer morn,
And listened to my mother's voice.
She spoke such words as mothers speak—
Of cheer and hope—and all the while

The tear drops glistened on her cheek.
And soon she turned and plucked a rose
That grew beside the cottage door,
And, smiling, pinned it to my coat,
As she had often done before.
I went away: 'twas long ago,
Still ever, till my life shall close,
The dearest treasure I can know
Will be a faded little rose."

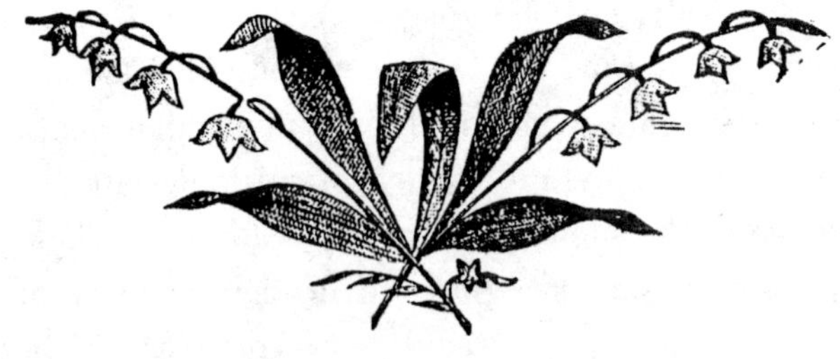

MEMORIES OF HOME.

DEAR to us still are the friendships we formed at the public schools, and hard was the breaking of those ties, yet we cherish no such memories of our school-mates as we do of home and mother.

If we have not already sundered the ties of home, the time will come all too soon when the silken cord must be severed. This thought should make us eager to enjoy all we can the sweet dream of childhood. If we are making preparations for a new home which the poetry of youth has painted with brilliant colors, we should not forget that the walls of that new home must be forever decorated with the picture of the old one. You may place the wide expanse of ocean between the two homes, but memory will paint the home of your childhood, and whatever you may say or do, will persist in hanging the picture on the walls of your parlor, your chamber, and your library. We may make our new home all that wealth and taste can produce, we may lavish upon it all the rich accumulations of youth and manhood, but beside the costly paintings that adorn the walls of its parlor, there must hang that old picture. Do what you will, it must hang there forever. If you take it down, an invisible hand rehangs it. It is a magic picture, and it requires not the light of day to see it. You can see it better in the hushed stillness of the night than in the light of day. If the associations of that old home have been unpleasant, if there is in that picture a mother, who, in the little room you used to occupy, sits weeping over your waywardness, with the dark autographs of sorrow written across her brow, if there is a sister with downcast look, a father sitting by the fireside with his head resting upon his hands, prematurely old because you broke his heart, how will that picture haunt your guilty soul in the night, how will its sadness embitter every cup of joy, and turn to wormwood every pleasure.

You cannot ask that father's forgiveness, it is too late. You cannot go to mother, whose loving hand might, perhaps, put a veil over that hateful picture, or hang in its place a more beautiful one. It is too late for this, for you helped bring a coffin to that old home, long, long ago, and be assured that coffin will be painted in one corner of the picture. You can go to the old home, but the shed where you played with your little sister will be torn down, the house will be changed, everything will look strange except, perhaps, the old orchard. But this will revive no pleasant memories, nothing but the sad day when you quarreled about picking the apples, and struck your little brother, who is now sleeping just back of the house in the garden beside his mother. You can go out there and call his name, but he will not hear you. You may strew with flowers the grave of father, mother and brother; you may erect costly stones, but these will not atone.

No: do not wait for that sad day, but while mother and father are still alive, and your little brother is with you, make home cheerful. Keep mother's forehead smooth, and father's hair unsilvered just as long as you can.

If you cannot love mother and make her happy, you cannot truly love and make happy the heart of any woman.

We exercise the greatest care in selecting the real pictures with which we adorn our homes, and if we do not afterwards like them, we can dispose of them and forget them. Why should we not, then, be infinitely more careful concerning the character of that picture on which we shall be compelled to gaze through life?

Through the power of memory the influences of home again become active in our lives. The peculiar circumstances of any particular portion of our lives after we have left the old home, seldom produce lasting impressions upon our minds. We are not likely to remember vividly our experiences between the ages of thirty-five and forty, at least, not in such a way that the remembrance exerts an influence over our lives and thoughts. But by a wise and beneficent plan we are so constituted that the memories of our early home, the memories of that period in which our characters were shaped, shall be influential through life. There seems to be a subtile and peculiar propriety in this fact.

The ordinary influences of life leave a sufficiently deep impression upon our characters as they pass without being repeated, or, at least, not oftener than their periodical nature may ensure. But here we find a special provision made to meet a required exception. Just at that period in our lives when the good and kindly influences of home are supposed to mold into consistent form the chaotic elements of our character, a principle is introduced whereby those influences are made to be self repeating through life. The instrumentality through which this is effected is the spirit of poetry which pervades the memory of these early years. No other period of our lives so lends itself to the play of our own imaginations.

There is nothing in life's experience that so quickly and effectually awakens in the heart those better elements that ally us "to angels and to God" as the sacred memories of home. This fact constitutes a positive power in our lives, and growing out of this fact is the highest duty of life, the duty to make the character of our home such that its cherished memories shall be a developing and gladdening influence through life.

"O memory, be sweet to me—
Take, take all else at will,
So thou but leave me safe and sound,
Without a token my heart to wound.
The little house on the hill!

"Take all of best from east to west,
So thou but leave me still
The chamber, where in the starry light
I used to lie awake at night
And list to the whip-poor-will.

"Take violet-bed, and rose-tree red,
And the purple flags by the mill,
The meadow gay, and the garden-ground,
But leave, Oh leave me safe and sound
The little house on the hill!

"The daisy-lane, and the dove's low plain
And the cuckoo's tender bill,
Take one and all, but leave the dreams
That turned the rafters to golden beams,
In the little house on the hill!

"The gables brown, they have tumbled down,
And dry is the brook by the mill;
The sheets I used with care to keep
Have wrapt my dead for the last long sleep,
In the valley, low and still.

"But, memory, be sweet to me,
And build the walls, at will,
Of the chamber where I used to mark,
So softly rippling over the dark,
The song of the whip-poor-will!

"Ah, memory, be sweet to me!
All other fountains chill;
But leave that song so weird and wild,
Dear as its life to the heart of the child,
In the little house on the hill!"

TRIALS OF HOME.

WE shall consider in another chapter, under the head of sorrow and its meaning, those great sorrows which sometimes visit individuals, but which are not universal. They constitute the heroic treatment of the few who languish in the silent and more terrible wards of earth's great hospital.

But by the trials of home we mean those thousand little annoyances of life whose sphere of action is for the most part home. In their individual capacity they are insignificant, and perhaps unworthy of notice, and yet their aggregate significance is written in dark and heavy lines on many a mother's brow. They are the crosses from which none escape, the inevitable experiences of every human being. Those who scorn them as unworthy of notice do not understand their meaning.

If every human desire were adequate to its own immediate gratification, there would be no such thing as trials and disappointments. But every want of humanity is separated from its gratification by the length and breadth of an effort, and the greater the want, the longer and broader the required effort. And it often happens that the effort is too short to span the chasm. There is no system of measurement by which we can adapt the effort to the intervening chasm. Every effort of man is an experiment. It is like building a light bridge on land, with which to span a stream, the breadth of which we have not measured. When we come to lay it across the stream it may be too short.

Trials and disappointments for the most part owe their origin to this fact, that human effort is found falling short of its goal.

The path of life runs so crooked that we cannot see around the curves. Then there are so many junctions that the time tables are forever getting mixed up.

Under these circumstances life can never run smoothly. There will be trials as long as humanity exists.

The mind desires ease, and only so much exercise as is prompted by its own spontaneous impulse. When it is required to step aside from the path of its own preferences there is a spiritual resistance, and a tendency to chafe and fret. These little tendencies and influences are what we mean by the trials of home.

One has said, "It may not seem a great thing to have a constantly nagging companion, or boots that always hurt your corns, or linen that is never properly starched, or to have to read crossed letters, or go to stupid parties, or consult books without indexes,—but to the sufferer they are very tangible oppressions, and in our short space of working life not to be made light of."

No truer words were ever uttered. Who has not noticed the almost absolute control which an uneasy boot will sometimes assert over the whole mind?

A sermon to-day may sound almost divine to us in a pair of slippers, but yesterday, in a pair of new boots, we should have regarded the same sermon as intolerably stupid.

A star actor, if thrown suddenly into the presence of his lady love, in a pair of overalls, will appear awkward in his movements.

How fretful we sometimes feel when we are hungry. A baked potato will produce such a change in us that we hardly know ourselves. The toothache has been known to transform in half an hour a saint into a sinner. How quickly will music calm an angry child.

> "The trifles of our daily lives,
> The common things scarce worth recall,
> Whereof no visible trace survives,
> These are the mainsprings after all.
> Destiny is not without thee, but within,
> Thyself must make thyself."

All these facts only show what a powerful influence little things may have over us. Our lives are made up of moments, and the character of each moment depends upon the influences of that moment; and it requires but a very small influence to change the character of a moment.

All growth is but a perpetual conquest over opposing forces. There can be no growth, physical, intellectual, or spiritual, except through the resistance to that element in which it grows. It is not necessary, however, that these conquests should come as the issue of great efforts or overwhelming sorrows. The triumphs of life are those which we win over self, and these are won on little battle fields; in the kitchen, in the nursery, at the breakfast table, on Mondays at the wash-tub, in the stable with a fractious, exasperating horse, in the field with the cattle, or amid the little vexations and annoyances of every day; as the breachy sheep, the broken mowing machine, or the disappointment of a rainy day.

It is by trifles like these that human souls are tested.

In overlooking these little trials, we overlook a very important principle along with them. It is that principle which distinguishes the effects of little sorrows from those of great ones. Simultaneously with the great sorrows there is developed in the soul a power of heroic endurance. Most of us have experienced at least one great stroke of grief, one which we had contemplated with such a shrinking that we believed it would be impossible for us to stand up beneath its weight; but when the blow came we were surprised at our own heroic calmness. This experience will always be found to accompany a great sorrow, and serve in part as a compensation. This arises from the sense of the inevitable which always accompanies a great stroke. There comes over every one in the moment of utter despair a feeling that approaches to satisfaction, and so strong is this tendency in some that when the despair has been found to be groundless, there has actually come with the first instant of relief a wish that it might have been otherwise, that they might have seen the worst.

The testimony of Du Chaillu concerning his feelings when he had been stricken down by a lion confirms the existence of this principle in human nature. He expresses his feelings as those of perfect satisfaction and resignation to his fate. Edgar A. Poe, with his almost divine intuition, makes one of the characters in his "Descent into the Maelstrom" experience something of this same feeling.

These feelings of course are but momentary flashes of insanity, but they show that God has implanted in us an instinctive satisfaction with the inevitable, however deeply it may involve our own souls in pain and sorrow. When one refuses to be reconciled to a great bereavement, there is still in his heart a secret feeling of rebellion. It may be because he possesses this instinct in a less degree than others, since all the instincts of human nature vary in different individuals; but in most cases it will be found that his sorrow is superficial and does not take hold on the depths of his nature.

In the little sorrows of life this principle is seldom manifested. This is why small troubles weigh far more heavily upon the heart in proportion to their magnitude than the great ones. We are of the opinion, however, that it was the divine plan that this principle should manifest itself even in the smallest sorrows and trials of life, but that through constant rebellion the race have come to that condition in which they do not experience it except in the emergency of great sorrow or danger.

But however this may be, the cultivation of that instinct in us can do no harm, and if we can so cultivate and develop it that we shall feel a sense of acquiescence and resignation in every little trial of our lives, till the gnat and the mosquito shall seem to us to have rights equal to our own, we have surely won a triumph that would become an angel's crown.

This, then, is our advice to those who are weighed down with the little trials of life: cultivate the instinct of resignation, try to feel satisfied with every fate that befalls you. This is not an impossible task. Your efforts will be rewarded. It will become easier and easier for you to attempt to do it, until at last your trials will become joys. If you cannot feel that God ordained your trials, if you cannot regard them as a part of the infinite plan, you must certainly consider them as the just penalty for your own transgressions. In either case you can reason yourself into a feeling of satisfaction.

Little sorrows, like the great ones, are disciplinary in their nature, and if the sufferer does not degenerate into a fretful and irritable being, they will develop his spiritual health. If he keeps ever in mind that he suffers chiefly because his soul is divinely receptive, that his very suffering but measures his spirit's capacity for joy,—his character will in the end blossom forth and bear fruits all the sweeter for the trials.

"What's the use of always fretting
At the trials we shall find
Ever strewn along our pathway?
Travel on, and never mind.

"Travel onward, working, hoping,
Cast no lingering look behind
At the trials once encountered;
Look ahead, and never mind.

"What is past, is past forever;
Let all the fretting be resigned;
It will never help the matter—
Do your best, and never mind.

"And if those who might befriend you,
Whom the ties of nature bind,
Should refuse to do their duty,
Look to heaven, and never mind.

"Friendly words are often spoken
When the feelings are unkind;
Take them for their real value,
Pass them on, and never mind.

"Fate may threaten, clouds may lower,
Enemies may be combined;
If your trust in God is steadfast,
He will help you,—never mind."

SORROW AND ITS MEANING.

WHETHER sorrow should be regarded as possessing a rightful place in the economy of being, or simply as an intruder, for whose stealthy entrance into the halls of joy and beauty man is wholly responsible, is a problem which many regard as too difficult for solution by finite mind, and which it is blasphemy to attempt to solve.

Yet we cannot help asking: Why the mighty wail of anguish and pain that goes up unceasingly from the lips of Nature? Why does the rose conceal a thorn? Why blossoms the loveliest flower just where the deadly-nightshade distills its poison dew upon its snowy petals? Why are the heavens deaf to the cry of wounded innocence? Why are the fairest and the loveliest in the armies of the just and good permitted to fall like withered roses before the iron hail of treason's hosts? Why has all that is good and lovely in human history been bought with blood, while virtue's victorious shout is preceded by the martyr's shriek? Can an agency so wide-spread and vast in its relations as that of pain and suffering exist in nature, and implicate no higher instrumentality than human folly?

It may be said that, since all suffering comes from the breach of natural law, and since God has given us the faculty of caution, by which we are enabled to guard against danger and accidental suffering, it cannot be true that sorrow and suffering are natural, and hence divinely sanctioned, but, on the contrary, they must owe their origin wholly to the voluntary action of man.

But God has given us no faculty by which we can predict an earthquake. He placed us upon the earth before he had finished it, while yet his engines were roaring, and his furnaces glowing, while the deadly sparks were still flying from his mighty anvil.

Now, in order that man should be wholly responsible for pain and suffering, he should have faculties sufficiently powerful to grasp and analyze the divine plan, so that he might anticipate and make provision for all possible movements in the universe. The fact that man cannot thus anticipate the changes of direction in the universal movement, proves danger and pain and sorrow to be divinely appointed. The ant cannot anticipate the movement of the foot that steps upon its little mound.

Is it not possible, after all, that history with all its crimson blots, with all its agony uttered and unuttered, with all of that which we call evil, but which to God may be but a necessary and momentary discord in the tuning of being's mighty orchestra,—is it not possible that all this, just as it is, constitutes a mighty whole, of whose sublime and infinite meaning we catch as yet but a feeble hint? Does not any other philosophy necessarily assign to the human will the power to intercept at any desired point the Divine plan? Is not the highest and grandest philosophy after all, that which lays the human will itself in the hands of God, the only "Uncaused Cause," and acknowledges the endorsement upon the parchment of human history, of him who holds in his volition the potentialities of all history?

Sorrow and pain when projected into the atmosphere of divine and eternal significance may lose the superficial qualities that we assign to them, and find their places in the "eternal fitness of things."

Perhaps, if we could see creation in its entirety, and know the inter-relations of its myriad parts, we should rejoice over that which now causes us sorrow. To us, the grandeur of the ocean is marred by the sight of a wreck, but to him who holds that ocean in the hollow of his hand, the wreck, the pale lips and the despairing cry may be necessary to the expression of a higher and grander meaning. The toad sees evil and only evil in the crushing wheel of the fire-engine as it flies on its errand of good. So we, in our worm-like ignorance and isolation can see nothing but evil in the engines of sorrow that pass over our souls, where they must pass, since our souls lie across their path.

The universe is all of one purpose, "so compact" that if we could know perfectly any nook or corner we should know all, for the awful secret of the Absolute is concealed in every finite entity. If we could read all the meaning there is in a single strain of music, we could translate the infinite harmonies of the universe. Could we tell why an atom of oxygen prefers an atom of potassium to one of gold we should know not only the secret of love's caprice, but the essence of the Divine Fatherhood.

"Flower in the crannied wall,
I pluck you out of the crannies;—
Hold you here, root and all, in my hand,
Little flower,—but if I could understand
What you are, root and all, and all in all,
I should know what God and man is."

Human knowledge cannot reach the essence of things. We cannot know our dearest friend only a few manifestations of him. The ulterior essence that makes all things a unit, we can never know. We are like insects viewing the motions of a machine. To them each wheel moves independently and from its own caprice. So we regard each movement in the universe as separate and independent. The belts and bars and gears by which each and every movement is linked with every other, lie beyond the horizon of our vision. If we could but discern the inter-relations of things, we might learn that the grandest event in human history is linked in sequential relation with the flutter of an insect's wing, and that the annihilation of an atom and a star would be equal catastrophes. Perchance we might see, in the ineffable light of that awful vision, how potential joys unspeakable have been born in darkened chambers; how every wreathed casket bears a universal ministry, and that,

> "The brightest rainbows ever play
> Above the fountains of our tears."

But sorrow has a more obvious ministry than that which is discerned only by such generalization. If, then, sorrow is a natural agency; that is, if we have been made capable of sorrow, and then placed in a world of danger and disaster where the causes of sorrow cannot be anticipated, surely this sorrow and affliction must have an individual ministry commensurate with its cost, or the wisdom of Him who ordained it is implicated. We may rest assured that sorrow serves some purpose in the economy of being, as definite as that of magnetism and light. We cannot reach the secret of its deepest meaning, and yet there seems to be within us a spiritual instinct that seeks to justify its existence and to find in it a ministry.

> "The gods in bounty work up storms about us,
> That give mankind occasion to exert
> Their hidden strength, and throw out into practice
> Virtues that shun the day, and lie concealed
> In the smooth seasons and calms of life."

Pain and sorrow are wasting processes of the soul, just as labor is a wasting process of the muscles. But who does not know that this very waste is the only condition under which a muscle can grow strong? If you wish to strengthen any muscle, the first thing to do is to weary that muscle by labor. A muscle grows strong only in the process of recuperation, the act of recovering a loss. It is a universal law of nature that every loss is just a little more than repaid.

Now sorrow is the labor of the spirit. It is the instinctive struggle of the spirit against the effects of maladjustment, and sustains to it precisely the same relation that physical labor sustains to the muscle. Every adult soul that has never known a pang of sorrow has long since ceased to grow.

It is true that the soul does not require pain with that degree of regularity with which the muscles require labor, but it is simply because, through memory and reflection, the influence is distributed. A single great stroke of sorrow will often soften, subdue, and ripen a whole life, for, since it is lived over and over again in the silent solitude of thought, it becomes life-long in its ministry. Who has not read this sacred ministry of sorrow on those brows of saintly triumph,—the thrones of peace?

We have not yet, it is true, caught the divine secret of how justice is maintained in the unequal distribution of human suffering.

We must, at once, and forever, abandon the idea that it can be found along the narrow line of individual merit. The world has sought it there long and diligently, and found it not.

One student is compelled by his instructors to practice

more hours a day in a gymnasium than another. The practice is irksome, and the other is allowed to sit with folded arms in smiling complacency, while his companion toils at the rope and bar. To this young toiler there could be nothing more unjust, for, like most students, he does not look forward to the effects of the discipline to which he is subjected. And yet in the future years his proud physique and glow of health beside his friend's puny form and pale cheek, may prove that the injustice was on the other side. There may not, however, be injustice in either case.

Perhaps the gymnasium is not the treatment best adapted to the weak student. Perhaps his constitution is such that he is incapable of developing a strong physique, and, perhaps, he could more surely reach the height of his physical capacity through the ministry of some gentler exercise. It is wisest to allow the physician under whose superintendence he is placed to decide these questions. Perhaps, again, these physicians may see in the stronger student the germs of a possible ministry, whose fruition will require the fullest development of all his physical powers. It may be that the forces of creation have conspired to make him by nature a performer of great physical deeds, a builder of bridges, and a leveler of mountains. One, at sight of whose mighty achievements, his fellows will bow in the willing acknowledgment of conscious inferiority. All these conditions and qualifications may have been discovered by those having charge of the two students.

Now let us suppose the students actually incapable of perceiving the reason for the difference in treatment to which they have been subjected. They cannot understand that the purpose which nature intended them to serve in the economy of being has any relation whatever to this problem of justice which they are trying to solve.

Does not this illustration cover all phases of the great problem of human sorrow? Are we not all in a vast gymnasium, under the superintendence of one who not only is the architect of the gymnasium, but who has adapted its every appliance to the requirements of our spiritual muscles? Every obstacle to our spiritual progress, every temptation, every pang of sorrow, is a weight or a crossbar in that great gymnasium, and we in our infinitesimal knowledge and prescience can weigh only the justice or injustice of apparent discrimination. We murmur as we bend beneath the weight of grief, and bitterly complain as we are made to revolve in agonizing contortions around the cross-bar of adversity. Yet could our eyes be tempered to the light of an universal sun, and we permitted to pierce the starry vistas of infinite meaning, with one glance through the lens of infinite intelligence, beneath the burning focus of that lens how would the nebulous haze burn from off the shining disk of this great problem, Justice.

Perhaps the divinest ministry of bereavement and sorrow is seen in the lofty moods that grow out of it, and that lift the soul above the reach of its own discipline; till it can stand with face wreathed in the smile of peace, subdued and tender and god-like, while with never a sigh it beholds the waves of desolation sweep over its fondest hopes. Thousands of souls have been educated in sorrow's school till they were able to do this. Almost every one has experienced certain exalted moods in which he has felt himself above and beyond the reach of all outward conditions; and clinging to the one fact of his existence and its inward relations, he has felt that he could smile at every possible catastrophe. It is sorrow alone that gives us the capacity for this the divinest of moods. How weak and *useless* are those "pulpy souls" that never have known affliction! Such are the ones that cover their faces and flee from the scene of suffering. They are the feeble characters that tremble and fall when shaken by great emergencies. But who are they that stand calmly and firmly against the fiercest charge of calumny. It is they who know the meaning of midnight watching and buried hope. It is they who have put the cup of sorrow to their lips and held it there till they have drained the bitter dregs.

> "The grape must be crushed before
> Can be gathered the glorious wine;
> So the poet's heart must be wrung to the core
> Ere his song can be divine."

We cannot doubt that every pang, every disappointment,

every blinding stroke of grief, holds in potentiality, a blessing that in some way follows a law analogous to that physical law of recuperation by which wasting, wearying toil ministers to muscular strength. The blessing may not always be immediate and visible, it may not, indeed, always be to our own selfish selves, but somewhere in eternity to the sum of all being. It would be impious to attempt to trace its divinely appointed course. It may require eternity to solve the problem of a blighted hope. We are silent when they ask us to point out the hidden blessing in war's dread scourge; or when the scorpion lash of pestilence smites the back of dying Memphis; or when the brilliant foot-lights with fiery fingers have caressed the oily scenery and the public hall becomes a tomb for charred and unknown corpses. We are staggered by the awful mystery when the light-hearted girl steps from out the merry throng, and reappears in sable drapery with a story on her brow. It requires a quick ear to catch the secret from the frozen lips of death, when the fair youth who but yesterday plucked the wild roses to twine in golden hair, comes to-day to those same woodland haunts to gather roses for love's speechless tribute, that he may lay them on the pulseless bosom of the maiden he adores.

But notwithstanding all this, we cannot resist the conviction, which comes to us with the force of an instinct, that sorrow is a natural phenomenon and bears the endorsement of the Divine hand. How else can we explain the philosophy of that instinctive acquiescence in the inevitable, of which we have spoken in the preceding chapter? Why, when the shadow of the angel's wing falls on the face of one we love, do we almost instinctively turn to the physician to learn if no power could have saved? and why that sigh of relief when he assures us that the result could not have been otherwise. The inevitableness of a friend's death will partially reconcile us to our bereavement. When one *knows* that he must die, he is usually calm and resigned, but he is wild while there is hope. Why is this? Why does utter despair always gives birth to calmness and resignation? Is it not a hint from the infallible book of human instinct, that whatever may be true of moral accountability and free agency, it is not inconsistent with a higher and grander truth that, in the infinite altitude of divine meaning, "Whatever is, is right?" We cannot see the purpose that is subserved in the universal economy by the poisonous plant, by thorn and sting, and deadly fang, yet the highest philosophy assigns to them a consistent meaning, even while it acknowledges that meaning to be above and beyond the proudest effort of human analysis. I cannot say that I ought not to suffer, till I am able to analyze every relation of my being. This I can never do. I cannot find in the great machine a single gearing by which one wheel is connected with another.

"Yet I doubt not through the ages one increasing purpose runs,
And the thoughts of men are widened with the process of the suns."

Is it not possible, nay, probable, that the same great principle in the universe which creates the deadly nightshade, and arms the insect with a fatal gland, also arms even ignorance with that which slays the objects of our fondest love?

The mother who bends over a little casket to leave her triune gift of roses, tears, and kisses, upon lips that never more will lisp her name, may yet perceive, in the light of a higher revelation, that though the rose-wreathed casket bears the ashes of her cherished hopes, it is also ministrant to a need she knows not of.

"Who knows of this inward life of ours?
Of the pangs with which each joy is born?
Who dreams of poison among the flowers,
Or sees the wound from the hidden thorn,
O'er which we smile when most forlorn?

"Who knows that the change from grave to gay
Was wrought by the deadly pain we bore,
As we lay the hopes of years away,
Like withered roses, to bloom no more
Upon life's desolated shore?

"Who knows, as we tread these careless ways,
That we think of our sainted dead the while,
That the heart grows sick, in summer days,
For a blessed mother's tender smile,
That held no taint of worldly guile?

"Who knows of the tremulous chords of love,
To the lightest touch that vibrate still,
As under her wing the stricken dove,
Unmurmuring folds—although it kill—
The cruel mark of the archer's skill?"

THE WIDOW'S HOME.

A WORK treating of home and the various phases of the home-life, could not be considered complete, were no chapter devoted to the widow's home. For the widow's home finds its justification in the normal and primitive constitution of things, as proved by the undisputed facts that marriage is an institution of nature, and that no organic law demands the simultaneous dissolution of husband and wife. Indeed, such a coincidence is of remarkably rare occurrence.

Widowhood, then, is an ordinance of nature, and perhaps the strongest evidence that sorrow holds a rightful place in the universal economy is to be found in this fact.

If, then, widowhood is inevitable, it seems right that provision should be made for its possible occurrence, at least, in so far as occasional and wholesome contemplation can so dispose our minds that the dark angel cannot come to us or ours by absolute surprise. We do not mean by this that husbands and wives should perpetually dwell upon the possible catastrophe of each other's death. This would be entirely unnatural. Indeed, nothing so surely indicates a morbid condition of the whole being as a constant tendency to dwell upon the possible death of ourselves or our friends. It indicates a disordered state of the nerves to be unable to sleep in consequence of a constant dread of fire. And yet it is surely the duty of all to make due provisions for such a catastrophe by way of fire-escapes. So while we should not allow ourselves to be in constant dread of bereavement, we should in our thought and meditation frequently acknowledge to ourselves the possibility of such an event, with an effort to realize that which we acknowledge. In this way we may prepare ourselves for almost any affliction, so that when the alarm comes we may not be suffocated and bewildered in the blinding smoke of our own grief.

But the liabilities to widowhood impose the duty of a more substantial provision. This affliction falls most heavily upon her who has leaned with the most childlike dependence upon the support of her husband. It is, perhaps, natural for woman to look to her husband for support and protection, but that complete surrender of her individuality which makes her a mere household pet, is to be condemned, not only as unnatural, but as a sin against herself and society.

Those who wear the badge of widowhood with the most heroic fortitude are those who, in the stern battle of life, have stood abreast with their husbands, who have never shirked the awful responsibility of womanhood, wifehood, and motherhood. When the fearful summons came that left them to fight alone, it found them with weapon in hand. And it was then that the glory and majesty of their womanhood shone through a veil of tears with a beauty that was divine. It is not the bereavement alone that lends sadness to the thoughts of widowhood, but it is the fact of added responsibility. There are often young children dependent upon their sorrowing mother, and no matter how nobly that mother may have performed her part in the conflict of life, in the present conditions of society there are few in whose homes would not be felt the sudden interruption and suspension of the husband's business, though it were preceded by years of industry and economy.

It requires something of a fortune, at least more than most men possess, in order that the interest alone may be sufficient to maintain the home, and to feed, clothe and educate a family of children ; so that some form of remunerative labor often becomes necessary even for the mother. And this adds to the sadness of the scene, for if there is a scene on earth that is sad, it is that of grief struggling in the toils of want.

But we would not be understood to mean that the widow's home is always and necessarily the scene of want, for it is not always, by any means, that there is a family of young children dependent on the mother's efforts for the supply of all their varied needs. It is, perhaps, as often that the children are able to support themselves and their mother. Nor is the widow's home ever the abode of unmitigated sorrow. We cannot, it is true, from the very nature of the case, eliminate sorrow from the widow's home, yet God has so constituted the human heart that even amid the darkest scenes of sorrow and affliction there come to it hours of mirth and joy. And, perhaps, the widow's home, where the necessary conditions of love and confidence exist, is not less potent in its formative influences upon character, than those homes where sorrow has never come. There is something beautiful as well as pathetic in the family scene where loving children recognize mother as the head. The sons and daughters who come from families of this kind are usually noble and generous. They have learned to be unselfish not only from the heroic discipline of their own lot, but from the tireless example of a mother's denial and self-sacrifice, qualities which belong emphatically to the widowed mother.

The angelic qualities of a mother's love never fully reveal themselves till the wand of sorrow touches her heart and writes a story on her brow.

"Arise and all thy tasks fulfill,
  And as thy day thy strength shall be;
Were there no power beyond the ill,
  The ill could not have come to thee.

"Though cloud and storm encompass thee
  Be not afflicted nor afraid;
Thou knowest the shadow could not be
  Were there no sun beyond the shade.

"For thy beloved, dead and gone,
  Let sweet, not bitter, tears be shed;
Nor 'open thy dark saying on
  The harp,' as though thy faith were dead."

HOMELESS ORPHANS.

A TREATISE upon the home life would be incomplete without, at least, some mention of the homeless. We cannot exhaustively consider any fact without also considering its negative.

The word orphan is one of the saddest in human language. It is a word at sound of which the gayest hearts are sad. It brings to our minds a lone wanderer who finds no object on earth to evoke a smile. When the child that has a happy home and loving parents imagines himself deprived of them, he experiences an oppressive feeling that may be likened to that of suffocation. It is probable, however, that the actual suffering of the homeless is far less than one would naturally suppose, for that principle in us which tends to makes us satisfied with the inevitable doubtless asserts itself here.

When we look upon the cripple who is obliged to substitute a wooden crutch for a leg, our hearts are moved to pity, and we feel that in some way we owe him something. We cannot feel at ease when we look upon him, while we ourselves enjoy the free use of our limbs. But the cripple himself has no such feelings. He feels that the wooden crutch is his other leg, and he in turn pities his unfortunate neighbor who has lost both limbs. And so it is with life. He who dwells in a palace pities him who dwells in a cottage, and he in turn pities him who dwells in a hovel. In the working of this principle may be discerned that law of compensation which underlies all human affairs.

But this fact does not justify selfishness nor allow us to neglect the rights of the unfortunate. For in spite of all compensatory tendencies the world is full of suffering. The air is rent at noonday and at midnight with the wails of sorrow and the shrieks of agony. What if every wave of sound around the earth could reach our ears! Think how the stifled sob of sudden sorrow would blend with the music where beauty moves to the pulses of the viol, and where in the great orchestral movement of human life could be found a place for the weird, discordant note of orphaned anguish. How the thunderous discords of that mighty orchestra are reduced to harmony by the dullness of our ears!

Pity is an element of human nature that, in many respects must be considered as distinct from the disposition to help. It is true that they both originate in the primitive faculty of benevolence, but this faculty seems to have these two closely related functions. The feverish and extravagant desire for wealth that the indolent pauper experiences originates in the same faculty as the thrift and honest effort of the industrious man, and yet these two products are not equally meritorious. Pity in its ultimate analysis is doubtless selfish. It is the pain that we experience on witnessing pain in others. Of course its chief tendency is in the direction of help, just as any pain leads us to remove the cause. But in the case of pity, the tendency does not always produce this result. Indeed, it often produces an opposite result, as when a lady through excess of pity flies from the scene of suffering. After the close of a certain battle, Florence Nightingale was called upon to witness the most terrible suffering in the hospitals, and to yield her tender ministrations to the shrieking and the dying. She had under her charge several young ladies as assistants. As they approached the couch of one mortally wounded, torn and mangled and writhing in the awful throes of the death agony, these young ladies covered their faces and fled from the place. The noble woman with a majesty almost divine, with no agitation, no weakening tears of pity, turned and rebuked them, and commanded them to return. Who of those ladies, think you, possessed most of that god-like love that dares to do and die for others? This act on the part of the young ladies, however, was not a selfish one in the popular sense of the word. They desired to aid the sufferers, they were there for that purpose. They were noble and generous, but they could not match the great soul of Florence Nightingale, and in their comparative weakness they gave way to pity. Neither was Florence Nightingale destitute of the power to pity; she was capable of deeper pity and more copious tears of sympathy than her assistants, but she crushed down her selfish pity, in order to give free scope to the grander sentiment of help. She knew that pity's tears could not heal those awful, gaping wounds, and that the hour demanded a higher ministration than tender words of sympathy.

But not alone in such an hour does the grandeur of human love display itself. The principle of benevolence is represented by two classes, the pitiers and the helpers. The pitiers are represented by the sentimentalists, who speak in touching generalities about the sufferings of humanity; the helpers, by the asylums and homes, the public and private charities of the land. One class is represented by words and tears, the other by the wordless energy that feeds, clothes and protects. One orphans' asylum is worth more than all the tears of pity ever shed. The grandest ministration is that which gives with a heart too noble to express its own pain. The divinest love is that which builds its own monument, of brick and mortar, with dry eyes and lion heart.

But how shall the homeless orphan profit by what we have said on the subject of home and its advantages? Surely, if he have no home, there can be no relations between himself and that institution except negative relations. The first thing to do, then, is to seek some place where he can eat and sleep, and this place he should call home, even though it have no other characteristic of home than that it affords him a secluded place in which to eat his crust, and a protection from the dew and rain at night. He should never change his quarters unless he can change them for the better. This rule should be observed as far as circumstances will permit. Perhaps the poor reader into whose hands this book may chance to fall may not understand the force of this advice. But when he subjects it to the light even of that rude philosophy of life which he has developed upon the street, we trust it will appear plain to him. He should call the place where he eats and sleeps home, in order that his heart may not lose that sacred word from its vocabulary. He should persist in eating his meals and spending his nights in this one place, in order that he may not lose that divinely born home instinct in which the institution of home has originated. If you are a bootblack upon the street, with no parents and no home that you can call your own, you must surely have some place in which you sleep at night. This you can call home, and it will soon come to be in some sense a home to you. And if, by blacking boots, you can earn a living, you can without doubt earn a little besides, and with the saved nickels and dimes, that nobody supposes you possess, you can buy good clothes, and thus appear to better advantage on the street and in that society in which you move: In this world of unjust discriminations, fine vestments are often mistaken for hearts, while real hearts wrapt up in rags are often carelessly thrown away. So if you have a good heart it is well to wrap it in as fine a piece of cloth as you can afford.

There are few orphan boys or girls who cannot obtain good situations, either in the city or in the country, where they may be clothed and fed, and be allowed to attend school, and to pay for such guardianship with moderate labor, in the same condition as the children of the household.

It is no disgrace to be sent to an "orphans' home." Of course such a home cannot be a perfect home, for it lacks the elements of "the fireside" and parental love. But it has enough of the essential elements to entitle it to the name of home. If the semi-public life which is inevitable is displeasing to the unfortunate one, let him remember that in all institutions of the kind the merits and demerits of the inmates are considered, and those who have proved themselves most worthy are the first who are permitted to avail themselves of the situations in private families that are constantly presenting themselves. Officers are employed expressly to search out such situations. And an orphans' home may be regarded as a kind of temporary accommodation where orphans are provided for until their applications for situations are successful. We believe that the active, benevolent element of society, if properly reminded of its duty, is capable of absorbing the entire element of the world's orphaned ones.

"Only a newsboy, under the light
Of the lamp-post, plying his trade in vain:
Men are too busy to stop to-night,
Hurrying home through the sleet and rain.
Never since dark a paper sold;
Where shall he sleep, or how be fed?
He thinks, as he shivers there in the cold,
While happy children are safe abed.

"Is it strange if he turns about
With angry words, then comes to blows,
When his little neighbor, just sold out,
Tossing his pennies, past him goes?
'Stop!'—some one looks at him, sweet and mild,
And the voice that speaks is a tender one:
'You should not strike such a little child,
And you should not use such words, my son!'

"Is it his anger or his fears
That have hushed his voice and stopped his arm?
'Don't tremble,' these are the words he hears;
'Do you think that I would do you harm?'
'It isn't that,' and the hand drops down;
'I wouldn't care for kicks and blows;
But nobody ever called me son,
Because I'm nobody's child, I s'pose.'

"O men! as ye careless pass along,
Remember the love that has cared for you;
And blush for the awful shame and wrong
Of a world where such a thing could be true!
Think what the child at your knee had been
If thus on life's lonely billows tossed;
And who shall bear the weight of the sin,
If one of these 'little ones' be lost!"

HOMES OF THE POOR.

HISTORY records no great reforms, no rare efforts of philanthropy and love, whose actors have not felt the restraint of at least moderate want. Out from the ten thousand unpainted cottages that dot the land have stalked forth the great thoughts and the mighty deeds.

Luxury is the concave lens which disperses the rays of human energy, while poverty is the convex lens which causes them to converge, often bringing them to a powerful focus, and like the mirrors of Archimedes burning the fleets of the enemy.

Let no young man despair because he is poor. As well might the engine despair because the iron bands confine the restless energy of the steam. The engineer computes the resistance to physical force in what he terms foot-pounds. So poverty is a term that simply designates the resistance to the divine energies of a human soul. There are two indispensable conditions to the development of power in the engine; first the application of heat, and second the outward resistance to confine the force generated. So in the soul these same two conditions must exist;

the heat of a persistent volition, of a dauntless purpose, must be applied, and also the outward resistance of circumstances to confine and concentrate the power thus generated.

The gigantic power of the engine is obtained by confining those restless particles of steam which are struggling for release, and which, if they do not soon obtain it, will burst their iron bands asunder.

How impotent is the most terrific heat if the steam which it generates have no resistance to overcome. Just so with the most gigantic volition and the grandest purpose, if they are not hedged about by some awful resistance. If they have no fetters, either seen or unseen, in some way proportionate to their own strength, they will be dissipated as harmlessly as the vapor which rises at its leisure from the open boiler.

By poverty we do not mean the condition of those who moan with hunger and shiver with cold, but more particularly the condition of that great class whose desires and needs are separated from their gratification by the breadth of a wearying effort. In this sense we attach to the word the significance of a natural law, obviously designed and ordained by the Creator to meet the necessary conditions of human development.

If we would trace the proudest achievement of human genius to its origin, we must follow it back through winding pathways, from the brilliant hall, from the deafening thunder of human applause, to the silent, dim-lighted cottage of poverty. If the gratification of every want lay within the leisure grasp of that want, the very atmosphere of human society would become pestilential with stagnation. Go to the sunny tropics where nature with curious caprice empties her lap of spoils in the presence of men, and behold the weakness, the languor, and the inanity. Humanity there has just activity enough to be vicious. Where must we go to hear the hum of spindles, to feel beneath our feet the jar of rushing trains, and to see the smoky signals of human industry waving over a thousand hills? We must go where winter, the genius of poverty, throws up his icy bulwark between the wants of man and their gratification.

Force and resistance constitute the eternal polarity of existence. The one cannot exist without the other, any more than there can be boreal magnetism without austral; any more than there can be action without reaction.

In order for force, either physical or mental, to be cumulative the resistance must exceed the force so as to elicit the increase. Hence the mission of poverty.

Not only is poverty necessary to develop human nature and make its forces accumulative, but it is necessary to prevent the extravagant and irregular expenditure of those forces. It may be that human nature absolutely perfect would be self-regulating, even when all its desires could be gratified without laborious effort; yet under present conditions it certainly requires resistance in certain directions. The son of affluence soon runs the rounds of all possible pleasures, and then life becomes insipid. We enjoy life's blessings just in proportion to their variety and the effort that they cost. All pleasures are enhanced by preliminary effort. This fact explains the adage that "stolen fruit is always sweetest." It is because of the exciting effort which accompanies the unlawful procuring of it. That fruit, however, which is bought with honest labor should be sweetest, while the most insipid is that which lies within the reach of the appetite without the aid of labor. When will men learn that ease and rest and luxury are misnomers? It is the subtile and divine alchemy of sweat which transforms sorrow and languor into joy and peace.

Homes of the poor! Sacred shrines of earth where the altar fires of genius have been lighted. May the world forever be blessed with moderate want. The human mind is never whole till it has suffered, and it is better that the angel of poverty should mete out the required suffering in the form of a perpetual restraint, than that it should burst like the thunder storm from the azure sky of luxury, darkening with its baleful clouds the sun of life. The home of the poor is the only home in which disinterested love can dwell, for the pride that inevitably accompanies wealth is in its very nature selfish, and thus usurps a place in the mind that might be occupied by a nobler sentiment. Nearly all the common interest there is in the rich family is simply the pride that they take in each other's display, and this feeling usually engrosses most of the time and energy of the rich. That pride which delights in the family wardrobe and equipage is simply the pride of the several individuals aggregated, and as such pride is the excuse of selfishness it is, of course, incompatible with true affection; and if affection among the members of the family cannot exist with this pride of wealth, surely affection for mankind cannot. This fact is what closes the doors of human sympathy against the rich man, and compels him to live alone in his glory. Hence it is that philanthropic movements and institutions almost always originate among the poorer classes.

The home of the poor man does not necessarily mean a home of suffering, save in that humiliation and restraint to which it is necessary for all souls to be subjected in order to develop. The poor man's home need not be devoid of a certain degree of luxury. Beautiful pictures and works of art can no longer be monopolized by the rich, for the busy brain of invention has brought them within the reach of all. The price of ten cents worth of tobacco smoke saved each day for fifteen or twenty days will purchase a fine book. The very poorest of men find no difficulty in purchasing this amount of tobacco smoke each day. Only think how many days there are in a lifetime. Three hundred and thirteen working days in a year at ten cents a day would give $31.30. Twenty years would give $626.00, which would purchase at least five hundred volumes, a library of which most men should be proud. For five hundred volumes of the best books comprise nearly all there is of pre-eminent worth in literature. What an inspiring thought for a poor boy! the gist of all literature purchased with the little self denial that it costs to refrain from making bacon of one's self.

Young man! promise us that as soon as you have read this chapter, you will begin to lay up ten cents a day, and if you will smoke cigars, then be a little more economical in other things, and lay up at least five cents. You have your life before you, and it would soon be so natural for you to lay by the small amount daily, that you would drop it from habit into your private treasury almost unconsciously. Try it, and reap the harvest.

"He sat all alone in his dark little room,
His fingers aweary with work at the loom,
His eyes seeing not the fine threads, for the tears,
As he carefully counted the months and the years
He had been a poor weaver.

"Not a traveler went on the dusty highway,
But he thought, 'He has nothing to do but be gay;'
No matter how burdened or bent he might be,
The weaver believed him more happy than he,
And sighed at his weaving.

"He saw not the roses so sweet and so red
That looked through his window; he thought to be dead
And carried away from his dark little room,
Wrapt up in the linen he had in his loom,
Were better than weaving.

"Just then a white angel came out of the skies,
And shut up his senses, and sealed up his eyes,
And bore him away from the work at his loom
In a vision, and left him alone by the tomb
Of his dear little daughter.

"'My darling!' he cries, 'what a blessing was mine!
How I sinned, having you, against goodness divine!
Awake! O my lost one, my sweet one, awake!
And I never, as long as I live, for your sake,
Will sigh at my weaving!'

"The sunset was gilding his low little room
When the weaver awoke from his dream at the loom,
And close at his knee saw a dear little head
Alight with long curls,—she was living, not dead,—
His pride and his treasure.

"He winds the fine thread on his shuttle anew,
—At thought of his blessing 'twas easy to do,—
And sings as he weaves, for the joy in his breast,
Peace cometh of striving, and labor is rest:
Grown wise was the weaver."

HOMES OF THE RICH.

IT is the duty of the poor man to live within his income, but it is no less the duty of the rich man to make his expenditures proportionate to his income. People sometimes hold up their hands in holy horror when they read or hear that some millionaire has spent an enormous sum on his buildings, his wardrobe, or his garden; but they do not stop to think that he is thereby discharging a duty which he owes to society. He is redistributing the money that he has gathered. The great mass of the people must earn their daily bread by performing labor for others, but only the wealthy can hire people to labor for them. Hence those who possess wealth and will not spend it in being served, are the thieves and robbers of society. No wealthy man has any business to live in a cottage. There are poor people enough to live in cottages. It is his business to live in a palace, and to hire those to build it who live in cottages.

We have, perhaps, used the word *served* unadvisedly. We do not mean that the wealthy man discharges his obligation to society when he expends large sums to increase his personal comforts. He should make his wealth serve himself by first making it serve society in the promotion of legitimate business enterprise. Nor do we mean that he should expend upon his dwelling and for his own personal gratification more than can normally and lawfully minister to his comfort, convenience and æsthetic faculties.

And yet there is concealed in the very sentiment of extravagance to which wealth prompts, a kind of compensatory principle; one of nature's curative efforts, by which the economic interests of society are made self-acting. The world's wealth cannot be hoarded by individuals save for a brief period. All attempts to do so are thwarted by nature herself through instrumentalities so cunning and subtile as to deserve our applause. She has three processes by which she robs the rich man of his unjust acquisitions and gives back the spoils to the poor. The first process she employs when she deals with the *miserly* rich man, the man who has sacrificed all other sources of enjoyment to this one instinct of hoarding. She has so constituted him that this sacrifice, this concentration of all the energies of his being upon the one organ of acquisitiveness, necessarily results in the withdrawal of potency from the intellectual. The miser's intellect, accordingly, is never broad and comprehensive. He has, it is true, a certain degree or kind of intellectuality, but it is for the most part of the same nature as that of the fox. He makes a use of his intellectual powers that is below their normal function, and hence tends to weaken them. This is the process by which organs and functions become "abortive," as the evolutionists would term it. When the wings of the bird are used chiefly for a purpose below their natural function they are becoming "abortive." We see the result of this process in barn fowl that use their wings only to aid their running. Hence hens and turkeys are unable to fly any considerable distance without great exhaustion.

Just so the intellectual wings of the miser are becoming abortive, for he uses them not to fly with but simply to aid his running. In very many cases we have only to wait one generation to see this abortive process completed. The children of the miser rarely have the executive force to keep the lock upon the father's chest. Thus nature, by a process subtler than the necromancy of the Egyptian wizard, gives back to the world that which has been taken from it.

Nature makes use of her second method when dealing with the energetic, active, shrewd, and executive rich man, the accumulator rather than the hoarder. The two are in many respects opposite in their characteristics. The merchant, the manufacturer, and the railroad king show no tendency toward the abortive intellect. Indeed, their function is usually such as to develop great strength and activity of intellect. But the miser proper is one whose motto is, "a penny saved is a penny earned." His sole delight is in the consciousness of his possessions, and in counting and sorting his valuable papers. His money is all in bonds and mortgages, hence he lives in idleness and gloats over the self-accumulation of his wealth.

Now this second method which nature employs in her ceaseless effort at equalization is simply this: she has made human nature such (and consequently society, which is but an outgrowth of human nature,) that the individual want cannot be met except by a contribution to the general good. Wealth is simply potential gratification. But it cannot minister to the desires of him who holds it save as it yields a secondary ministration to the general interest, whose relation with it is the sole source of its potentiality. The natural wants and desires of man lie within comparatively narrow limits. Bacon wisely says, "The personal fruition in any man cannot reach to feel great riches." A very moderate income will meet all the personal wants and desires of man. He cannot want or desire anything outside the bounds of his nature. He desires food, but the quantity has a very obvious limit, and there must also be a comparatively moderate limit to its costliness. He desires raiment, but, even if his caprice demands golden garments, the inevitable limit is easily reached. All the potentiality, then, which his wealth possesses, beyond a small per cent., must redound to the general good in spite of him. The rich man is the smallest stockholder in his own wealth.

Two men were once conversing about John Jacob Astor's property. One was asked if he would be willing to take care of all those millions merely for his board and clothing. "No," he indignantly replied, "do you take me for a fool?" "Well," said the other, "that is all Mr. Astor himself gets for taking care of it; he's *found*, and that's all. The houses, the warehouses, the ships, the farms, which he counts by the hundred, and is often obliged to take care of, are for the accommodation of others." "But then he has the income, the rents of all this large property, five or six hundred thousand dollars per annum." "Yes, but he can do nothing with his income but build *more* houses and warehouses and ships, or loan money on mortgages for the convenience of others. He's *found*, and you can make nothing else out of it." The world ought not to complain so long as it gets ninety-nine per cent. of the rich man's income. If the rich man uses his wealth in building tenement houses to rent, he not only furnishes remunerative labor to the workmen who build them, but by his competition he lowers rent and thus confers a general blessing. The same is true if he invests it in railroads, for the more railroads the more competition, and hence the lower the rate of transportation. There is but one thing he can do with his money that will not yield the general good a much larger contribution than himself. He can lock it up in his own vault. But in that case it not only yields himself nothing, but nature will make use of her first method and will take the money herself and leave his children or grandchildren penniless.

Nature's third method is a modification of her first. She uses it in her dealings with the *children* of the active rich man. It is simply that law of which we have already spoken in our chapter on "Homes of the Poor," by which restraint upon desire develops executive power. In the children of the rich we see, perhaps, little if any tendency to the abortive intellect, but the abortive tendency is chiefly or wholly confined to the executive powers. There is much difference between earning a dollar, and asking papa for it. The boy who toils all day for a dollar and brings it home at night, hungry and tired, not only knows the value of that dollar, but by such a practice he is developing in his soul a power of action that will enable it to laugh at every obstacle that earth can offer. Take the wealth from the children of the rich and they become objects of charity. This is especially true concerning the daughters of the rich. Little *pretty* things! what can they do? What are their lives worth to their kind? One good, noble factory girl, who has earned her daily bread amid the roar of machinery, who knows what it is to "breathe the factory smoke of torment from the fuel of human lives," and on whose heart is stamped, with the die of agony, the value of a penny, is capable of yielding a higher ministration to the world than a thousand of the pulpy daughters of luxury and ease. God bless the toiling factory girls! And may the time shortly come when Social Science shall solve the great problems of hunger, and cold, and want, and shall release them from their menial thrall, and place in their hands the golden key to the secret of a nobler life.

We would not be quoted by the poor in justification of their poverty. Poverty is unnatural and undesirable to all, and there is little excuse for most people to remain in its fetters, making due allowance, however, for exceptional cases. Poverty, like temptation and sin, yields its ministry only in the process of being overcome. The tribute we have paid to poverty in the preceding chapter would be almost as applicable had our theme been temptation, yet we would hardly advocate exposing ourselves needlessly to temptation for the sake of its *possible* ministry.

All normal action is disciplinary, for every possible gratification implies an aggressive movement. The eternal warfare between want and satisfaction is a natural warfare, and one which cannot cease till the army of creation shall give the signal of surrender. And he who refuses to engage in this warfare is a traitorous deserter, and deserves the deserter's fate. He who is contented with poverty, and seeks not to subdue it, must be reckoned with this class; he has mutinied against the generalship of his Maker.

Wealth, then, if it be the representative and co-relative of service done to mankind, so far from being an evil or a necessary accompaniment of moral demerit, is a badge of honor. It is the war record which shows how far one has triumphed over the divinely appointed opposition to his progress; and in this sense may even justly be compared with the moral virtues, which are the spirit's war record, and show how far it has triumphed, in the spiritual warfare, over the forces of temptation and evil. Wealth is an evil only when it is allowed to release its owner from honorable and worthy labor. No possible condition of life can release one who is physically and mentally able, from the moral obligation to toil.

But suppose one inherits a million. Shall he toil for his daily bread? No! not for his daily bread, but in behalf of mankind. We have but a secondary claim upon our own powers. Wealth augments our natural endowments. Two men with equal talents, the one poor and the other rich, possess very unequal power for doing good. So that the man who inherits a million should begin life as though he were penniless. We do not mean, of course, that he should chop wood or learn the blacksmith's trade. But that he should regard the million simply as a re-enforcement of his faculties. He is by so much, a more talented man, or rather his natural talents are supplemented by that which virtually makes them more powerful.

The rich in the majority of cases violate the laws of the home life, from the fact that they allow their wealth to release them from toil, the only thing that can render the "earth-life worth living." Indolence will render every possible joy insipid.

We have said, in the early part of this chapter, that those who possess wealth and will not spend it in being served are the thieves and robbers of society. But that service should be simply for the purpose of releasing them from a lower duty in order that they may perform a higher duty which their wealth enables them to fulfill. Hence, if the wife and daughter will not engage in some form of service to their kind, they have no moral right to hire a servant to serve their food for them. Indeed, they have no moral right to the food itself. Labor is a natural ordinance, and riches cannot release one from the obligation to a universal law. It is as binding upon the millionaire as upon the pauper, and he who seeks to evade this law is a criminal according to the statutes of the universe.

Let every rich man's daughter engage in some regular and useful vocation; and thus bless herself by the labor, and mankind with the product. Not that we would impose upon her, simply because she is wealthy, the somber duties of a nun. But we would have her labor daily in order that she may fulfill the mission of her life, in order that she may develop in herself and entail upon the coming generation that which labor alone can develop. The wife who does not, at least, exercise a general supervision over her own household affairs is a drone in society.

There is, however, no objection to the employment of

domestic servants, provided it be necessary; but that law of the home life which demands seclusion, privacy, and personal management of one's own affairs, releases the rich from any obligation to furnish employment in this way, and, all things considered, renders it far better, both for themselves and for mankind, that under ordinary circumstances they should not do so. In very many rich families the position of servant is but little better than that of a slave, so that the employment which such rich families furnish to the poor is of slight account. And in those families where the servant is treated approximately as an equal, she usually, either through the ignorance or indolence of the wife, has the whole management of affairs, which makes the home a kind of boarding-house or hotel, so that the home-life becomes semi-public. Yet if the wife will treat her servant as her equal, and at the same time exercise a general supervision over her own household, both these evils may be obviated. And if the employment of a servant will thus afford the wife leisure to engage in some higher service to her kind, it is surely her duty to employ one. But she should consider herself as truly a servant as the one she employs, only in a higher capacity, for when wealth makes one anything but a servant of humanity, it makes him a robber and a thief.

The only absolutely selfish motive that the highest morality permits in the accumulation of wealth, is the normal desire for independence in all the relations of life;

and if beyond this, nature has endowed one with a special capacity for acquiring wealth, the product of that capacity, like the product of every other form of genius, is mankind's and not his.

The home of the rich man should represent as much wealth as, thus expended, will have a tendency to increase the comfort and convenience of his family. Beyond this, however, he has no moral right to lavish wealth upon his home for the mere gratification of his vanity. He should invest it in some honorable and useful industry, where it will yield humanity a higher rate of interest than that of mere taxation.

Burns has given us the licenses of wealth in the following lines:

"But gather gear by every wile
That's justified by honor;
Not for to hide it in a hedge,
Nor for a train attendant,
But for the glorious privilege
Of being independent."

THE OLD-FASHIONED HOME.

FASHION holds a legitimate place in human affairs. It is based in a constitutional peculiarity of human nature, which is a sufficient guarantee that it has a right to be. It is only the abuse of fashion that makes it repugnant to the better instincts of man. When the proper definition of fashion is presented to the mind it meets with an instinctive approval.

We would define true fashion as the uniformity that results from the conservation of truth and beauty. That which is true and beautiful is naturally conserved, while that which is false and ugly contains the seeds of its own dissolution. This necessary uniformity resulting from a constant law is natural fashion.

The fashion of the world, for the most part, is artificial and false. It is simply a temporary uniformity resulting from caprice. There are two elements that enter into the composition of the fashion sentiment, and the virtue or vice of the fashion is determined by the proportion of these elements. First, a love of the beautiful and true, and second, a love of novelty. Any given fashion is capricious, short-lived, and generally absurd, just in proportion as the latter element predominates over the former.

There is no more appropriate sphere for the display of legitimate fashion than the home world, which, perhaps, in part accounts for the fact that in all ages architecture has stood foremost among the arts. And, perhaps, it is in this field that fashion has maintained itself purest from the adulterations of caprice. Few houses or buildings in the construction of which there is any pretense to architectural skill, exhibit a serious violation of natural and wholesome taste. Unlike the varying patterns of ladies' bonnets and gentlemen's coats, which vibrate from extreme to extreme, the architectural ideal seems to recognize certain fundamental and unchanging laws of taste and harmony.

It is true that there have been marked changes in architecture. It has grown with the race from the rude structure of the savage to the imposing palace of the nineteenth century.

But in every period there has been an evident tendency to abide perpetually by principles, as fast as men have been able to develop them.

Each decade witnesses modifications in the details of

architectural adornment, but this does not touch the fact of permanence in the architectural ideal.

It is, in part, such permanence that makes the old-fashioned houses seem beautiful to us, for these houses, with their well-sweeps, huge chimneys, and naked gables violate no essential law of beauty.

To be beautiful and tasteful a thing must violate no law of its relations. So essential is this that some have defined beauty as "superior fitness." According to this definition a thing may be beautiful to-day and otherwise to-morrow. When it loses its fitness it loses its beauty. But no argument of fitness or unfitness can take away the beauty from the old-fashioned fire-place with its cheerful flames, which like a band of gold-capped spirits, half in earnest, half in jest, chase each other up the broad chimney. No person of sensitive mind can sit without emotion beside those century-old hearthstones and watch upon a stormy night "the great fires up the chimney roar."

We seem to see reflected from the ever changing golden sheen of the blaze the images of merry boys and girls at play, or with their slates and pencils solving by the flickering light the problems assigned them by the old schoolmaster who long ago dismissed the school for the last time. Oh! the visions that we see in the fire, visions of the forgotten long ago, of joys and sorrows strangely blent; visions of romping boyhood and laughing girlhood, visions of love's first dream, of eyes that caught the broken story from trembling lips that could not speak it; visions of the bridal queen crowned with coronet of maiden blushes; visions of life's stern battle; visions of sorrow's first shadow, of red-eyed grief and midnight watchings; visions of all life's checkered pathway, as it winds through flowery fields or over pain's hot desert sands, through the fragrant spice groves of joy or over sorrow's mountain crags.

We would not proclaim ourselves "fogies"; far from it. We are enthusiasts in every conceivable species of human reform, and yet we are compelled to consider the old-fashioned home as the typical representative of the natural institution of home. We speak now, not so much with reference to the mere outward difference of architectural designs, etc., which superficially distinguishes the old from the new-fashioned home, but more particularly with reference to those inner and vital differences that distinguish the two modes of home life.

It is painful to know that the modern home life differs from the old-fashioned chiefly in its departure from the standard of nature.

There is hardly a feature of the modern home that does not proclaim itself to the most casual observer a defiant breach of natural law. Let us imagine ourselves members of the board of health, and in that capacity let us inspect a typical modern home. A servant responds to the ringing of the bell and informs us that "Mrs. —— is not in," meaning simply that she has not yet—at ten o'clock—risen. This is simply a patent process of elongation, to which the truth is subjected to meet the demands of fashionable society. Of course it is not at all *injurious* to truth. When we make known our official business we are admitted, and the servant shows us to the kitchen, where we learn nothing in particular except the most approved process of shortening human life, and of destroying the teeth, morals, etc., of the next generation. We next enter the sitting-room. We are almost nauseated by the sickening odor of coal gas that is fast escaping through the open door of the coal stove while the back damper is closed. The servant assures us, however, that it is nothing unusual, and declares she "can't smell a thing." We go to the window and try to raise it unobserved, but to no purpose. There are two windows, and the outside one doesn't "shove up." The house, of course, has all the modern improvement, including that beautiful invention of double windows, which has perhaps lengthened the "consumption column" in the statistics of human mortality more than any other invention of man. "There is a register in the chimney, but Mrs. —— says the room doesn't heat up so well when it is open, so we keep it closed all the time."

Do the children frequently have colds with sick headache? "O, and to be shure they do most all the time, but Mrs. —— thinks it is because the house isn't war-rm enough, and shure it looks rasonable. She's put a coal stove in their slapin' room." As we find it impossible to answer Bridget's argument, we will proceed to inspect the parlor. As we enter we shudder with a sensation of dampness. Bridget draws aside the curtain, and raising the window a few inches turns the slats of one blind on the north side. "Mrs. —— says we mustn't let the light shine in the parlor, because it fades the car-rpet. There ain't been no drop o' light in the room afore since six months ago."

Let us leave the parlor in its darkened beauty and go to the children's sleeping room, where the coal stove has been set up to keep the little creatures from "catching cold." We find a room nine feet by twelve with one window. Of course the door must be kept closed during the night that the coal stove may be effectual in preventing the children from taking cold. Economy dictates that it isn't necessary that the coal stove should do it all, so a double window is put on and cotton is tucked in around the joints; anything to keep the "cold air out."

One of the most ingenious and economical inventions of modern times is the process of warming our dwellings with our own breath. Air that has been breathed once or twice is apt to be a little unwholesome; but then it saves coal, and so we can afford to have sick headaches, and to rise in the morning with heavy, dull spirits, with furred tongues and yellow skins.

We have not overdrawn our picture of the modern home. Nor have we selected one of the fashionable homes of the rich; for these, indeed, in many respects, approach the old-fashioned home. They generally have more spacious sleeping rooms, and the greater size of such houses secures better ventilation throughout. It is the average home of the great middle class that we have described, though, perhaps, we have made a freer use of hyperbole than is consistent with ordinary descriptive writing. We do not hesitate to express our conviction that the unhygienic principles involved in the construction and management of the modern home are the prime causes of consumption and dyspepsia, those two fell scourges to the human family, from which probably a far greater number perish than from the stereotyped curses of "war, pestilence, and famine."

If society has a moral right to compel men to train themselves in the use of sword and musket, in order that they may be able to meet and repel the onslaughts of war and conquest, and thus save their children from bondage and disgrace, why has it not also a right to compel them to so train and govern their bodies hygienically as to repel the fiercer onslaught of foul disease, and thus save their children from the darker bondage of inherited weakness and premature death? There may be a shade of the ludicrous in our claim, but we believe that society has the same moral right to prohibit, in the construction of all new dwellings, the nine by twelve "bed room" that it has to prohibit the grog-shop; the same right to enforce ventilation and all the general laws of hygiene in our private dwellings, that it has to make laws for the prevention of suicide and infanticides.

Such an exercise of civil authority would violate no natural right of man. Man belongs not to himself, but to the world. The wheel is not its own but the engine's. We possess but one natural right vouchsafed to us by our Maker, the right to make the most of ourselves, and all sub-divisions of this one great right are inseparably connected with corresponding duties. Indeed, one can have no natural right to perform a single act which it is not his duty to perform. This may not at first receive the ready credence of the general reader, especially of the American who has been accustomed to give such extravagant definitions to the word liberty. But upon careful thought we trust that all will assent to its truth. Probably no human being is able at any time to tell just what kind or extent of action is allowed by his natural right, or demanded by this natural duty. We surely have a natural right to eat just that quantity of food that will meet the requirements of our physical nature, no more, no less, and no one would contend that the verdict of duty, if the exact bounds could be ascertained, would not be precisely the same.

This illustration is no more obvious than that which it is intended to illustrate, viz., the application of this principle to every function and relation of life. When one ceases to act in accordance with this principle, and in so doing falls below the aggregate intelligence of society, he becomes a proper subject for civil guardianship and governmental regulation. Few question the right of society to prevent a man from taking into his stomach poison liquid in the form of alcohol, but why should they question its right to prevent him from taking into his lungs poison gas in the form of air that has been robbed of its oxygen and charged with carbonic acid by the vital demands of half a dozen persons in a tight, unventilated room, its atmosphere, perhaps, still further vitiated by the liberal contributions of a kerosene lamp or two? Are fluids and gases so different in their nature that society has a moral right to prohibit the use of the poison fluid of the grog-shop, while it has no right to prohibit the free use of the deadly gas of the small, unventilated sleeping-room?

Our condemnation of the unhygienic features of the modern home may seem somewhat strange, but while we acknowledge the views to be radical and the language strong, we are sure they do no injustice to our convictions.

While we believe emphatically in all the civilizing forces; while we would bid God-speed to every useful invention; and while our faith in man's progression and ultimate achievements amounts almost to fanaticism,—we must still contend that the modern home in most of its features is a retrogression and not an advancement.

Yet this is not necessary. Nor is it due to the refinement of the modern home. It is not attributable to the piano and the cooking range, to the fine pictures, the decorations, the drapery and the beauty, but to the unhygienic influences, the carbonic acid and the enervating luxury. The people of America need entertain no fears from the frequent ebullitions of political passion. They are the necessary accompaniments of self-government. But on the garnished walls of ten thousand private houses there appears, to him who can read it, a handwriting that hints at possible doom. In the dim, uncertain shadows of the hour a finger points to the deserted banquet halls of Nineveh and Babylon and Persia, and in our languid luxury there is a sickening suggestion of the feast-couch, Rome's death-bed. The same spell of public and private effeminacy seems to be settling over us that has prefaced the doom of every perished empire whose pathetic wrecks now strew the shores of time. Physical weakness, especially of women, in every age has been the almost invariable prognostic of national downfall, and who will deny that there are indications in this direction that may justly excite alarm? We have no sympathy with those mournful, dyspeptic alarmists who are forever sounding the signal of "trouble ahead," for the mere pleasure of listening to the music of their own blast. And yet we believe there are forces at work in American society that should cause thoughtful men and women seriously to reflect. We have not criticised the modern home thus severely *because* it is a modern home. We condemn only those evil features that constitute no necessary part of the home.

The more modern the home the better. The world's latest thought is its best, and we can truly say from our heart, God bless the noble inventors of our land who are lifting the burden of drudgery from the shoulders of women. We are glad that the old-fashioned loom has been used for kindling wood. We are glad that spinning no longer constitutes the chief occupation of our girls; and yet if this release from the bondage of labor results only in idleness, as it does in too many homes, better a thousand times that the hum of the spinning-wheel should again be heard!

If the modern home with its many true improvements would conserve the naturalness of the old-fashioned home, we should have one that would be typical of all that hope points to in the great hereafter, but until it does this we must regard the old-fashioned home of our fathers as the best and truest type of that which we hope awaits us.

"Isolated, bleak, and dreary, stands the old house on the hill.
Rooms that rang with mirth and music now are empty, silent, still.
Desolation reigns supremely, and the old house bare and lone
Stands with many a broken window, through which cheerful lights once shone;
Wrapped in dust and hung with cobwebs, how each empty, low-ceiled room
Seemingly resents in echoes every loudly spoken tone.
Houses old and bare and lonely, thickly o'er this land of ours,
Stand, like long-forgotten headstones, 'midst their tangled growth of flowers.

* * * * * * * * * * * * * * * *

"Never then forsake the roof-tree, from its shelter do not roam;
Like a sacred shrine of incense, keep the altar fires of home.
For of all the piteous ruins, not one comes so near my heart
As some old deserted homestead where once life and love had part."

OUR LAST FAREWELL OF HOME.

ON the programme of every human life is written "final scene"—monitory of the hurried farewell, the choking sob, and the parting forever. No matter how bright has been the rainbow of youth's promise, no matter how fair and serene life's course has been, the end of that life shall be sobs and tears. But one is never called from his earthly home until he is willing to leave it. He is persuaded, instead of compelled to seek another home. We refer, of course, to the process of a natural death, resulting simply from old age. No provision has been made to lighten the agonies of suicide, or an untimely death. The principle, however, which we shall mention, seems even in these cases to act to a certain extent, but it is only during the actual process of death. It does not lessen that instinctive tenacity to life that makes the very thought of death a source of sorrow.

It has been said that one may live as long as he chooses, and as a rule this is true, for as a rule one may, by temperance and moderation, die a natural death; that is, by the gradual decay of all the powers. When this is the case the instinct of life is one of the first to die. Hence when one cannot live any longer, he will not choose to live. This is the means by which God persuades us to leave our earthly home. He convinces us and makes us feel that it would be better for us to leave the home that no longer has any charm for us. He takes away the instinctive love of life and transfers the home love.

We have said that the love of life is one of the first instincts to die. It would, doubtless, be the first were it not for the fact that nature preserves it as long as it can be of any use to us. It is this same instinct that gives the power to resist death, and to live amid influences that tend to destroy life. Without this we could not live an hour. Now it would not be wise in nature to allow this instinct to die so long as we are capable of living any longer. But no sooner has this stage been passed than all dread of death at once ceases, and the person softly sinks into the arms of death as the child sinks into slumber.

The death of this instinct is not instantaneous, for it is subject to the same law of decay as the other powers. But its death always precedes that of the general system.

The testimony of the old will confirm this doctrine, that the love of life and the fear of death gradually vanish as they approach life's goal. The poet has said, "There is a beauty in woman's decay." But this beauty of decay is not confined to woman. There is a beauty in the decay of humanity. The law of beauty is the law of completeness. It is embodied in the principle of the circle. All forms of beauty may be reduced to this principle. Hence old age must be the very symbol and embodiment of beauty, for is it not the typical example of completeness? It represents the completion of a life's experience. It is the triumphant period in which the arcs of the great circle are closing with a divine beauty that appeals not to the eye, but to the soul. It must be felt by the spirit that can perceive a beauty in the universal plan.

We are so constituted that in any given period of our lives we are best satisfied with the conditions and circumstances that naturally surround us at that period. The youth wishes that he might always be a youth, the young man wishes that he might always be twenty-five. The mature man thinks he would like to stop just where he is, and forever remain at the height and glory of his powers, but the old man thinks the best time to stop is when the labor of life is done and he can sit down and enjoy rest. It is the old man alone whose wish is granted. He is permitted to rest, and as he has nothing to do but rest and feast his soul on divine beauty, he is not particular whether he takes that rest and drinks in that beauty while gazing at the sunset of this life or the sunrise of the next.

Contentment is the natural condition of the human mind. Discontent is an abnormal condition, and the tendency to be satisfied with present conditions and circumstances descends into the minuter relations of life. In summer we feel that we could not possibly endure the winter, but when the winter comes there comes with it new pleasures and delights which we would not exchange for those of the summer. Even on a beautiful morning we are apt to wish it would always remain morning, and when enjoying ourselves at some evening entertainment we think the evening the most delightful part of the day.

This principle in our nature manifests itself still more forcibly in old age. When we reach that period we are in that condition spiritually as well as physically in which the only pleasures that we can enjoy, or that we desire to be able to enjoy, are just those which are given us.

In the process of death we see that the lowest powers die first. If the face of the dying be watched there will be seen to play over it, in regular succession, the expression of the various faculties in the order of their rank. The last to die are the moral and religious.

These leave their divine impress upon the countenance, hence the calm, holy and serene look so often seen upon the faces of the dead.

The terror of death recedes just as fast as we approach it, and when we reach the last stage of decay the dark river is found to be illumined by the mirrored stars of faith.

There are joys in age which youth cannot know. They

come not as miserable compensations for infirmity, but they are the ones which approach nearest to perfection. They come as a free gift; those of youth and manhood must be won by toil. The youth finds no joy in rest nor in meditation, for his history is unwritten and he has nothing to meditate upon. A feverish ambition burns in the brain of the young man, for he feels that he has everything to accomplish in a few short years, and whatever joy he receives he must receive it discounted at the bank of toil.

Youth and manhood have their joys, pure and deep and holy. Joy is the only natural and normal condition of every human soul through every hour of its being from the cradle to eternity, and yet we must draw this wide distinction between the joys of youth and those of age. The former have in them the element of exhaustion, and are allied to those of intoxication, while the latter seem in their very nature strength-giving. Age derives no mean joy from tracing through their complex evolutions the great events of human history. It is to age alone that these great events are visible from their inception to their completion. Where age beholds beauty, order and divinity, youth beholds but fragments, chaos and chance. The old man derives a conviction from his long experience and observation that "there's a divinity that shapes our ends." He sees, as youth cannot see, the beauty and significance of a life completed. To him death is but the crowning act in life's great drama, the opening of a golden gate at the end of life's narrow lane.

Life and death are counterparts of each other. There are those, however, who believe that physical death came to man as a punishment for sin, and that had it not been for sin, all mankind would have lived eternally upon the earth. But the law that dooms man to physical death is the same which dooms the animalcule. If the coral reefs were in process of formation when the first sin was committed it was because the corals were dying then. Did not death obtain among the finny tribes of the ocean, perhaps a single year would be sufficient to crowd the deep to overflowing; but if the animals were dying, then must not all which is subject to the organic law have died also? Man is as subject to the organic law as any other member of the animal kingdom. He eats and drinks and breathes and sleeps as they do. Some of these animals are not only made on the same general plan as man, but they possess every physical organ corresponding in position and action, and both animals and man owe their lives to the vital action in these organs.

Now can any one believe that the great process of vital action in man, of digestion and respiration, was governed by some other principle before he did wrong for the first time, and was afterwards changed? Of all the outgrown doctrines of dogmatic theology, this must be regarded as the most childish and unscientific. We must not be misled by creeds which are at variance with natural law. We must not regard death as a penal expedient. It can afford us no hope or consolation to regard it as such. Human death is as much an ordinance of nature as the fading of the rainbow or the withering of the rose. The doom of eternal change is written with a pen divine upon all that lives. We can regard death only as a voyage that separates us from those we love. We gaze upon a face while over it there falls a stillness deeper than slumber, and the last smile that reaches us from that receding spirit is like the waving of a kerchief far out at sea. The ship sinks beneath the horizon into the unknown beyond, and with sad steps we move away from the dark wharf, not knowing whence our friend has gone.

The doctrine which teaches that physical death is a punishment for sin, we believe, has done much to weaken the faith of mankind in the doctrine of immortality, by giving to it the air of superstition. A genuine outgrowth of man's nature cannot be at variance with the highest philosophy. Man is the highest specimen in the great cabinet of natural history, the chrysalis that holds a prophecy of higher environments.

We must look beyond the fact of death for hope. We must look to the analysis of that which suffers the change, and see if its nature and relations be such that death can doom it to oblivion.

In our next chapter we shall try to show that man's

nature itself holds the credentials of his immortality, that just as the nature of the lungs would prove the existence of air, so man's spiritual organization proves the existence of God and the fact of immortality.

But in this chapter we are considering only the midnight tragedy of death, in which the scenery is dark and the actors are cruel. We have reason to believe, however, that the curtain falls before the play is ended, for the last scene is too stupendous for the stage appliances of earth. The lights are too dull to represent the glory of that sublime tableau. Hence the cunning plot, that makes the curtain fall with a rush that extinguishes the lights and leaves the death-bed watchers frantic and bathed in tears —a wailing audience in a darkened theater.

"Lo! 'tis a gala night
Within the lonesome latter years!
An angel throng, bewinged, bedight
In veils, and drowned in tears,
Sit in a theater of hopes and fears,
While the orchestra breathes fitfully
The music of the spheres.

"Mimes, in the form of God on high,
Mutter and mumble low,
And hither and thither fly;
Mere puppets they, who come and go
At bidding of vast formless things
That shift the scenery to and fro,
Flapping from out their condor wings
Invisible woe!

"That motley drama! ah, be sure
It shall not be forgot!
With its Phantom chased for evermore,
By a crowd that seize it not,

Through a circle that ever returneth in
To the self-same spot;
And much of Madness, and more of Sin,
And Horror, the soul of the plot!

"But see, amid the mimic rout
A crawling shape intrude!
A blood-red thing that writhes from out
The scenic solitude!
It writhes!—it writhes!—with mortal pangs
The mimes become its food,
And the seraphs sob at vermin fangs
In human gore imbued.

"Out—out are the lights,—out all!
And over each quivering form,
The curtain, a funeral pall,
Comes down with the rush of a storm—
And the angels all pallid and wan,
Uprising, unveiling, affirm
That the play is the tragedy 'Man,'
And its hero, the Conqueror Worm."

HEAVEN OUR HOME.

WE have thought it expedient to consider this chapter wholly in the light of reason. And should the devout Christian feel that the coldness of its logic is inconsistent with the subject, we assure him that it is not because we are not in the fullest sympathy with the Christian ideal, but because we have purposely aimed to treat the subject from the standpoint of science.

This is why we have avoided all reference to Scriptural authority, even where such reference would seem peculiarly appropriate.

It is the skeptic who most requires to be convinced of the cardinal truths of religion. But with him Scriptural evidence has little weight, while he is usually proud of his scientific attainments. So we believe the thoughtful Christian will rejoice in the method we have chosen.

It is not our purpose in this chapter to attempt any description of that place or condition toward which the instinct of faith in all ages has pointed mankind. Our efforts will be simply to satisfy enquiring minds that the objective of that universal instinct through which humanity looks Godward and heavenward, is real and not a delusion. The great need of our age is a firm belief in the reality of man's religious nature. The most pernicious effects of modern skepticism are seen in its attempts to undermine this belief. Let mankind once be firmly convinced on scientific grounds that man is a religious being, that there is a real significance in his religious intuitions, that these intuitions spring from faculties that correspond to objective realities, and that his earthly home foreshadows an eternal home, and the question of creed will take care of itself.

However painful may be the fact, it cannot be denied that the startling interrogations of the present age mean something more than can be answered by the old time exhortation. The problem of human destiny is one that deepens with the evolutions of history. The hour has come when the great question must be discussed in prose instead of poetry. The awakened spirit of doubt to-day confronts religion with the awful questions: "Is there a God?" "Is there a heaven?" "Is it true that the earth-home is but a type, a working model of 'a home to be?'"

The answer to these questions must be accompanied by reasons that appeal to human logic, for in the flashing revelations of modern science, the eye of faith has seemed to grow dim.

And yet it is but the clamor of the immortal instinct

itself that gives rise to these questions, for the belief in God and immortality is as universal as that in obligation and human rights. Every human heart is the theater of this immortal instinct. We care not how the heart may be blinded with the self-deception of atheism,—and atheism is always and necessarily self-deception,—when the mask is torn off we find immortality written there.

We do not mean that the human heart has not also been the theater of doubt and fear. God seems to have ordained that in every department of life we should find the hand of truth and grasp it in the dark. Into the unanswering ear of the ages man has poured his wailing cry. Through the dark gorges he has climbed to the star-lit height whence a struggling beam has fallen upon the midnight of human history.

He has listened in the darkness
To the music of the spheres,
He has solved night's awful secret
Through the alchemy of fears.

From the dawn of time he has been trying to say father; and shall we say that his lisping annuls the infinite argument of instinct? Who would question the reality of the parental instinct when once he had heard the unsuccessful attempt of the little child to speak the honored title?

As the child instinctively questions his father concerning the great untried future of his life, so humanity with the same instinct pours its anxious yearnings into the ear of the universal father.

Shall man live beyond the grave? was the involuntary question of startled humanity in the shadow of the first death. That question was asked, not of the empty air, not of the silent wood, not in the forgetfulness of self-communing curiosity, but beneath the eternal stars, upon the waiting knee of faith, it was whispered into an unseen ear. "'If a man die, shall he live again?' is a question older than Job, newer than the latest grave." Formulated theology has entertained it as the fundamental problem, but cannot settle it. Science has grappled with it in vain. Above the proudest flights of reason, above the sweep of tube and lens, beyond the language of the spectroscope, where human eye has never rested, lies the mysterious realm through the silent gate of death.

The instinct of immortality was not born of any creed. The church cannot claim it as her offspring. It is the necessary outgrowth of the human organization. It was old when love for the first time bent over the couch of death and left its roses and kisses there. In spite of conflicting creeds and dogmas, the universal soul of man rebels against oblivion with an instinct that implicates nature. Either love and devotion and honor and heroism and genius are immortal, or nature, at whose hands we receive the unanswerable instinct, is false. The argument of instinct is in its very nature conclusive. It is of the same nature as that of sense.

This is an age peculiarly sensitive to the charge of superstition. Skepticism is rife among the masses, but this fact is itself fraught with a weighty meaning. "History repeats itself" is an adage, but its vast significance is understood and felt by few souls. The life of nature is but the ceaseless movement round a spiral, a circle with an ever increasing diameter. Through doubts and questions the world crept into the light of faith. One grand revolution of the divinely ordained process has been completed and doubts and questions now begin again, but this time farther from the center, on a grander scale.

These doubts and questionings will lead humanity to prouder heights and more glorious beatitudes when they shall have completed another revolution. The world's highest faith to-day began in the doubts and questions of brutal ignorance. What, then, shall be the issue of those which were born of the telescope and the laboratory? The proud champions of unbelief are doing a grand work. Every triumph of Ingersoll will in the great revolutions of God's design be found to be a sermon for the truth. He is fast defeating his own ends by hastening the world over its second desert of doubt.

Science will struggle on with glass and lens till it learns that love gives no lines in the spectroscope, that honor is without physical properties, and conscience is unaffected by the galvanic current.

Skeptical scientists object to the doctrine of immortality, because they cannot demonstrate it with their science.

We cannot scientifically demonstrate that we love our friends, but we know we love them. We cannot prove that beauty exists, yet do we not know that it exists? It may be that the scientist is unable to prove the existence of God, but every spirit knows that God is. No mathematical formula can prove the immortality of the soul, but the unformulated science of intuition assures it.

The conservatism of the universal mind retains the achievements of science, and will, by and by, use them in the demonstration of those very truths which now they are used to disprove.

Whether against the will of science, or in accordance with it, her grandest revelation is that the Christian religion is based in the organic constitution of man.

Every element of the soul, every faculty of the mind, has its mate in the form of a cosmical law. We possess the faculty of reason, and accordingly there exists the law of causation. We possess an instinctive love of music, a distinct and separate faculty of the mind, and there exists the law of harmony. Our mathematical instinct finds its counterpart in the eternal relations of time and space, number and quantity. There are just as many faculties of the mind, hence functions of the brain, as there are laws in the universe. No more, no less. There is no universal principle that has not its representative organ in the human brain. Hence the mental faculties and the natural laws are mutual keys. We believe that the evolutionists have unnecessarily weakened their own cause by a false definition of faculty. They would make the primitive faculties of the mind only so many habits. But the question arises, whence the first impulse that was the necessary antecedent to the first act of the faculty? Acts cannot become habitual nor hereditary until they have been performed at least once. But it requires a faculty to perform them for the first time. Hence the essential characteristic of the faculty,—the power to give impulses and the skill to perform,—must have existed prior to the influences of habit and heredity. The fact of manifestation through the instrumentality of a cerebral organ is the one and only unmistakable evidence of a primitive faculty.

Light is doubtless the natural agency by which the power of vision has been developed. Yet light could no more *originate* that germ of a distinct mental faculty that lies behind all phenomena of vision, and by which we translate those phenomena, than it could create the acorn whose *involved* potency it simply *evolves*. The eye existed potentially or the light could not have developed it. Man is *as he is* because of his environments, but we cannot say that *man is* because of his environments. We are *at least* driven to the assumption that matter held a human potency independent of all environment. That potency was the germs of human faculties, God-created and God-implanted. The magic finger of the sunbeam touched them and they awoke, and hammering upon the anvils of matter began to forge, from the materials of their environments, the only weapons they can use,—organs. Thus we see why an organ is the only infallible criterion and credential of a faculty. And we see the force of the foregoing reasoning when we remember that the human brain holds an organ whose function is Divine worship. Environments could not have created that organ. They could only have developed it. Its "living germ" lay back of all environments, as a divine prophecy, and proof of the reality of that to which it corresponded.

Since faculties are as their organs, and since organs are formed by the living principle, out of the material of their environments, it is not wonderful that man should be as his environments. Different environments would doubtless have caused a different mode of action in the faculty of Divine worship. Indeed, we have a proof of this. In the heathen mind this faculty gives an instinctive desire to find an objective in idols of wood and stone. Yet after all the essence of its action is Divine worship. And there is a limit beyond which environments cannot produce modifications. They may, however, thwart the effort of the faculty to forge a material organ, hence the significance of extinct species.

The atheist tells us there is no God, but science puts its finger on the God-organ, an organ whose function it is to produce that moral sensation known as reverence for God. It produces this effect invariably in savage and in civilized man. Has nature thus erred? Has she given us a God-organ, and no God to meet its demand? A stomach forever doomed to hunger in the presence of imaginary food; lungs strangling for air in the depths of a universal vacuum; an ear forever straining to catch the voice of harmony while nature shrinks beneath the wing of everlasting silence; an eye forever gazing into the blackness of universal night, while no wave of ether touches with its trembling fingers the bosom of the stars.

What should we say of such inconsistency in nature? And yet to give us a love of God, when there is no God to love, would be as base a falsehood. Every one believes in the eternal consistency of nature. The atheist has but transferred his worship from God to nature, and no argument can convince him that she would for once be inconsistent, but he must tell us why she gave us a God-organ and no God.

Every precept and every exhortation of the Christian religion is the recognition of some particular function of our being, and every prohibition is the recognition of its liability to perverted or diseased action.

The ethics of the Christian religion is based on the principle of right and wrong, and science lays its finger on the organ of conscientiousness. Prayer is as much an organic function of the soul as digestion is of the physical system, and for the same reason there is a prayer organ.

Will the atheist tell us that nature has given us a prayer-organ and has given us nothing to pray to? One has said that "if there were no God, it would be necessary to invent one," for the prayer-organ demands a God as much as the lungs demand air.

Christ said, "Love thy neighbor as thyself," which was only the organic language of benevolence. He taught the doctrine of spirituality, and science points to the organ of spirituality. And so it is that every teaching of Christianity responds to an organic necessity of our being. The decalogue is written on every human brain. Immortality is an organic instinct. As the migratory bird flies toward the south guided by the faultless pilot instinct, so the soul flies heavenward by an instinct as faultless.

Christianity is a reality or our instincts are false. God lives or nature lies. We leave our earthly home but to find a better and a brighter one, or over all that is there hang the spectral lenses of deception, and falsehood's elements were blinded in the womb of being.

Whether heaven be a material place or a spiritual condition is a problem that falls outside the pale of our intuitions. For aught we can know, it may be the grand center of centers around which revolve in eternal gyrations the unmeasured systems. Or it may be that it exists independently of space, that its place is wholly spiritual, and that just under the thin veil of materiality around us, above us and beneath us lies the ineffable realm of the Eternal.

Whatever may be the essence of heaven, we may rest assured that it will afford the opportunities and conditions of eternal soul growth. The buds that on earth have fallen before their time shall blossom there in fadeless beauty. Genius shall exhibit its divine allegiance, and love shall be crowned the eternal queen.

There comes a time to the reverent soul when the veil is lifted, and in the awful hush of that moment we call death, when the fetters are falling from the spirit's limbs, amid strains of music soft as the rustle of wings, it is permitted to look upon the unveiled splendor. And often, very often, it beckons to us and whispers with its latest breath, "I hear them *now*," always laying peculiar stress upon the word "now," which indicates that through the presence of this divine instinct it had been listening. On how many a dying couch have the sacred words, "The pure in heart shall see God," found their last and best verification!

But science cannot reproduce the vision of the dying. Their own faint whispers cannot portray it. We must go down to the dark water. The details of the passage are known only to those who embark in the unseen ship. We cannot tell how, nor when, nor where, nor amid what sights and sounds we shall enter the unseen realm. We only know that while beyond the chill flood silence reigneth and

No sound of gently dipping oar
Hints to us of the other shore,

there is still the voice of a divine fact within that whispers, "It is well." The spirit lays its listening ear against the great heart of being, and learns an awful secret that it cannot tell. A secret, at the sound of which it leaps triumphant from the arms of pain, flame-wreathed and singing, thorn-crowned and rejoicing.

> "It must be so: Plato, thou reasonest well,
> Else whence this pleasing hope, this fond desire,
> This longing after immortality?
> Or whence this secret dread and inward horror
> Of falling into naught? Why shrinks the soul
> Back on itself, and startles at destruction?
> 'Tis the divinity that stirs within us;
> 'Tis heaven itself that points out an hereafter
> And intimates eternity to man."